My Reign in Spain

A Spanish Adventure

Rich Bradwell

To my wife, for always being there, and for (nearly) always smiling. Much love.

Follow Rich at www.twitter.com/richbradwell

Like Rich at www.facebook.com/RichBradwellAuthor

Email Rich at richbradwell@gmx.com

Contents

Chapter 1 – Madman or genius?

The plane passed over the sprawling city thousands of feet below, then out over the glittering Mediterranean before turning back in a wide arc and beginning its descent. This felt good; it was February and it had been months since I had seen sunshine. Back in England I had passed through another interminable winter: dark on the way into work, dark by the time I left the office, and the weather set to that most English of settings: "drizzly". But here, instead of the usual perma-blanket of grey cloud, I could see the sun bathing the land below and the waves foaming gently on the beach. I had escaped! It felt as if I was getting away with something; like finding out at the till that your full price jeans are already discounted, or waking up, realising the clocks have gone back and you've won an extra hour in bed. Yes, I felt happy. Perhaps even verging on smug.

I had three months off work and would be travelling around Spain, enjoying the country and trying to learn Spanish. I'd dabbled with language-learning CDs and books in the past, but had never progressed beyond a few basic phrases. It had only ever been a hobby of mine, nothing serious. Until now. Now it was *very serious* indeed, because something big had just happened, something completely unexpected.

I hadn't seen my best friend, Jack, in a couple of months. We were living on opposite sides of the country and we were both busy with work and our own lives. We messaged each other frequently, but it was fair to say I learnt precious little about developments in his life from the jokey messages, cat memes, and crudely drawn pictures of me that he liked to send.

Despite the regular contact, it was rare for him to call unannounced. So when my phone lit up with his name, and his gurning photo, I wondered if it was something important.

"Rich, have I got some news for you, boyo!" he practically shouted down the phone.

Jack was getting married. I didn't even know he had a girlfriend. Apparently it had been a whirlwind romance and now they were engaged.

"Who is she then?" I asked.

"Sofía! She's amazing, gorgeous, really funny, and kind. I met her in a bar and then I don't know. I just completely fell for her. And guess what? She's Spanish."

I was taken aback, "How long have you been dating?"

"Two months. I know it's not long, it just feels right, so I asked her to marry me."

"Yes, but are you sure she knew what you were asking? This could all just be a horrible misunderstanding."

"Oh shut up!" He laughed, and then took a breath, "I want to ask if you'd be my best man. The wedding is going to be in Spain, but I really want you to do it."

"Sure, no problem, of course I'll do it," I said instinctively, but then something dawned on me. "I guess I'll have to do a speech?" I said tentatively. I didn't like public speaking. I was already dreading it, and I had only been aware of it for five seconds. I wondered vainly if Spanish weddings might not require speeches, or if the women gave the speeches.

"Yeah, you will," Jack said, crushing what hope I had, "And there is one other thing," his voice was uneasy now.

"Another thing?"

"Yes. Well, all of Sofía's family will be there, and most of them don't speak English…," he trailed off.

I shrugged, "So you're going to have a Spanish best man as well?"

"Almost," he paused, "We were kind of thinking you could do the speech half in English and half in Spanish."

I didn't like the sound of this at all, "What? Are you sure you weren't *kind of thinking* about someone else, because I don't speak Spanish."

"Come on! You've got ages to learn, and you're the *best* man now," said Jack. I shook my head and sighed, but said nothing. Jack spoke again, brightly. I could tell he was smiling, "So, it's agreed!" And that was that.

Before long, the idea to spend three months travelling in Spain and learning Spanish formed in my mind. It would be a big challenge, but I'd always wanted to learn Spanish. Besides, I was looking forward to traveling again. It had been a long time since my epic road trip around the USA. I would have a great time soaking up the sun and sangria and I would finish at the wedding in Andalusia, no doubt fluent in Spanish and ready to knock their *calcetines* (socks) off.

I was starting off with a month at a language school in Barcelona before travelling around and my first task was to find the apartment where I would be living. I made my way out of the airport, took the metro and headed into the centre of Barcelona. An hour or so later I got off in the *Plaza de Cataluña*, the huge square at the top of the famous street, *Las Ramblas*. There were at least eight roads I could see, spanning out in every direction from the corners of the plaza. I was disoriented and reluctantly unfolded my huge map. Still I couldn't quite figure out which direction was which. I rotated the map as I tried to get my bearings. I may as well have lit a neon sign above my head saying, *"I am a tourist and it's my first day here"*, but I didn't need to, because I was too busy desperately twirling my map around, and slowly turning through 360 degrees. Eventually I picked a side street, oriented myself and walked the few blocks to my apartment building. I entered, hauled my bag up the stairs and knocked on the old wooden door. I could hear footsteps shuffling inside, and after a moment, I was greeted by my new landlady, Luisa, a woman of about 60, she was wearing an apron and had bright pink lipstick on. It was a strange combination.

"¡Hola!" she exclaimed, beaming. "Rich?" she said, nodding at me.

"Si! Rich," I said, pointing at myself. This was good, I could manage this. And I *could* manage it. Until the moment she started speaking again - at a speed and complexity that I distinctly could not manage. Any feeling of smugness I had evaporated instantly.

"*Por favor, lento,*" (Please, slow), I said in my broken, child-like Spanish. She nodded enthusiastically and said three words at a pace slow enough for me to be able to recognise that I didn't know them, and then proceeded to speed back up to her normal pace – she was like a rapper in a hurry. I knew I couldn't ask her to slow down again, and it wouldn't matter even if she did. I decided to go with just nodding. Nod and smile. Just nod and smile.

After she had shown me around the apartment I took my bags, put them in my room and closed the door. I sat down on the single bed, and looked at my spartan surroundings. There wasn't much more than a small desk, chair and wardrobe. There was a window, but when I looked through I saw that it faced onto a small internal courtyard. The waning dusk light faintly illuminated the scene, and almost immediately my attention was drawn to the window opposite. An old man was sitting in a large comfy chair, looking directly at me. *How long had he been waiting there?* I felt like I was intruding, drew the curtain back and made a mental note never to look through the window again. I cast another glance around the room, I wasn't downhearted. I wouldn't be spending that much time in here. I had a city to explore and people to meet. Soon my thoughts were interrupted with Luisa calling my name. I could smell food; it was dinner time.

I entered the kitchen and to my surprise there was another guy sitting at the table. In his early twenties and square-jawed, he looked like a young Arnold Schwarzenegger. I approached, and he acknowledged me with a nod of the head. My head ran through the options of what he could possibly be doing in this strange household. *Family friend? Her strangely Germanic-looking son? Toy boy, 30 years Luisa's junior?*

As if reading my mind, Luisa, gestured at the stranger, *Es Nils, es estudiante como tú.* (This is Nils, he is a student like you). Of course, that explained it. I hadn't expected her to be hosting any other students, but it made sense.

I introduced myself and Nils replied in decent English, but with a thick German accent.

"How long are you in Barcelona for, Nils?" I asked.

"One month. But I ask you somezink," he paused, "I zink it is better for you to call me Miguel," he said rather cryptically.

"Miguel?" I asked in surprise.

"Yes. Zis is my Spanish name. Miguel," he nodded, seemingly pleased with the name. "And for you, Rich, I call you Ricardo," he paused, and then added unnecessarily, "Your Spanish name."

Hmmm, is it worth protesting? I asked myself. *He might just do it regardless. Best to go with the flow. When in Rome do as the Romans do.... Or in this case - When in Spain... do as the strange German man tells you to.* I nodded, "Ok, Ricardo it is," I said half-heartedly. Miguel beamed happily and began tucking into his food.

The next day was a Sunday and I was free to explore. I walked out of the apartment in the bright morning sunshine and strolled through the *Eixample* district (which literally means extension in Catalan), a residential and commercial district just to the north of the old town. It was built in the late nineteenth and early twentieth century and marks the point where Barcelona's twisting, narrow gothic lanes open up into huge straight avenues, arranged in a grid and then crisscrossed in perfect diagonal symmetry. The architecture is modernist, with vast four or five storey buildings joined together to form a single structure that runs uninterrupted along each block. I was looking for a building designed by Barcelona's favourite son, the acclaimed architect Antoni Gaudí. There are few cities so closely-linked with just one architect, particularly one whose style is so unique and immediately identifiable. After a couple of minutes, I found what I was looking for - *Casa Batlló*. To be honest it would have been hard to miss it. Completely distinct from the neighbouring buildings, it was covered in a shimmering green, blue, brown mosaic mix. The roof looked like the scales of a giant dragon, and the prominent balconies that jutted from the front of the building resembled the bones and skeletons of whales, or some other creatures of the deep. It was arresting, intriguing and appealing in equal measure.

I entered and saw why the house is nicknamed the *Casa dels ossos* (the house of bones). The pillars and inner sculpting of the house brought to mind a skeleton, and the light filtering through the stained glass heightened the otherworldly feel. I continued my walk around, noting the unique features in every corner. When Gaudí was commissioned to redesign the house in 1904 he wanted to tear it down and start again. Instead he was persuaded to renovate the existing building that had been built thirty years before. By this point in his career Gaudí had started to make his mark on Barcelona through several high-profile projects.

Gaudí had graduated from the Barcelona school of architecture in 1878. When the Dean of the school signed Gaudí's diploma he famously remarked, *"Who knows if we have given this diploma to a madman or to a genius. Time will tell."* (Unfortunately, there's no record of Gaudí's response). Gaudí began his career by designing small additions to churches, and furniture. In fact, furniture design was something he kept up, and each piece in the house I was looking around was individually designed by Gaudí himself. Each item was unique, but the whole set was characterised by curving, dark wood.

By the 1880s Gaudí began to design whole buildings, firstly in an oriental style and then later in the neo-gothic style. By the 1890s Gaudí really hit his stride. He became increasingly interested in nature and religion and began to draw inspiration for his designs from the natural world. He largely abandoned straight lines and angles in his projects as they were not found in nature. His work was instead recognisable by curving, swirling lines and a more organic appearance.

I finished up in the *Casa Batlló* and decided to continue my Gaudí tour by heading north on the metro to one of his other masterpieces: *Park Güell*. The park lies a few miles out of the city centre and was originally envisioned as a commercial housing development, based on the current vogue of the time (English garden cities), hence the use of the English word "Park" in the original name. The development was set on a rocky hill with views down to the city below, and well above the smoggy air that plagued the city at the turn of the twentieth century. Despite the lofty ambitions, only two houses were ever built, and Gaudí himself moved into one of them.

I exited the metro station and started the climb up towards the park. It was surprisingly steep, and I stopped to catch my breath. Steps were cut into the pavement - it seemed to be rising at an almost 45 degree angle. I looked back down the street and saw the centre of the city and the sea beyond. After a moment I headed off again, continuing the steady climb towards the Park. Like *Casa Batlló* Park Güell was also constructed in Gaudí's heyday, (1900-1914) under the direction of Count Eusebi Güell, a longtime patron of Gaudí. Güell was a successful industrialist, having made his money from textiles, and met the young architect not long after Gaudí had graduated. They got on well and shared common interests including a deep devotion to Catholicism. Güell commissioned Gaudí to design a series of buildings and by the turn of the century, when Güell conceived of his new luxury housing development in a park, it was Gaudí he turned to.

I approached the entrance and could see at once why Park Güell wasn't quite the commercial hit that Count Güell was hoping for. The gatehouses looked like something from Hansel and Gretel. They reminded me of two gingerbread houses, with brown crazy-paving like brickwork and roofs that looked like icing. Fun - certainly, but considerably less practical than a nice three-bed semi with a garage. I wandered in to the park, past the twin gatehouses, and was confronted by a massive stone staircase, flanked by crazy mosaic walls with turrets. It lead upwards to a forest of huge pillars. Resting on those pillars was a massive flat terraced area overhead. Even more than at the *Casa Batlló* Gaudí was showing his fantastical, mythical and playful side in this design. Reportedly on one occasion Gaudí said to Güell, "Sometimes I think we are the only people who like this architecture." Güell replied, "I don't like your architecture, I respect it." I've tried to find the context for that quote, but couldn't. It's hard to know if it was meant as a sharp rebuke – a cutting remark which left Gaudí smarting - or whether it was just classic late 19th century banter, and the two men shared a good laugh over Güell's cheeky zinger. I'd like to think the latter, but I guess we'll never know.

I climbed the staircase and wandered through the pillars. The undulating roof, supporting the terrace above, was decorated in more mosaics. Towards the centre, the columns thinned out creating a natural space and calm. It didn't surprise me to learn that Gaudí had designed this section to replicate the high vaulted ceilings of a church. I passed through more columns and out the back, up against the rock face of the hillside. Immediately to my left was a natural looking corridor, but slanted, and formed from a wall of uneven rocks on one side and pillars built from rough stones on the other. The whole corridor of rock was leaning over to one side as if it was rolling. Gaudí had designed it to look like a great wave. As I rounded the corner I was aware how keenly I was looking around for more interesting little details - they seemed to be everywhere. I knew the terrace, back above the pillars, was the centrepiece of the whole design and decided to head off into the depths of the park first.

The sun was shining and I was happy to be walking: in the way that being outside on a sunny day makes you feel. It's pretty much the exact opposite feeling to knowing that it's a sunny day, but you are going to stay in anyway and *not* make the most of it because you're too tired/hungover/can't be bothered/halfway through binging the latest TV drama series. I walked along the rocky paths and past one of the viaducts that Gaudí had built in to the park. Out here the scenery and landscaping were much more natural. There were rock formations and sculpted rock pillars but generally the vegetation had been allowed to grow, and I noted that I was essentially walking around a fairly rocky, sandy hillside. There were trees, but also lots of scrub, brush, much of which masked some steep drop-offs.

Once I'd reached the park's eastern edge I circled back around. Out here there weren't many tourists. As is usually the case, while the selfie-stick-wielding hordes were clogging the entrance I didn't have to walk far to find a bit of peace and quiet. My feet crunched on the sandy path and I saw the odd cactus dotted amongst the palm trees. It reminded me that I was in a different ecosystem now. I knew Barcelona was in the Mediterranean-Subtropical zone, but I was still surprised to see the cactuses.

After a little while I reached the large stone terrace. Known as the Greek Theatre it was originally envisioned as a place where cultural events, open-air concerts and the like would take place for the entire community. It now served as the seating area for Park Güell as a modern-day tourist attraction. Most people were sitting around the edge on a balustrade which ringed almost the entire terrace. It doubled up as a single continuously curving bench and was covered in blue, green, yellow and white mosaics. It was designed to look like a sea serpent and it provided an intriguing border to the open space of the terrace. I noted the stone of the bench was moulded into a strange curved dipping seat, rather than a flat surface as you would expect. Legend has it that in order to make the stone bench comfortable Gaudí had a workman drop his trousers and sit in soft plaster in order to record the correct anatomical posture – foreshadowing the emergence of ergonomic chairs by

17

more than 50 years. What I didn't understand about the story was why the workman had to drop his trousers. Who knows? Who am I to question Gaudí's architectural genius?

Beyond the twisting sea serpent bench was a fine view of Barcelona. A panorama of the city was spread out beneath me, running down to the sea which stretched on and met the horizon in a blurry haze. Amidst the patchwork of buildings stitched together in the quilt of the city was one that was immediately recognisable. The *Sagrada Familia* (the sacred family) church was Gaudí's final, and crowning, masterpiece. It is unlike any other building on earth. It mixes gothic and art nouveau styles, with fantastically detailed sculpting and carving inside and out. Eight huge spires sprout from the central section and huge naves push out to both sides. It has a capacity for 9,000 people. Incredibly, despite being started in 1882, it is not yet finished, and won't be for at least another 10 years. It is popularly thought of as a cathedral, but since it doesn't have a resident Bishop (as it's not finished yet), it isn't technically a cathedral (there you go fact fans). However, the Pope did consecrate it as a *minor basilica* in 2010 – which is not really the same. It's a bit like getting a "well done for trying" medal.

Gaudí got involved in the project in 1883, after the initial architect quit, and he worked on it for almost his whole professional life, at first in tandem with other projects and eventually concentrating on nothing else. The *Sagrada Familia* has divided opinion from the start. It's such an outrageously unusual building that it's not surprising. The architect Louis Sullivan pronounced it *"the greatest piece of creative architecture in the last twenty-five years. It is spirit symbolised in stone!"* But not everyone was so complimentary. The writer George Orwell described it as *"one of the most hideous buildings in the world."*

Gaudí became increasingly fixated on the *Sagrada Familia* and in 1910 he gave up all his other work for it. After the death of his father and then niece in 1912 Gaudí lived alone (in Park Güell) and lived a life revolving around his faith and his dedication to the *Sagrada Familia.* In 1925 at the age of 72 he moved into the workshop on the construction site in order to be closer to the project. A year later he was killed when he was hit by a tram. When he was struck, he lost consciousness, and despite his fame in the city, passersby assumed him to be a beggar, owing to his shabby and unkempt appearance - consequently he didn't receive any immediate help. Eventually someone called for a taxi to take him to hospital where he received basic care. The following day, when someone finally recognised him as the internationally-renowned architect and sought additional care for him, his condition was too severe to save him. Thousands turned out for his funeral which was held at a chapel in the *Sagrada Familia.* By the time of his death, the project was still only a quarter completed.

I took in the rest of the view. The hills rose up behind Park Güell, hemming in the city to the coast. Down at the shore I could see the port area and just in front of it a prominent hill, Montjuïc, where Barcelona's stadium from the 1992 Olympics is situated. I could see the Nou Camp too, the home of Barcelona's famous football team. In the far distance I could even see a strip of beach. This city seemed to have it all, but I was done for the day and the rest of it would have to wait. It was getting late in the afternoon and soon Luisa, my landlady, would be preparing dinner. I strolled back off the terrace and down the stone staircase, noting an enormous mosaic-covered lizard that I'd somehow missed on my way up.

Güell and Gaudí's plan to develop the park as a housing development never materialised and in 1922 the city council agreed to purchase it, opening it as a public park four years later. Judging by the happy faces eagerly photographing the various wonders all around, the fact this project was never finished (and therefore is open to everyone, not just sixty lucky households) seems to have worked out for the best. I'm not sure what the excuse for the *Sagrada Familia* is though. Gaudí's been dead for nearly 100 years and it's still nowhere near done. However, as Gaudí once famously joked, he wasn't concerned at the pace of construction, since his client, God, was not in a hurry.

Chapter 2 – Independence!

Monday morning, and as I blinked awake I realised it was back to school time. *Back to school?* How strange. It was something I hadn't experienced for close to 15 years, and this time it was voluntary. I didn't mind though. My days would be short, only four hours of lessons, in order to have time to explore the city. Then after a few weeks of lessons to get my Spanish up to speed I would be ready to tour the country.

I went into the kitchen for breakfast. There was a choice of two cereals and milk laid out on the table. Miguel wasn't there and it looked like Luisa had gone out too, which was good. I struggled to understand almost anything she said, and I think she felt the same way about me. The previous evening I had returned home for my dinner and found her and Miguel sat at the table watching the TV in the kitchen. Luisa greeted me enthusiastically as usual, inquired about my day, which I just about managed to comprehend, before the language barrier became insurmountable. She got up to prepare the food, clattering around with a few frying pans. From what I had gathered, all food in the household came via a frying pan filled nearly to the brim with oil. She brought over three plates: some kind of fried ham on one, two fried eggs on another and fried vegetables on a third. It was like she was running a greasy spoon cafe. I half expected her to bring out fried bread, black pudding and a big mug of tea. Instead I got wine, which is perhaps an idea greasy spoons could adopt.

She sat back down and the three of us settled into an agreeable silence, broken only by the sound of the TV murmuring away. The programme appeared to be a Spanish version of popular quiz show, *Who wants to be a millionaire?* We watched as a contestant made their way through some of the early rounds towards the bigger money. I found it almost impossible to follow when the presenter and contestant were speaking. But since the questions and multiple choice answers were displayed on the screen I realised I could make sense of what was going on. The contestant spent so long umming and ahhing over their answer that I even had time to work out what the question meant, and could just about figure out which answer they were leaning towards. I was starting to feel pretty pleased with myself and, eager to practice some more conversation, I decided to comment to Luisa. I constructed a sentence in my head and mentally double-checked it before unleashing it.

"*¡Esta es mi programa favorito!*" (This is my favourite programme), I said, looking happy with myself.

Luisa turned to me, "*¿Qué?*" (What?)

What does she mean *what?* I thought to myself and tried again, "*¡Esta es mi programa favorito!*"

She looked at me blankly. She thought for a moment and went with "*¿Qué?*" again. Miguel, who was watching our exchange, began to stifle laughter – clearly he could understand what I was saying.

I didn't know how there was confusion here. It was a statement of such blinding simplicity that I didn't really know how to simplify it further. There was nothing for it but to press on. I was committed, so I said it again and I could see her visibly wincing as I mangled the words. She looked like she was about to say *"¿Qué?"* again, so I searched desperately for any other relevant Spanish I knew. Quite simply, I had not prepared a back-up line. But suddenly the words, *"Me gusta,"* came to me, which means *I like*, and just to make clear I gestured at the television and repeated it.

Her face lit up in relief that she had finally understood something I said. *"¿Te gusta?"* (You like it?).

Sí, I said affirmatively. She nodded and smiled at me as if I was a halfwit. I nodded back and stayed quiet for the rest of the programme, puzzling over the misunderstanding. I couldn't figure it out, after all it was a perfectly constructed sentence. To be fair to her, perhaps saying it was my *favourite* programme was a stretch. It was patently obvious that I'd only watched half of one episode and it was being broadcast in a language which I clearly couldn't understand. Perhaps her confusion was justified after all.

That was yesterday though, and today I would be learning some Spanish in the school. No doubt I would be a sparkling conversationalist in no time. I finished my breakfast and walked to the school building. It was only a five-minute stroll through the *Eixample* district and it was another fine morning. I entered on the ground floor and climbed the stairs to the second floor where the school was located. It was a light and airy space and I was welcomed by the receptionist. I say welcomed - she said hello and handed me a test paper in one swift move, which is a pretty unwelcoming way to greet someone.

I went through to a room with a few desks; some of my fellow students were already scribbling away. I took a desk and turned the paper over. It was a test to determine my Spanish level and ensure I was allocated to the correct class. The first couple of questions were easy enough, although pretty soon I noticed a pattern emerging, with questions like "Why do you want to learn Spanish?" and "Why did you choose Barcelona?" It was starting to feel more like market research than a language test. Soon the grammar questions came, and they were much harder, but at least they were multiple choice. *Good old multiple choice, pretty much a guaranteed 25% on that section,* I thought to myself.

I handed in my test and waited for it to be marked which turned out to be surprisingly quick. Unsurprisingly I found I had been assigned to the beginners class which took place at 4pm-8pm every day. I had most of the day free, so I decided to wander down to the old town. I left the school, passed through the huge Plaza de Cataluña where I'd arrived a couple of days before, and then down *Las Ramblas,* the main boulevard that runs through Barcelona's old town. The centre of the street is pedestrianised and tree-lined, so it provides a pleasant amble of more than a kilometre down towards the sea.

I strolled along, once again enjoying the feeling that I was wandering in the sunshine on a Monday morning when I could easily be in work. I took in my surroundings: the pavement cafes, with people drinking their espressos and the kiosks selling papers and magazines. I had been to Barcelona once before, some years ago, and I remembered being somewhat shocked to see a market with birds and other small animals right here on *Las Ramblas*. The sight of hundreds of live animals in small cages on the street was as unpleasant as it was unusual, and I wasn't upset to find that it had been shut down in 2010. The other thing I recalled were the various street performers who ply their trade up and down *Las Ramblas.*

Like many other touristy places, *Las Ramblas* has its fair share of entertainers: playing guitar, dressed-up like robots, holding statue-esque poses and so on. However, on my previous visit I remember the fun we had watching one particular guy. We were sitting at one of the pavement cafes and saw a mime artist holding a frozen statue pose. His trick was simple: as people passed by he would suddenly jump out at someone, and make a loud "snarf" noise. The unsuspecting person would scream or shout in shock before laughing at the strangeness of it all. It was a simple and very repetitive trick, but was nevertheless hilarious. Strangely he kept doing it without ever seeming to stop and approach the customers watching in the café for tips. Perhaps he was simply doing it for the love of jumping out on people. Perhaps he wasn't even a street entertainer.

I kept my eyes peeled but unfortunately didn't see him. There was another reason to keep my eyes peeled. Regrettably, one of the many things that Barcelona is famous for is pickpocketing. In a survey of the worst places in Europe for pickpocketing Barcelona was no. 1 and *Las Ramblas* is renowned as the riskiest place in the city for it. I wasn't worried, I just needed to avoid being distracted, and so long as I wasn't ambushed by a man in a mime outfit making a snarfing noise in my ear, I knew I would be fine.

I took a rest at a café and consulted my guidebook. Apparently, *Las Ramblas* derives from an old Arabic word "ramla" which means sandy riverbed. It was originally a sewage-filled stream which drained water from the hills behind the city into the Mediterranean Sea. The stream served to separate the Gothic Quarter to the east from the *El Raval* suburb on the western side. Eventually the city began to expand and in the 14th and 15th centuries new city walls were built and the stream was diverted around them. *Las Ramblas* was converted into a thoroughfare, although it wasn't until the 18th century that trees were planted and it became the pleasant boulevard we know today. *Las Ramblas* still divides opinion, the Spanish poet Federico García Lorca called it the "only street in the world which I wish would never end". Yet for many Barcelona residents these days it's a tourist trap, suffering from pickpockets, and as day turns to night, prostitutes as well. However, on a fine morning, with sunny skies overhead it seemed a great place for people-watching, and I passed an enjoyable hour sipping a *Café con leche* watching the world go by.

I decided to head into the Gothic Quarter and was soon picking my way through a labyrinth of twisting streets. The area is the centre of the old city, dating back to Roman times. By the medieval age Barcelona had grown into an important city and there are a few buildings from the period still standing, including the original Barcelona Cathedral. I found it by chance, walking down a street which came out almost directly on to one of its huge, looming sides. It was as if I'd stumbled upon the foot of a giant. I looked up, and then had to look up some more, craning my neck back to see the top. It really is a massive, hulking building and the rest of the Gothic Quarter is built in close around it on three sides, so there's no standoff space to step back and admire it. I wandered round the front where the steps lead out into a square, and finally I was able to take it in. For such an old building, its scale is impressive - they broke ground on the project in 1298. Fortunately it wasn't built by Gaudí or there's a chance they might still be going.

I passed through more narrow streets, happy to wander aimlessly. Although there were a few very old buildings about, most were more modern. Classical and neo-gothic architecture predominated, the majority constructed from the 19th century onwards. After a little while I came to the *Plaça Reial*, a magnificent square, hemmed in by four-storey buildings on every side. Around the square were covered passages, with arches that opened onto the square itself. There were plenty of cafés offering seating in the sunshine, so I decided to stay and order lunch. In the afternoon I continued wandering through the Gothic Quarter. A lot of the buildings were three, four or five storeys and I noted that some of the balconies had flags draped from them. Two designs predominated, one had horizontal red and yellow lines, while another was similar but incorporated a triangular blue section with a white star in the middle. I knew one was the Catalan flag, but the other I wasn't sure about. It certainly wasn't the Spanish flag. In fact, I hadn't seen a single one of those on my walk. It didn't surprise me; Barcelona is the capital of Catalonia (*Catalunya* in the Catalan language, and *Cataluña* in Spanish) and the home of Catalan nationalism. I didn't remember seeing all these flags last time I was here, and while that might be my memory, more likely it was due to the recent resurgence of Catalan nationalism.

Spain is made up of 17 autonomous communities, which are a bit like states. Catalonia is one of these autonomous communities and this gives it some powers to run its own affairs. As you've probably heard, there are many who would like Catalonia to be an independent country. The issue really came to a head in October 2017, following a disputed referendum. This spilled over into mass demonstrations, a smattering of police violence, politicians thrown in jail, and the re-imposition of direct rule from Madrid (temporarily removing Catalonia's autonomy.) But how did they get there?

The central government in Madrid, long fearful of the breakup of Spain, has always been adamant the Catalans will not become independent and therefore they have always forbidden a referendum on the subject. To be

fair, they are equally uncompromising with the Basques –
another region in Spain with separatist tendencies.

For many years support for independence in
Catalonia was fairly low (only 15% in 2006, according to
one survey). However, following the economic crisis in
2008, support for independence began to grow, and
Catalan nationalist parties did increasingly well in the
regional parliamentary elections. This is when the
problems really started, because if there's one thing that
Catalan nationalists like, *(the clue's in the name)*, it's
nationalism and independence (specifically the Catalan
variety). In defiance of the government in Madrid the
Catalan regional government started testing the waters,
trying to build support for a referendum on independence.
In 2014 - buoyed by the calling of the Scottish
independence referendum – the Catalans organised a vote
of their own.

The government in Madrid was clear that any vote
would be illegal, and the national constitutional court
confirmed the poll could not be called a referendum. It
didn't stop the Catalan regional government. They did
what any disobedient schoolchild would have done: they
held their referendum anyway, but gave it a different
name. It was not a *referendum on independence,* but a
"citizen participation process on Catalonia's future", *so
there*. In the end more than 80% voted in favour of
independence, although the turnout was low (only 40%).
Many who favoured staying part of Spain chose not to take
part, so it was difficult to gauge the exact level of support
for independence. However, the nationalists took

encouragement from the result and vowed to continue the fight.

When Catalan nationalists won the regional elections again in 2015, they promised to hold a real referendum, and on 1 October 2017 they did so. Unlike last time, where the government in Madrid ignored the poll, this time they reacted angrily and sent in the police to try and stop it happening. The resulting scenes of police removing ballot boxes and manhandling protesters were broadcast around the world. Mass demonstrations ensued, and the Spanish government re-imposed direct rule. The strange thing is that surveys conducted before the poll suggested support for independence in Catalonia was only 41%. Lots of commentators have said that the heavy-handed reaction of the Spanish government has only *increased* the support for independence. It has certainly increased the sense of grievance amongst those that already supported separation.

The idea of Catalan independence has a long history. In fact, the Catalans celebrate the "National Day of Catalonia" every September (glossing over the fact they aren't actually a nation and arguably never have been). The day marks the defeat of Catalonia in 1714 in the War of Spanish Succession which marked the beginning of Madrid's domination over Catalonia. Back then Catalonia was a principality (still not a nation) and was fighting alongside Charles VI (a man from Austria) against Philip V (a man from France) for the vacant position of King of Spain. The old King of Spain had died with no heirs and this had sparked a war between the two chief powers of

Europe, both of whom fancied the idea of owning Spain. Catalonia was keen to retain its status as an independent principality and judged that the Habsburgs of Austria would allow them to stay independent. Unfortunately, their side could not match the powerful French (the Bourbons) and eventually the Austrians gave up their claim. Various treaties were signed, and the Catalans were left high and dry.

The Catalans were faced with a decision: to keep resisting on their own or to surrender to the Bourbon forces. A war council met in Barcelona and after many debates they decided to continue their resistance. Their preference was to die fighting rather than live in oppression. One Catalan leader coined the phrase: "Let the nation end with glory". In 1713 Barcelona was put under siege and after eleven months the Catalan resistance (and the whole Spanish War of Succession) was brought to an end. The Bourbons overran the city, burned various buildings and their man, Charles VI, became King of Spain. Catalonia was subsumed into modern Spain and the rule of Madrid over Barcelona began.

It's worth lingering on this conflict for a moment because the story that Catalans tell about themselves (even today) is that Madrid has oppressed, or at least restricted Catalonia for centuries. Following the siege of Barcelona, and the conquering of Catalonia, Charles VI issued the "Decree of Nueva Planta". By this decree, all the historical sovereignty and rights of Catalonia were abolished, its local administration dissolved, and its language banned from being written or taught.

Fast-forwarding to the early 20th century (during Gaudí's time), there was a renaissance of Catalan culture, in literature, art and architecture, so that by the time of the Spanish Civil War in the 1930s, it was no surprise to see Barcelona lined up with the Republicans against Franco's Nationalists (or fascists). Following Franco's victory he sought to crush any separatist movements and eradicate regional differences in Spain. He was as harsh on Catalonia as anywhere. He banned the public use of the Catalan language and had all town, village and street names changed from Catalan to Castilian Spanish (i.e. standard Spanish). Education, radio, TV and newspapers were all strictly in Spanish, even children's names were strictly controlled. New babies had to be given standard Castilian Spanish names – Catalan names were expressly forbidden.

It's fair to say that a lot of hostility towards the central government has its roots in this period – after all this is living memory for a lot of people (Franco remained dictator of Spain until his death in 1975). Following the move to democracy in the late 70's the idea of the 'autonomous communities' emerged, and Catalonia and other places gained more control and freedom. Interestingly, one of the first things the new regional government of Catalonia did was create a public holiday for the "National Day of Catalonia" - despite it commemorating a defeat, and not independence (not that they are still sore about it, obviously).

As I walked around I was aware just how much Catalan language I could see on signs and shopfronts. It's similar to French and Spanish, but is distinct from both, for instance it uses a lot more x's than Spanish. I'd read that it is often a tricky decision for shops whether to write their sign in Spanish or Catalan (e.g. supermarket is *supermercat* in Catalan or *supermercado* in Spanish). Apparently it can be seen as a political decision about where the shop owners' loyalties lie. Catalan is spoken by about half of residents as their native tongue, and is associated with the independence movement. However, just as many people speak Spanish natively, and most people understand both. In a reversal from the Franco era, the Catalan regional government has instituted various laws to encourage Catalan, including mandating all schools to teach in Catalan and half of all films in cinemas be Catalan.

I learnt later that all those flags I'd seen had a special significance. While the red and yellow striped one is the flag of Catalonia itself, the one with the additional blue triangle and white star is specifically for Catalonian independence. Known as the *Estelada* (Lone star flag) it was created in the early 20th century as a flag for the nation of Catalonia. It's clearly an emotive symbol for both sides. In 2016 the Spanish government barred football fans from bringing the flags to a cup final match between Barcelona and Sevilla, held in Madrid. The government applied a law which prohibits the display of symbols that "incite, foment or help violent or terrorist behaviour." A judge later overruled the ban after Barcelona complained, citing freedom of expression.

2017 was the year that the issue sparked into life. Following the disputed and interrupted referendum in early October, the Catalan nationalists declared independence on 27 October 2017, but it did little to resolve the issue. Madrid's forceful response was to lock up several nationalist politicians, and to call fresh regional elections for December 2017, which the nationalists then won by the narrowest of margins. The only thing that's clear is that both the flag and the issue of independence itself continue to be divisive. And that's because there are a large number of Catalans (around half) who definitely don't want independence. They are proud to be Catalan *and* Spanish. As the Scottish referendum showed, those that shout the loudest are not necessarily in the majority. However, it's hard to see how this will be resolved until there *is* a proper referendum, and everyone has had the chance to have their say.

Chapter 3 – Back to school

That afternoon I returned to the school for my first lessons. I climbed the staircase and made my way back through reception and into my classroom. Around ten students were sitting in a semi-circle in chairs that incorporated their own desk. These chairs have always reminded me of a baby's high chair, and I wedged myself into mine awkwardly. I looked around. My class were a motley crew, mostly young adults, the odd teenager and middle-aged person mixed in. The teacher, in her thirties, was also in the classroom handing out papers. She approached me, and gave me a worksheet.

"¡Hola! ¿Cómo estás? ¿Cómo te llamas?" (Hello. How are you? What's your name?), she said brightly.

It took me a moment to process her questions, "Ummm, I'm Rich, and yeah I'm…" I replied, but she cut me off.

"¿Inglés? No. ¡Aquí, hablamos español!" (English? No, here we speak Spanish), she reprimanded me. And with that she proceeded on to the next student.

That was how I learnt that English was prohibited in the classroom. Occasionally the teacher allowed us to ask a question in English, but her response was always in Spanish. I found it exhausting to listen to nothing but Spanish for four hours, even if the teacher did have to speak almost comically slowly at times. Occasionally she had to resort to so many gestures that it felt like we were playing charades.

As part of the introductions the teacher made us play a simple game - we had to write down four things about ourselves, one of which was a lie, and then tell them to the rest of the class, whose task was to spot the fib. It was a good way to get to know and to size up my classmates. There was a young Portuguese man who was a dead-ringer for champion-biter and sometime footballer Luis Suárez, an American guy who was so young that he was named Chandler, after the character in *Friends,* and an older engineer from France, Yann, who looked permanently bewildered -he seemed continually surprised to be addressed in Spanish - and a German girl whose main characteristic seemed to be "pouty".

The other students took it in turns to present their facts (and lies) to the class. Fortunately, their Spanish was as bad as my own and I could understand them. It was an entertaining game, although some of the lies were so preposterous that they were easy to spot – *No, Chandler, I don't believe you are a professional balloon artist who specialises in doing rhinos.* Others were subtler, and gave the class more work to do, but soon enough their web of lies and untruths tended to fall apart. It was an amusing start to the class, and certainly a lot better than studying verb tables, which was what I had feared. At the end I was given homework – something I hadn't experienced in many years – before we packed up and I wandered home.

I arrived back at the flat and Luisa was already preparing dinner, Miguel was nowhere to be seen. I sat down and she brought out Gazpacho, the cold tomato soup popular in the south of Spain. I'd learnt that Luisa was originally from the South, so I wasn't surprised she was serving it, but she had served it the previous day, so I asked her about it.

"*¿Gazpacho otra vez?*" (Gazpacho again?) I asked, unintentionally bluntly.

If she thought I was being chippy or complaining, she didn't show it. "*Sí. Es bueno y saludable.*" (Yes! It's good and healthy) she responded brightly. "*¿Te gusta? ¿Verdad?*" (You like it, yes?).

I wasn't sure if that was a question or an instruction, so I nodded.

She continued in slow Spanish so I could understand, "There are some villages in Andalusia, in the South of Spain where they eat Gazpacho every day." She paused and for effect added, "365 days a year!"

I wasn't sure if she was implying that *I* would be eating Gazpacho every day, so I commented tentatively, "*¡Eso es mucho! ¡Es demasiado!*" (That's a lot. It's too much).

She shook her head, and firmly replied, "*No. ¡es bueno!*" (No. It's good!). With that she turned and went back to cooking, and I stared at my gazpacho, wondering how many more bowls of the stuff I would have.

***

The first week passed by pleasantly. I explored Barcelona in the mornings and afternoons, wandering further afield and eating leisurely *Menu del días* (set lunch menus) at restaurants. I spent an enjoyable couple of hours at Gaudí's masterpiece *La Sagrada Familia.* It was as impressive, intricate, mystical and beguiling on the inside as it was from the outside. It was surrounded by cranes and scaffolding, but I couldn't see anyone working - no wonder they had been building it for over a hundred years. I visited the Picasso museum (he lived in Barcelona during his youth) and went shopping in the stores off *Plaza de Cataluña.* I was also reading "Homage to Catalonia", George Orwell's classic account of his involvement in the Spanish Civil War. He had come to Barcelona to volunteer to fight, and it was fascinating to be walking through so many of the places he had described 75 years before.

In 1936 Spain was suffering from the Great Depression and Europe was being buffeted by extreme political ideologies. The Nazis had taken power in Germany and the Fascists in Italy. Meanwhile, communists, socialists and anarchists were organising across Europe (well, perhaps not the anarchists, they tend to be rather averse to organising). Nevertheless, an atmosphere of change was in the air and Spain was no different. In 1931 anger at the widespread poverty and incompetence of the government led to the abolition of the Spanish monarchy and a republic was declared. Unfortunately, the new republic immediately faced significant problems. Both Catalonia and the Basque region wanted independence, something which would have led to the break-up of Spain itself. Meanwhile the government and the Catholic Church were very hostile to each other, and the government was suspicious of the army, who they believed had too much influence in politics. The divisions between political ideologies, church, state, military and regions set the stage for civil war. In summer 1936 the General of the Army, Francisco Franco, led a coup by the Nationalists, a broadly right-wing group. They swiftly took control of half the country (more or less the western half). The eastern half, including Catalonia, remained loyal to the left-wing leaning Republican government that had been deposed in the coup.

Confusing matters further were other countries who got involved to support their favoured sides; the Communist Soviet Union supported the Republicans, while the Nazis supported the right-wing Nationalists. Increasingly the fight was seen as an ideological one between left-wing and right-wing beliefs. Across Europe idealistic foreigners were attracted by the idea of defending socialism, and some, including George Orwell, went to Spain to fight.

Orwell arrived in Barcelona at the end of 1936, determined to see some action defending the socialist ideals of the Republicans from the Nationalist-fascists. Orwell described the Barcelona he found, walking up and down Las Ramblas and through the *Plaza de Cataluña*. When he arrived he wrote, "The anarchists were still in virtual control of Catalonia and the revolution was still in full swing ... It was the first time that I had ever been in a town where the working class was in the saddle ... every wall was scrawled with the hammer and sickle." As you can imagine, the anarchists did not run a tight ship: they discouraged people from sticking to one-way systems, and abandoned the use of submissive forms of speech, such as "Señor" or "Don". Their armed units were often a rabble and regarded by other Republicans as close to useless. They had no rank system, no hierarchy, no salutes, and their "Commanders" were elected by the troops. Unsurprisingly Orwell grew weary of the conflict, finding war to be much more mundane than glamorous and returned to England in 1937. At the same time Franco's nationalists (who controlled much of the regular army and enjoyed support from the ruthless Nazis - who used the Spanish Civil War as a practice run for World War 2, launching bombing raids and so on) began to crush the Republicans. In early 1939, Franco captured Catalonia, one of the last leftist strongholds and his dictatorship of Spain began in earnest.

In the evenings of that first week I hung out with Miguel, my German housemate. We would walk down *Las Ramblas,* into the Gothic Quarter, finding ourselves in small, dark bars, or if the evening was mild sitting out in the *Plaça Reial*. Miguel seemingly had two main interests in life – learning languages and unsuccessfully hitting on women. He already spoke German, English and French and now he had his sights set on Spanish. One evening, sitting at one of the outside tables of one of the cafés that stayed open serving beers he told me why he was keen on learning Spanish.

"Ricardo, languages are like tools. Ze more tools you have, ze more you can achieve in life," he nodded sagely. It was like listening to the Terminator give his life philosophy.

"But tools for what? I mean I like to travel, and it makes sense to learn a language, particularly one that's used in several countries, but what are you planning on doing with it?" I was genuinely interested.

"It could be anything. It may be useful for business, for instance. Or for women."

Of course, women - everything seemed to come back to this, his favourite subject. I wanted to see where he was going though, "With women?"

"Yes, women!" his eyes lit up, "Being successful wiz women is a skill. It takes tools and of course, practice," he said.

If I hadn't known he was talking about women, I would have guessed he was describing electrical work or carpentry. "Go on, explain."

"It is simple, Ricardo. I used to be like every other guy, like you, no good wiz women," I rolled my eyes, but he didn't notice, "but I learnt somezing important. You *can* be good if you practice. And if you change your attitude." He paused, "I took ze red pill."

"Red pill?"

"Yes, like in ze Matrix. He can take ze blue pill and go back to ze fake world, or ze red pill and wake up to ze real world. Zis is me now – living in ze real world, Ricardo."

"Right, and what does that involve?"

41

"It means nice guys finish last! You do whatever it takes to impress ze women! Magic tricks, psychological games, impress zem in zeir own language. Say what zey want to hear, whatever," he waved his hand dismissively.

I laughed, "Right, so doing magic tricks is living in the real world?" He didn't seem to understand and I pressed on, "So when I asked why you were learning Spanish, it was actually about women?"

He weighed it up for a moment, "Yes, I zink so. Many reasons, but zat is ze best one."

I rolled my eyes again and laughed, "Why don't I get us another beer, and when I come back you can show me a magic trick?" his eyes lit up like a puppy, and I wandered inside to fetch more drinks.

Chapter 4 – Presenting...

The weeks in Barcelona passed by; my daily diet of fried food and gazpacho continued unabated and little by little I began to understand some of what Luisa said to me. I continued to explore the city by day, went to class in the late afternoons and drank with Miguel in the evenings. My Spanish was improving: lessons were generally fun and my vocabulary was expanding. Yet learning grammar was a real slog. However, unless I wanted to spend my time talking solely in the present tense, unable to refer to the past or future, like an amnesiac just woken from a coma, then unfortunately grammar was essential. I studied the different verb endings, drawing up complex tables with the present, past, future tenses and the rather baffling subjunctive form. I also found that I was learning interesting cultural titbits in class. One day we did a lesson on *los refranes* (sayings or proverbs). In English we're so familiar with our sayings that we forget how metaphorical and obscure they can be e.g. "Too many cooks spoil the broth," (I can't remember the last time I had broth, spoiled or otherwise. And I don't believe I've ever seen more than one person attempting to cook any kind of broth or soup.) Or "don't look a gift horse in the mouth" (I don't think I've ever looked at a gift horse, or its mouth).

In Spain they have just as many proverbs and some are directly equivalent to ours e.g. *Más vale tarde que nunca* (Better late than never).

Some are completely unique e.g. the refreshingly abrupt: *Zapatero, a tus zapatos* (Shoemaker, to your shoes.) This means go back to what you know.

Intriguingly, some sayings are essentially the same, but expressed in a subtly different way: *A falta de pan, buenas son tortas* (If there's no bread, cakes will do) which is similar to Beggars can't be choosers.

Spanish proverbs strike a similarly cautious note to many English proverbs, often advising prudence, forethought and vigilance, yet I couldn't help but notice there were far more rural, religious and food based metaphors. The proverbs seemed to reveal something about Spanish culture, history and the rural society they must have emerged from. Interestingly, just as English draws many proverbs and sayings from Shakespeare (e.g. to wear your heart upon your sleeve), Spanish is just as influenced by the seminal text Don Quixote by Cervantes e.g. *Mientras se gana algo no se pierde nada* (As long as something is gained nothing is lost.)

On another day, in another interesting, illuminating, but not particularly useful lesson, I learnt that Spanish animals do not make the same noises as English animals. I was surprised, to say the least, as I hadn't realised that there was such variance between, for example, the dogs of the world. While English speakers think that dogs "woof", the Spanish believe it as a *"guau"* or *"guau guau"* pronounced like "wow" or "wow-wow". This seems to be due, at least partly, to the structure of the language itself. This framework seems to affect more than just the words, but even the perceptions of external sounds. As the teacher explained, very few, if any Spanish words end in "f", so the sound of "woof" just doesn't sound right to Spanish speakers, as they wouldn't interpret a sound as ending in an "f". But in other cases, the noise an animal makes is simply perceived differently e.g. sheep. We think we hear "Baaaa", but the Spanish hear "Beeee". The teacher struggled to explain why, other than to say that if that's what you are taught you are hearing as a child, then that's what you believe you hear, and for her the idea of "Baaaa" was just as strange. However, she reassured us that some sounds were universal, even if written slightly differently e.g. "oinc-oinc" for a pig, or "mu" for a cow.

Outside the classroom I continued to discover new sights in the city. One day I wandered up Montjuïc, the sizable hill that looms over Barcelona. Montjuïc, which translates as "Jew Mountain", is only a kilometre or so from the centre of the city. It rises up 200 metres and looks directly down on the port area. A cable car ran high above me, but I decided to walk up it instead. While it was a strenuous effort, it felt good to be slowly climbing out and above the hubbub. I passed through gardens and pressed on up the relatively steep incline. The sides of the hill were fairly clear, affording increasingly impressive views back down on the buildings below.

In centuries gone by the hill was wooded, and it was used by the townspeople to graze animals and grow crops. Owing to its strategic location it was also the ideal site for fortifications, and the Castle of Montjuïc, which still stands, was built in the 17th century. I came across it as I climbed and went inside to explore. An impressive stone arched bridge lead over a grassy ditch, presumably where the moat must have been centuries earlier. I wandered around, admiring the size of the castle, but what really impressed me were the views of Barcelona on one side, and the vast Mediterranean on the other. It was a fine day of blue skies and the sea seemed calm, so I strolled leisurely round the outside walls, stopping at some of the old cannon dotted around. It was easy to see why the fort was located here: it enjoyed a commanding position and would have made an assault from land or sea very difficult indeed.

Inside there were a few displays and I learnt that the castle played a role in both the War of Spanish Succession in the early 18th century and the Napoleonic invasion of Spain in the early 19th century (although not much of a role as the castle defenders surrendered to Napoleon's army without a shot being fired, following orders not to resist). The castle was used well into the 20th century, when it functioned as a prison.

The castle gained its sinister and forbidding reputation around the time of the Spanish Civil War when political prisoners were held, tortured and sometimes executed there. The leading Catalan nationalist, Lluis Companys, who had helped found a semi-autonomous Catalan state and was elected its president in the 1930s led Catalonia to fight with the Republicans against Franco when the Civil War broke out. As Franco closed his grip on Barcelona in 1939, Companys went into exile in France, but he didn't remain there long. Following the Nazi invasion of France in 1940 he was arrested by the Gestapo, and the Nazis, who were on good terms with Franco, sent Companys back to Madrid. He was interrogated and tortured for a few weeks before he was sent to Montjuïc castle to be executed. By sending him back to Barcelona Franco was trying to make a point about what he would do to Catalan nationalists under his new regime.

At his execution, Companys, who refused the offer of a blindfold, was taken before a firing squad of Civil Guards. As they fired, he reportedly cried *"Per Catalunya!"* (For Catalonia!). Interestingly, Companys takes the "honour" of being the only incumbent democratically elected president in Western European history to have been executed.

It all made for grim reading, but as I went back outside I was immediately cheered by the fresh air, and I turned to start climbing the hill again. I passed the Botanical Gardens and took in the view of the city once more. As Barcelona began to expand in the late 19th century – the same time as Gaudí was toiling away designing his buildings - Montjuïc was cleared for parkland, and it became a popular recreational spot.

A couple of decades later the hill was selected as the site for the 1929 World's Fair, an international exposition which demonstrated Barcelona's intention to market itself as a great global city. The exhibition was a gathering of people from many parts of the world, and comprised displays promoting products, arts and culture of the different countries that participated, almost like a cultural Olympics. Many of the buildings on Montjuïc date from the Fair, and soon I approached one of the more famous ones: the *Palau Nacional,* meaning the National Palace in Catalan. It's a huge, fabulous construction, built in the renaissance style, resembling a grand parliament building. It was the main exhibition centre for the Fair, and now hosts the National Art Museum of Catalonia (again missing the point Catalonia is not *really* a nation, not yet at any rate). I didn't have time to go in though, so kept walking until I arrived at the Olympic Stadium.

I walked inside, rather surprised to find the stadium not locked. I passed through the concourse, behind the stands and looked out past the track into the centre to the sports field. It was rather strange being in a completely empty stadium, like seeing behind the curtain in a stage show. I stood for a moment contemplating all the great sporting achievements that had taken place here through the ages. The Olympic Stadium was built for the 1929 World's Fair, and was the basis of Barcelona's bid to host the 1936 Olympics. However, Barcelona lost out to Berlin. In the interim the Nazis took power and an international protest movement against them hosting the games swung into force (even as early as 1936 Hitler had got himself *a bit* of a reputation). Barcelona volunteered to host an alternative "People's Olympics"; an idea which won support from several left-leaning countries. However, the outbreak of the Spanish Civil War scuppered these plans. Following the war things didn't get any better for Barcelona, and it endured several dark decades under the dictatorship of Franco. And interestingly, Barcelona's resurgence eventually *did* come thanks to the Olympics. In 1986, a decade after the death of Franco, the return of democracy, and Catalonia's regaining of autonomous status, Barcelona was awarded the 1992 Olympics.

I went back outside and took a final look down on the city before I started the climb back down. Under Franco, with his preference for Madrid, Barcelona had become an industrial backwater, but in the mid-80's preparations for the Olympics began and a massive investment and regeneration of the city was launched. New roads, improved sewage, new green areas and new city beaches were developed. That's right, pre-Olympics there were no beaches in Barcelona - and now they have two miles of them. In a rather visionary move the city made the decision to tear down worn-out industrial buildings at the waterfront, replacing them with beaches and a massive new marina. The economy improved, unemployment halved and tourism surged. Meanwhile the stadium, which was disappearing into the distance as I descended, was completely gutted and refurbished for the showpiece event. A few years later, in 2001, it was renamed as the *Estadi Olímpic Lluís Companys* in honour of the Catalan leader who was executed and buried on Montjuïc sixty years earlier.

***

I didn't have long left in Barcelona, and I was looking forward to moving on. A few weeks had passed and I was definitely in a routine, not an unpleasant one, but I was getting itchy feet. Miguel continued to irritate, confuse and amuse me in equal measure, but I appreciated being able to get out and discover the bars and nightlife of the city with him. Occasionally we were joined by other friends – classmates from school typically, but often it was just the two of us. On one such evening, a few days before my departure, we were in the Gothic Quarter. At Miguel's insistence we were talking to each other in Spanish – broken, halting, grammatically incorrect Spanish, but Spanish nonetheless. Miguel could barrel along at a decent speed, although everything he said was in the present tense, and peppered with errors.

"Hoy estudio cuatro horas y volver a casa para estudiar mas. Me gusta. Tambien, corro cuarenta minutos para ejercicio. Me gusta." (Today I study four hours and to return home to study more. I like it. Also, I run forty minutes for exercise. I like it). It sounded like the garbled ramblings of a drunk, but I had to admire his tenacity. It was better than I could do.

After a little while I grew tired of speaking Spanish, and also of trying to understand him, "Miguel, can we switch to English instead?" I asked, cleverly already switching to English. He looked disappointed, like a child who'd had his lollipop taken away, so I continued. "I had a question to ask you, and it would just be too complicated to do it in Spanish."

At this his eyes lit up, "Ok, what is it?"

I racked my brain, since I didn't have a question, but then one came to mind. "Miguel, where do you see

50

yourself in five years?" *Hmmm, sounds like I'm interviewing him, little bit strange.* But he didn't see it that way, in fact he appeared to take it at face value. And I was genuinely interested. For all the difference in the way he and I saw the world, I always appreciated how much he thought about the future and his efforts for self-improvement.

"This is a good question Ricardo," he paused for a moment. I don't know why, but I rather enjoyed being called Ricardo now. He continued, "Ok, well first, ze most important is my business success," he said definitively. I raised my eyebrows in question and he carried on, "Yes, when I return to Germany I will do my MBA. Then I will start a business. In five years it will be making money," he said confidently.

"What type of business?"

"Pets. I have some new ideas for ze dog products."

"New products for dogs?" I was genuinely intrigued.

"Yes," he said and tapped the side of his nose conspiratorially, as if it was a great secret. "People love zeir dogs."

Unsure if I could get anything more out of him I changed tack, "What else will you have done in 5 years?"

"I zink two more zings are important. First, I will get ripped."

I interrupted, "Get ripped? What do you mean?"

He rolled his eyes, "Get ripped! Muscles, big muscles. Zat is ze plan."

"It doesn't sound like much of a plan," I said, sarcastically.

"I cannot live my life as a puny weakling! I am already putting on muscle mass." It's true, he was always drinking protein shakes and taking supplements, "In five years, no, in one year, I will be, how do you say, hunky beefcake."

"No, I would never say that," I said, honestly. "And what else, you mentioned another thing."

"Yes, also I will have a harem."

I almost spat my beer out, thinking I'd misheard him. "A harem?"

"Yes, I will have many girlfriends. You know."

"No, not really. You don't mean a group of live-in concubines?" I asked jokingly. He looked at me baffled, and I explained. "A harem is a place where a sultan or king kept his many wives and mistresses. They all lived in a special part of his palace and were at his beck and call. I'm guessing that isn't what you mean?"

"No, it means a man who has several girlfriends, like in a rotation, and how do you say, plays ze field. I read about it on ze internet. It sounds good, why not?"

"Well, firstly because it sounds like a huge amount of effort. And besides, how many are we talking about here: more than three? More than six? Double digits?"

Miguel tried to justify himself, "I don't know, but I am young, and I want to be top of ze food chain."

I laughed out loud, "You're not a jungle animal," I said and kept chuckling.

He looked displeased, "Zis is not a funny joke," he said, sounding more German than ever.

"There is another thing," I said and paused, "You do realise that in order to build a harem you'll have to get at least one girlfriend first," I said, laughing again. He screwed up his face, before allowing himself a smile, and then taking another drink. He was a funny guy, and who knows, maybe I would miss him when I left.

Not long later it was my final day of class. I'd mostly enjoyed my few weeks of language learning. The days were short, the classes enjoyable, and I'd grown to like the teacher, despite her refusal to answer any of my questions in English. It was less of an issue now that I was able to express myself in a basic way, even if I did sound like a confused two-year old. Our task on the final day's class was to give a 10-minute presentation on a topic of our choosing, followed by 10 minutes of questions. It was fairly daunting, but we were allowed notes and to show video clips if we wished. I was sixth or seventh up, so I had the chance to see the competition first. An Italian philosophy student called Giacomo, who I'd always been a little wary of, went first. His presentation was on hidden political satire in popular American cartoons of the post-war era. It was a new one on me and a tough start. I had to admit that I found his allegory of Donald Duck as an oppressed worker and his uncle Scrooge McDuck as an unscrupulous capitalist rather tricky to follow. It didn't get any easier when he started comparing the Smurfs to a communist collective. I think I, like the rest of the class, was pretty relieved when he sat down. Although I did at least learn the Spanish word for Smurf *(pitufo)*.

Chandler, the young American college student was next up. Suffice to say it was a sharply contrasting presentation. Chandler had picked the subject of American Football, specifically College (University) Football. He kicked off with a video clip called "Big Hits", which seemed to be a montage of burly men running full pelt at their opponents and cracking their helmeted skulls together. Invariably both men would end up on the floor (presumably with concussion). The running collisions were interspersed with clips of what could only be described as flying headbutts. Rock music blared and Chandler grinned, pointing out any especially big hits with an excited *"Muy grande!"* (Very large). He followed this with a handout depicting five different team uniforms, asking us to rank them in order of what we thought were his favourites. It was pure guesswork, and once again involved conspicuously little Spanish. The presentation did have a certain charm, even if the Belgian, Italian and French students looked completely perplexed. And it was infinitely preferable to hearing any more about the Marxist parallels hidden within *Tom and Jerry*. Chandler sat down, and presentations on the books *Game of Thrones* and the country of Cuba followed.

After the break it was my turn. Recently I had been reading about artificial intelligence and technological developments, so I decided to talk about that. I showed video clips of a driverless car predicting a crash on the motorway a couple of cars ahead and one of a fleet of drones flying in formation, both of which burned some time up. *Two can play at that game, Chandler.* I'd also written notes and partially memorised them, so I had a decent flow, even if I was making lots of mistakes. Next came the question section. Chandler asked about the possibility of flying cars, and I quipped that, "we aren't living in the age of *The Jetsons,* not yet at least." He looked at me blankly, after all he was only 19. I tried to explain who *The Jetsons* were, but it turned out that my Spanish was completely inadequate for such a task. The concept of an old cartoon about the future that had got lots of things wrong was too much for him, and I certainly didn't help matters by bringing up *The Flintstones* – that really did only serve to confuse things further. In the end I decided to cut my losses, and simply said *"Pero, para la pregunta. No, no coches vuelen."* (But, for the question. No, no cars fly.) Not particularly insightful, but it was the best I had.

After that the questions dried up and the teacher did the honours by continuing to interrogate me. Clearly she wanted me to keep talking for the rest of the allotted time, but I did rather get the impression she wasn't listening. She started off with some basic questions about what I thought would be the most important new technology and I blathered on about transport, driverless cars and hyperloop monorails – something I liked talking about since I could use the English word hyperloop as I assumed there wasn't a Spanish word for it yet. Every time I finished my answer she nodded distractedly and said, *"Hmmm, sí, bueno, correcto,"* (Hmmm, yes, good, correct). Still my time wasn't up and she kept asking questions, inquiring whether I thought there were any dangers in new technology. I hesitated. It was tricky: not only did I have to translate word-for-word into Spanish in my head which was a great effort, but I also had to think up a cogent answer to a tricky question.

I went with the "just-start-speaking" strategy which is always a risk. I started tentatively, *"Si... hay peligrosas. Tecnología no es todo bueno.* (Yes there are dangers. Technology is not all good). She looked distracted, so I carried on. After all I had a few bits of vocabulary in my notes that I hadn't used yet. *"Hay problemas en el futuro. Por ejemplo, cuando los robots son inteligente. Ellos quieren tomar el poder, y entonces ellos seran los jefes nuevos, en vez de los humanos."* (There are problems in the future. For example when the robots are intelligent. They want to take power and then they will be the new bosses, instead of the humans), I said. It was certainly a bold statement.

"Si, correcto," (Yes, correct), she said in a preoccupied manner, and went on to ask me a question about space travel.

I couldn't believe it. Did she hear me? The robots will take over and become our leaders? And that's "correct"? Very strange. Did she understand a word I was saying? Or more worryingly, perhaps she knew something I didn't.

Shortly afterwards she brought my presentation to an end. Two more followed (on horse-riding and Buddhism), and that was the end of the class. Those of us who were finishing the course were presented with a certificate. The teacher shook my hand, smiled warmly and said, *"Bien hecho Rich, tu progreso es excelente y has hecho una muy buena presentación."* (Well done Rich, excellent progress and a very good presentation). And that was it. But what was particularly strange was that she never breathed another word about the looming robot takeover.

It was my last morning in Barcelona. As a special treat, instead of cereal, Luisa was making me a fried breakfast. It was the last thing I wanted. It felt quite likely that my body would simply reject any more fried food. It was like a soaking piece of kitchen roll that couldn't absorb any more water. Except I was the kitchen roll, and the water was grease. I didn't want any more, but she was smiling and chattering away as the eggs were popping and the bacon was crackling. *Better to be polite and swallow it down than refuse it and risk being rude. Yes, that made sense. Unless I threw up on myself, which would be pretty much the height of rudeness. Hmmm. Whatever, I'd detox after this,* I thought to myself.

I wanted to say something to her in Spanish, but didn't want to risk anything complicated so tried, *"Mi último día, hoy,"* (My last day, today).

"Qué?" (What?), she barked from the stove.

Seriously? I thought. I repeated it, and thank goodness, she understood. She asked me where I was heading next. I'd given it some serious consideration, toying between various options. One possibility was to head straight to Madrid, but on reflection, having just spent so much time in a big city, I wanted somewhere smaller, and out in the countryside. I looked at the map of Spain. I was in the North East corner, not that far from France. Since I didn't want to go to Madrid in the centre of the country just yet, I had two options. I could track south down the Mediterranean coast, or I could travel north towards the Atlantic and head into the Basque Country. I was already in the North so it made sense to go that way first, then down through Madrid and finally push south and finish in Andalusia. I had a plan then, all I needed now was an exact route. With that in mind, I had visited the train station the previous day and bought myself a ticket to Pamplona, four hours to the north.

I told Luisa where I was headed later that day. She smiled, *"¡Ah, los toros!"* (Ah, the bulls!) she exclaimed. She was referring to the famous running of the bulls which took place through the streets of Pamplona every July. Fortunately it was March, so I had a very low likelihood of getting gored by a bull, but I nodded enthusiastically anyway. After I finished my food I went into my room to pack. A little while later I came back out to say goodbye to Luisa. Luckily Miguel had also finally woken up. He was staying for another week, so this was our goodbye. I gave him a hug.

"Goodbye Miguel, it's been..." He cut me off abruptly.

"Ricardo, en español por favor."

I made a mock sigh, and started again, *"Adiós Miguel, es especial para conocerte"* (Goodbye Miguel, it is special to know you). It wasn't quite what I wanted to say, but maybe it captured my feelings better than I realised.

He beamed, *"¡A ti, tambien!"* (And you, also).

I looked at Luisa, and she gabbled something at me, but rather fittingly I didn't understand a word of it. I wouldn't have had it any other way. I gave her a hug and opened the door of the flat, bag on my back once more, headed down the stairs and started walking to the train station.

Chapter 5 – The bulls

The train pulled away, and gradually we left the centre, then the suburbs of Barcelona behind us. We were speeding directly north-west towards the Atlantic; the Pyrenees (and the French border) were running parallel along our route 70 miles or so to the north. The train moved at a fair clip, and it wasn't long before we were leaving Catalonia and approaching the next state, or to give it its correct name, the "autonomous community", of Aragon. Spain comprises 17 autonomous communities (and two autonomous cities). Previously, Franco had centralised all power in Madrid (and into his own hands). Following his death and the transition to democracy, decentralisation began in 1978.

Each of the 17 communities were granted differing degrees of power through their own regional parliaments. Although this was a result of moving from dictatorship to democracy, it actually had its roots much further back - pre-16th century - when Spain was a series of kingdoms. The map of the autonomous communities bears a lot of similarities to the kingdoms that existed in medieval times. Intriguingly those communities that have a greater sense of national and linguistic identity (Catalonia, the Basque Country etc) have been granted a significantly higher degree of autonomy and independence than those communities thought of as more traditionally Spanish (Extremadura, Murcia etc.). And Spain *has* done a good job of decentralising power compared to most other countries – only 18% of government spending is directed from Madrid, and the majority of civil servants are employed by regional governments, not the central government. However, as we left Catalonia I wondered if it was really enough, and whether one day Catalonia would break free and claim independence.

We crossed over into Aragon. Undulating, verdant rural farmland with sparse clutches of houses here and there passed by my window. Population-wise Aragon is one of the smaller communities of Spain, (the biggest three are Andalusia, Catalonia and Madrid), but size-wise it is one of the biggest. The Pyrenees and its foothills occupy huge swathes of the north of Aragon, but the territory also extends hundreds of miles south and inland as well. More than half of the 1.3 million Aragonese live in the capital city, Zaragoza, probably because both the mountains and the baked interior have a tough climate, albeit in different ways. The train continued to speed through the countryside; my destination was still a couple of hours north. The scenery began to change, the dark green fields and outcrops of trees gave way to a patchwork of carefully-tended fields of gold and jade. We had entered Navarre.

An hour or so later we pulled into the train station in Pamplona, which was listed in my guidebook as Pamplona/Iruña. The second name, Iruña, revealed I was close to the Basque Country, albeit technically not yet in it. Navarre lies south east of the autonomous community of the Basque Country, but there are still plenty of Basque speakers in Navarre – around 12% having it as a first language, and a further 8% bilingual. However, for me learning Spanish was causing enough problems, and I didn't want to even consider getting involved with another language.

I left the train station and headed to my hostel, walking first through ordinary looking city streets, until I came to the impressive and imposing city walls. In the 16th century 5km of walls were built around the city to protect it from invaders. These walls were particularly important given Pamplona's strategic location close to the neighbouring kingdom of France. Throughout the middle ages Navarre went from independence, to rule by Spanish Kings, to rule by the French, and back again, with a dizzying frequency. Throughout this period Pamplona remained the key to both Navarre and the foothills at the bottom of the Pyrenees. I approached the walls and passed through a stone archway fittingly called the "Gateway of France", one of six entrances, and the one used by any travellers who arrived from that country in centuries gone by.

I walked the narrow, cobbled streets of the old town. The place had a quiet charm, very different to Barcelona. However, in a few months the town would transform. Pamplona is famous for the San Fermin festivities, when people run through these streets chased by six angry and dangerous bulls. The "running of the bulls" takes place every day for a week. It was crazy to think people participated in this activity voluntarily. Yet hundreds take part daily, and more than a million come to enjoy the festivities from the safety of the sidelines each year.

The festivities trace their roots back to the 12th century, while the running of the bulls supposedly began in the 14th century. In the middle ages the bulls were led from the countryside to the bullring for the afternoon's bullfights. Legend has it that as the bulls made their way through the streets of the town local youths showed their bravery by running amongst them. Now, as then, the six bulls that run through the streets in the morning are the same who fight (and are killed) in the bullring that evening. The only difference is that in the past the bulls only chased local idiots, whereas nowadays they chase idiots who have flown in specially for the occasion. And, obvious as it seems, it bears mentioning that it *is* dangerous. 15 people have been killed since 1925, which doesn't sound that bad, until you hear that on average 200 to 300 people get injured *every year.* And it's not just sprained ankles and broken legs; some of these people get badly gored. I would imagine any level of goring is bad, even a very light goring. Goodness knows what it's like to be unlucky enough to be *badly* gored.

I made my way to my accommodation, where I checked in and dropped my bag. I'd gone cheap by staying in a hostel (after all, I was travelling for three months), but I had at least booked a private room instead of a multi-person dormitory. I liked being around backpackers, but not *that* much. I relaxed in my room for a few minutes and then wandered through the common area, where I noticed some rather scruffy looking people. Clearly, they had just arrived as they had small backpacks at their feet. They looked exhausted and I realised they were hikers. They seemed too tired to chat, and besides there was still some of the afternoon left for me to explore the city.

I walked back through the streets, and passed some bars, most of them serving *pinchos*, which are the speciality of the Basque region. I stopped at one, ordered a beer and looked along the bar at the various offerings where a smorgasbord of little plates were laid out in two rows. *Pinchos* (or *pintxos* in Basque) are like tapas, but on a cocktail stick. Fittingly *pincho* in Spanish means spike, and curiously the individual *pinchos* themselves had strange names. I looked down the blackboard menu, unable to make sense of the strange metaphorical names. For example, *"Crujiente Ropa"* (Crunchy clothes), *"Come mis orejas"* (Eat my ears) and *"Migas con buenas recuerdas"* (Crumbs with good memories). A strange mix. The vague "crumbs" was the only word that even hinted at food. I ordered a couple at random and fortunately when the *pinchos* arrived they were delicious, perfect little bundles of food skewered together. Slices of ham, wedges of aubergine and cubes of cheese all impaled on a little stick.

I took to the streets again and went for a wander. I passed several hikers, all coming from the same direction, and all looking exhausted. They were easy to spot, carrying backpacks and walking sticks, halfway-to-filthy and nearly dead on their feet. As I walked I noticed various shops and services that seemed to be catering specifically to them: foot massages, blister treatments, foot baths and so on. The feet-based economy was clearly booming here in Pamplona.

I kept walking through the pedestrianised old town, observing the odd hiker and small groups sitting in the bars. Finally, I came around a corner and saw the cathedral at the top of a rise. I walked towards it slowly, suddenly aware how quiet it was. There was no one else around at all. I reached the top and took a closer look at the cathedral. It was square, with two flat fronted towers, and a small columned entrance. The sandstone looked attractive in the afternoon light, but the cathedral seemed a little squat, as though they had found this rather convenient spot on a hill, close to the centre of the city, and just perched the cathedral there.

I did a quick tour of the outside, before heading in. I passed through the nave of the cathedral and went immediately out the side to look at the well-preserved 13th century cloisters. They were very impressive and gave a wonderful sense of connecting the grand old building to its peaceful inner garden. I strolled through the passageway, walking slowly – something about the history of the place encouraged me to take my time. I re-entered the main chamber and noted the high vaulted ceilings and the gothic arches. It was peaceful inside in a familiar way, and I sat down on a pew to reflect for a moment.

I explored the back part of the cathedral and saw that a doorway led to a museum. It was well laid out and told the history of both the cathedral and Pamplona in general. Pamplona was founded by the Romans in 74 BC when their rule extended throughout the Iberian Peninsula, but was later sacked by the Visigoths, who also famously sacked Rome. They loved a good sacking. They were basically the management consultants of 5th century Europe.

Later rule of Pamplona passed between the local Basques, Navarrese Kings and the French. In the 8th century the Moors – the Arabic Muslims who had their base in Southern Spain (of which more later) – took Pamplona. During the 9th century the Basques and Moors intermittently held control of this key settlement. Pamplona and this part of Navarre marked the furthest extent of the territory held by the Moors. It's interesting to note that Pamplona lies only about 50 miles from the north coast of Spain and the Atlantic Ocean, and is even closer to modern day France, and at that time the writ of the Moors (under their Caliphate) encompassed everything south of there. All of that territory was ruled from their capital Córdoba in Andalucía. The museum laid it out in a neat timeline, and noted that Pamplona, which was mainly built around its fortress until the early middle ages, only experienced a boom when the pilgrimage - the Way of St. James *(El camino de Santiago)* – began in earnest in the late 11th century.

The Camino was described as having a resurgence in modern times. Presumably that explained all these hikers I had seen. Apparently, they were retracing the medieval pilgrimage from France all the way across Spain to the city of Santiago in the far West of the country, to see the bones of the apostle of St. James. The standard route from the French side of the Pyrenees to Santiago was over 800 kilometres. *Rather them than me,* I thought, *were there no buses in Spain?* I moved on to another room of the museum, empty, except for the sound of Gregorian chanting. I went to the far wall and saw that each individual voice of the Gregorian chant was coming from an individual speaker. I stood and listened for a minute and quickly realised I wasn't in to Gregorian chanting. *Was anyone? No wonder you never heard it on the radio,* I thought.

I passed back into the main part of the cathedral and took a final look around, before I walked back to the hostel. I entered the common room and sat down on one of the couches. The energy in the room was still low, people lounged around, one or two listlessly watching the TV and a couple more on phones and tablets. A few minutes later a pretty young woman with jet black hair wandered into the room and spoke to the girl who was sitting across from me.

"I just finished with the masseuse. You were next, yes?" the black-haired woman said. The other girl nodded in affirmation, rose and walked slowly out of the room. I could see she had blue sports tape bandaging her knee and her gait had the faintest hint of a limp.

I was intrigued, so I struck up a conversation with the black-haired woman, "So are you doing the walk...the pilgrimage?"

"The Camino?" she asked, I nodded, and she continued. "Yeah I've been going five days. I started in Saint Jean." She looked at me expectantly, and I realised she thought I was doing the pilgrimage too.

"Me? No! The pilgrimage? The Camino? Of course not." She looked slightly affronted, and I realised I had protested a little too much, so I backpedalled. "I'm travelling around Spain for a few months, and I've only just found out about it." She looked a little happier, so I carried on, "I'm really taken with it actually, and I was thinking I might do it in the future." It was a lie, but did that matter? *Was lying about pilgrimages more serious than regular lying? Seemed like there might be a rule about that.*

"Cool!" she said enthusiastically. "You know what? You should come out with me tomorrow and walk for a few hours, so you can get the feel of it, and see if you want to do it in the future!"

"Yeah. That could be great!" I said, thinking that it sounded distinctly un-great.

She'd really warmed up now, "I'm hungry, would you like to go for dinner? And I can tell you some more about it?" She flashed an attractive smile. *Now that did sound great,* I thought.

Chapter 6 – The Camino

The alarm clock showed 5.40am. I could hear people moving around in the hallway outside. *Why the hell was I awake?* I didn't want to be, but I had idiotically agreed to walk with the woman from last night, even though she had insisted on 6am. Considering it was a religious walk, that seemed like a distinctly unholy time. Letitia, from Lithuania, had seemed nice though, and like she wanted the company. So I thought, *why not?* But nice as she had seemed, right now bed seemed a whole lot nicer. I wanted to go back to sleep. I wondered if I'd ever agreed to meet someone at 6am before. *Doesn't sound like something I'd normally do.* But there was nothing for it. I'd agreed. It would be worse if she knocked on my door and I was still in bed. *It would definitely be awkward if she came in and saw me. Harder still for me to explain, "The lazy pilgrim, that's me! Just call me Mr Snooze Button!" I could say cheerily. No, that wouldn't go down well. Not at all.* Reluctantly, I swung my legs out of bed, sat up, rubbed my eyes, and finally staggered towards the bathroom.

I had a quick shower, dressed hurriedly, grabbed my small backpack, then left the room. She was already waiting in the lobby, walking boots on, trekking sticks in hand, medium sized backpack on her athletic, slender frame. She looked sprightly and happy. *Eurgh, was she a morning person?* I hoped not.

"Hi Rich! How are you doing this morning?" She asked in her typical smiley way. *Yes, she **was** a morning person.*

"Yeah. Umm good I suppose," I said, revealing myself to be the opposite of a morning person. I barely sounded human.

She laughed, "Don't worry, we'll get a coffee on the way to wake you up, sleepyhead!" I tried to smile, but I think it ended up somewhere between a grimace and a wince. She laughed again and punched me on the arm. She was making the best of it. *Why did people have to try and make the best of it at 6am? Why couldn't I just suffer silently for an hour or two?*

I followed her out of the hostel and on to the pedestrianised street. It was still dark and cold. I could see other walkers ahead of us in ones, twos and small groups. There was a surprising number about. I guess Pamplona was a common place to stop and this whole pilgrimage thing was more popular than I'd realised, but something still bothered me.

"Letitia, why have we started at 6am?" I tried not to sound accusatory. I needn't have worried though.

"Because this is the best time to start. Everyone starts early on the Camino!"

"Right. But why do they start so early? It's still dark. I can't really see where we're going. Do you walk so late in the day that you need to get started at 5.30am?"

"Noooo," she gave a short cheery laugh, "Normally I finish at about 2pm or 3pm." I was perplexed, she could sense it and continued, "You start early, so you can finish in the afternoon, and get something to eat, have a chat, rest and wash your clothes. I do that every day, as I packed light," she tapped her backpack. I hadn't realised, but I guess she had everything she needed for her five week walk on her back. Yet the backpack was surprisingly small.

"Seriously?" I looked again at her pack, "How many clothes do you actually have?"

"Two sets! Walking clothes and relaxing clothes." I was surprised, but she *was* a pilgrim. This wasn't a fashion show.

A few minutes later we found a café. I ordered a *café con leche* and a pastry, both of which were very welcome. The room was packed with other walkers and it was only 6.15am. I was surprised that the café was even open, but clearly it was another part of the underground pilgrim-based economy. I chatted with Letitia about why she was doing the Camino; she had just finished a long internship after university and would be starting work in the summer, so had some months off. However, she quickly moved on to the subject of her controlling boyfriend, who she claimed maintained an intolerable, yet conflicting, level of jealousy and distance. Her solution had been to put some real distance between them by going on this pilgrimage. I was surprised by how open she was. The issues came out, one after the other, but I appreciated her frankness. I didn't know whether she was just an open person or whether she was in a Camino mindset. Either way, having a coffee and listening to a Lithuanian lady tell me her about her boyfriend troubles at 6.30am was not what I'd expected to be doing when I pulled into Pamplona's train station the previous day.

Abruptly Letitia drained her coffee and stood up in one swift move, "Right, let's get going. Time to hit the road!"

I still hadn't properly woken up, and was acutely aware that my bed was still waiting - lonely and empty - and less than a 15-minute walk away, but there was no going back now. Well, not until the afternoon at any rate, so I too finished my coffee. I wanted to draw it out, but only froth remained and Letitia was eyeing me closely. I picked up my pack and we set off again.

The streetlights guided the way as we moved through the still and quiet city. Over the tops of the buildings the merest hint of morning light was softening the black sky at the edges. Letitia was confidently leading, which begged a question in my mind.

"Letitia, how do you know the way? Do you have a map?"

"A map? No! Of course I don't have a map!" She said, as though I'd asked a stupid question.

I thought for a moment. This was a woman who was walking more than 800 kilometres, on her own, in a country she had never been to before. *How the fuck, or more accurately, why the fuck, did she not have a map? Was she crazy?* "Ummm, Letitia, are you actually crazy? Why don't you have a map?"

"Because you don't need one. Look," she pointed. There was a small silver disc inlaid into the stone of the pavement. It had a drawing of a shell on it, "These markers lead the way."

"All the way to Santiago?" I looked closer. It was a little plaque, "But they can't have these for 800 kilometres."

"True, these are the official markers. Sometimes there are signposts, and often people paint an arrow on a wall or on the ground."

"Really?"

"Yeah, yellow arrows. Always yellow. They are everywhere." Sure enough, within a couple of minutes she spotted one on a wall. It looked like an insignificant piece of graffiti. I'm sure I would have never noticed it. "Those arrows are the most common signs. I think volunteers paint them. I've only been lost on the Camino once, and I've walked 100 kilometres."

"That's impressive," I said.

"Well, to be honest, you are always heading in the same direction! It's always due west, so it doesn't vary that much! Plus there are other people walking, so you can look for them." I looked around and saw a couple of pilgrims marching on in the distance. Evidently she was right, or at least not completely mad.

Around 7.30am we were on the very outskirts of Pamplona. In the early morning light, the houses rather

73

suddenly gave way to fields. It struck me that I had never walked from the centre of a city, through its suburbs to its outskirts, and then out into fields. *Of course I hadn't. I would, and should, have taken a bus today,* my mean-spirited conscience piped up. Clearly that wasn't the point, and I *was* enjoying it. However, I was conscious that every step I walked away from Pamplona was one I would have to retrace later.

"I don't know how far to go today. How far are you walking?" I asked Letitia.

"I don't like to plan too much, but normally around 25 kilometres," she said. I was impressed. That was considerably further than a half marathon, and she did that every day, and would do so for five weeks, with a pack on her back. "If you want to do the same, then I reckon we'll get to the halfway point in a couple of hours, and we can have a break there together."

"That seems like a long way. I'm not really sure I'm a 25 kilometre kind-of-a-guy. Maybe I'll turn around in a bit."

"Come on! You've only done 5 kilometres! And besides the halfway mark is a hill that is the highest point on this section of the Camino."

I was unsure, "Trying to convince me to walk further by explaining there's a huge hill at the end doesn't seem like a winning tactic. It sounds pretty tiring."

"Sorry if it's too much for you, Grandma!" she said, and laughed.

"No need to be sexist and ageist…" I muttered and kept walking.

Out in the countryside we passed through golden wheat fields. The sky was a pleasant light blue and dotted with clouds, the sun warming, but far from hot. Nevertheless, I removed my coat and jumper and put it in my small pack. I was pleased I wasn't carrying a bag as heavy as Letitia's. She shifted the shoulder straps, momentarily putting her fingers inbetween the straps and her shoulders, lifting the weight. *Maybe I should offer to carry it?* I wondered. *Don't want to appear sexist though. Good old modern day equality - fraught with the ever-present danger of a sexist faux pas, but at least I don't have to carry her pack.*

We continued walking and talking. I had to admit I enjoyed being out in the fresh air. An hour or two of pleasant hiking along the side of more wheat fields eventually finished when we began our ascent up the hill, the *Alto del Perdón* (the Mount of Forgiveness). It wasn't too steep, but it was relentless. Soon we stopped talking, instead giving in to the sole task of climbing. As we ascended the views of the plain beneath us began to open up and a collage of fields was visible. High above us, along the ridge line I could see wind turbines, like the spikes on the spine of a huge lizard. I focused on my feet again, putting one foot in front of the other, making the effort to keep up with the steady pace of Letitia. She was fit, no doubt about that, but I was stubborn. Which, while not technically as good, was enough for appearance's sake.

Eventually we reached the top. We could see over both sides of the ridge now. It felt like we were on the crest of two waves surging up to meet each other. On the ridge line the wind blew strongly, buffeting us as we stood and took in the view. Down below the plains and fields pushed out on each side. Calm, rural, unchanging.

I looked around the summit. There was a huge cast iron statue of 14 silhouettes, pilgrims leaning forward, braced against the wind. The silhouettes, some on horseback, some walking, were framed by the hills and fields in the distance. This place seemed majestic and grand, yet the sculpture placed the individual pilgrims at the centre of it. The inscription was dedicated "to the place where the path of the wind crosses that of the stars" and paid tribute to all the pilgrims who had climbed this hill over the centuries. Letitia read from her guidebook; apparently this hill marked the point on the route where pilgrims obtained forgiveness for their sins and their spiritual health was guaranteed, even in the event of their death on the Camino. I found that rather troubling. It seemed like a rum deal if you left your village in medieval France, walked hundreds of kilometres, but died earlier than this point - in the Pyrenees for example. Then you received no forgiveness at all. Yet if you made it to this particular hill suddenly everything was forgiven? It all seemed rather arbitrary. And what about me? I'd made it up the hill. True I'd started in Pamplona and was about to turn back, but you know, *I was* at the top of the hill, so I assumed it counted. The rules are the rules.

The Camino started in medieval times when word spread that the bones of the apostle James had been found. Various stories about the bones and their journey from the Holy Land to Spain perpetuate. Their discovery centuries later by a hermit in the far North West of the country is also steeped in legend, but we do know that in the 9th century the bones were declared real by the local Bishop. A cathedral was built in Santiago (literally meaning Saint James) and pilgrims began making their way there. By the late 11th century visitors from further afield were also journeying to Santiago. English travellers began making the pilgrimage to Santiago from 1092 using ships that left the south coast of England for a somewhat perilous crossing to the north coast of Spain. From there the pilgrims walked 100km inland to Santiago.

The fame of the Camino grew throughout Europe in the early 12th century. It fed the growing appetite amongst the pious population of the middle ages to prove their devotion to God. People did the Camino for multiple reasons: to get closer to God, to show their devotion or perhaps because of a vow. People who were ill or in danger often asked God or a saint to help them and promised to go on a pilgrimage if their wishes were granted. It would be foolhardy to go back on a promise to God after He had granted what you asked for. Some were motivated by a belief in miracles; the sick or injured thought a pilgrimage could cure them and started making their way to Santiago. This was one reason there were so many hospitals on the route, because so many people were already sick. Sometimes people even did the pilgrimage on behalf of a relative, as an act of supplication to God to request intervention for them to recover.

Around 1140, the Camino gave rise to the Codex Calixtinus, perhaps the world's first guidebook. The text, also known as the Book of St James, is actually five books, covering the story of St James, miracles associated with him, sermons and history. Book five, described as a guide for the traveller outlines towns and stages, "so that pilgrims setting out for Santiago, hearing this, can work out the expenses necessary for their journey." This strikes me as futile. Everyone knows the prices in guidebooks are always out of date, even more so when the original print run was in the previous century. The Codex also contained a section on the "Perils of local food" and even a guide to the local people pilgrims were likely to encounter. The French author didn't seem keen on the people of Navarre:

> They're malicious, dark, hostile-looking types, crooked, perverse, treacherous, corrupt and untrustworthy, obsessed with sex and booze, steeped in violence, wild, savage, condemned and rejected, sour, horrible, and squabbling. They are badness and nastiness personified, utterly lacking in any good qualities...Navarrese eating and drinking habits are disgusting. The entire family - servant, master, maid, mistress - feed with their hands from one pot in which all the food is mixed together, and swill from one cup, like pigs or dogs. And when they speak, their language sounds so raw, it's like hearing a dog bark.

I'm guessing that's a 1-star review. There are also some rather less heated sections in the book, including tombs to be visited, which rivers to cross and which to avoid, and a detailed description of the cathedral in Santiago. However, the majority of the Codex is concerned with the spiritual elements of the pilgrimage, as this was what the medieval pilgrim was seeking. As the Codex says:

> The pilgrim route is for those who are good: it is the lack of vices, the thwarting of the body, the increase of virtues, pardon for sins, sorrow for the penitent, the road of the righteous, love of the saints, faith in the resurrection and the reward of the blessed, a separation from hell, the protection of the heavens.

The Camino further gained in popularity in the 12th century when Popes Calixto II and Alexander III established the idea of the "Jacobean Holy Year". It was declared that all Christians who made the pilgrimage would have their time in purgatory reduced or eliminated altogether. Catholics (unlike other Christians) believe that when you die you enter the intermediate state of purgatory if you have not reached a sufficient level of holiness in life to enter heaven. However, any pilgrim who completed the Camino had their time in purgatory halved. In a holy year (i.e. when the festival of St James falls on a Sunday) pilgrims would have their time in purgatory completely waived. Understandably the number of pilgrims walking the Camino in a holy year was significantly higher than normal. The tradition persists to this day and the last holy year (in 2010) recorded the second highest number of pilgrims in the modern era - 272,000.

Letitia and I took in the view and went and sat down by a snack van that had made it up the hill. Perhaps it too had been granted forgiveness. I hoped not, as the food was awful, but who knows. We sat down together and looked out over the plains. She cast her glance west, she had nearly 700km still to walk. I had a rather less impressive 12.5km in the other direction, but it still felt far. I told her I was pleased she had encouraged me to join her.

She smiled, "Just another day on the Camino," and gave me an affectionate punch on the arm. After a while she said she had to leave and we hugged. We turned and went in opposite directions, both of us with a steep descent ahead of us.

It wasn't yet midday and I observed that, as Letitia told me, I was now walking into the sun. Before it had been directly behind us, casting our shadows on the path in front. Letitia had told me that modern pilgrims only tended to walk *to* Santiago, yet in centuries gone by, pilgrims had to walk back home again. Only the most traditional and/or masochistic pilgrims walked back these days. And all this walking *was* tough. It was hotter now, the sun was in my eyes, and I didn't have Letitia for company. Nevertheless, the exercise was good for me. I started to sweat and I imagined the daily fried feasts that I'd enjoyed at Luisa's house in Barcelona being worked off.

I got towards the bottom of the hill and pressed on past the same wheat fields I'd passed a few hours earlier.

There weren't many people walking in the opposite direction; there was no one walking in mine. The few people that did pass me offered the standard greeting of *"Buen Camino!"* One or two eyed me up, curiously, offering me a polite nod of the head. Clearly a few thought I had already walked all the way to Santiago.

"*Buen Camino!* Are you walking back now?" One young man asked me, not really stopping, swivelling to listen to my answer.

"Sure, I'm walking back now," I shouted, as the distance between us stretched out. He gave me the thumbs up. *Why ruin it? I was walking back, that much was true. I mean, yes, I'd only made it as far as the snack van on the top of the hill a few kilometres away, but yeah, I was walking back.*

The kilometres crunched slowly underfoot. I was tired now, and it was hot on the shadeless path. I wondered if I could ever walk the whole thing. It would be a challenge, although I had enough of that with the language. I also had a lot more of the country to see, but maybe one day I would. Eventually the outskirts of the city came into view. I drew it in slowly, each kilometre harder than the last. Finally, I reached the outermost suburb of Pamplona, and found a café. I hadn't seen another walker in an hour or two and I was glad of the rest. My feet were overheating and I was developing a blister, I could feel it. I sat for at least an hour, pleased not to be walking, until I realised I had to get back. I picked myself up for another tiring hour of walking. I'd had enough really: I was dragging myself through the streets of Pamplona. Eventually I started to see the familiar signs for massages and foot baths, and suddenly I could see the appeal. *No harm in seeing what it's like*, I thought, and made a beeline for the nearest place.

Chapter 7 – Surf's up

I passed another amiable day in Pamplona, resting up my tired legs and deciding what to do next. I took my guidebook to a bar, ate some *pintxos* and planned a route. I would keep going north - I wasn't far from the Atlantic and the Bay of Biscay. Due north was the Basque Country proper, and I could visit the fashionable seaside city of San Sebastián. After that I would turn west and visit Bilbao, the largest city and unofficial "capital" of the Basque Country.

The following morning I headed to the bus station in Pamplona. On the way I observed a few straggling pilgrims, backpacks on, walking sticks clicking on the pavement as they went by. I descended the escalator into the bus station which, rather strangely, seemed to be located wholly underground, and looked for the bus to San Sebastián. I walked along the line of buses and soon enough saw the one labelled "San Sebastián/Donostia" (which is the Basque name for the city).

The journey was an easy hour and twenty minutes through pleasant countryside which became more undulating, almost mountainous as we entered the Basque Country (*País Vasco* in Spanish and *Euskadi* in Basque). It's an unusual place; the greater Basque Country, as opposed to the official autonomous community (which is smaller), stretches across the North East of Spain from the coast in the north, to the region of Navarra in the south, and then over the Pyrenees into the very Southwest corner of France.

The Basque language *(Euskara)* is a complete outlier, bearing no resemblance to the Latin languages that predominate elsewhere in the region. Even now linguists and historians are at a loss to explain where it comes from or how it evolved. Languages in adjoining regions normally have a lot in common with each other. For instance, French, Spanish, Catalan, Portuguese, Italian and so on are Romance languages, all derived from Latin and all reasonably similar. However, Basque is completely isolated. It is one of the few remaining examples of a pre-Indo-European language (i.e. it pre-dates Latin and other ancient languages such as Celtic) in Europe. It also has seemingly nothing in common with any other living language, making it hard for outsiders to learn. It looks very different to Spanish and is immediately recognisable with its heavy use of the letters x, k, z which are found less frequently in Spanish. Basque has given many words to the Spanish language, and even a few to English, the most common two being: anchovy, which came via Portuguese, and bizarre, which came through 16th century French. Legend has it that this originated from the Basque word "bizar" which means beard, as the French supposedly found the marauding (and bearded) Basque warriors strange and odd-looking, and coined the term accordingly.

The Basque language had been declining over several centuries, but the arrival of the dictator Franco, who ruled Spain until the 1970s, provided it an unexpected boost. Franco was as intolerant of Basque as he was of Catalan. Public use of any language other than Spanish was discouraged and seen as a sign of separatism. However, in direct opposition to his rule (perhaps even because of it), public consciousness of the Basque identity and language started to grow. This legacy of repression continues to give Spain problems with its regions today, many of which have strong separatist movements. Yet the form and path that nationalism took in Catalonia is very different to what happened in the Basque Country. In Catalonia the movement was slower, subtler and very political, whereas the independence movement in the Basque Country exploded violently in the 1960s with the terrorist group, ETA.

As I pulled into the bus station in San Sebastián, that violent past seemed a world away. Instead I found a pleasant bustling city, with people strolling along and gliding by in the cycle lanes. I left the bus station, and walked along the wide River Urumea. I followed it towards the sea and saw that it split the city in two. It would have been an agreeable fifteen-minute stroll, if it wasn't for the fact I was rolling my suitcase behind me. I'm unsure why, but there's something revealing and awkward about having to wheel a suitcase around a city. It always feels desperately uncool, like strolling about after you have split your trousers. Yet logically, it's a perfectly natural thing to have just arrived with a case in tow. Infinitely worse, and probably ultimately less cool, would be arriving with no case or spare clothes.

The very worst experience of the rolling case parade is when your roll-y case meets cobbles. That really is embarrassing. It is so out of place – it's like a tractor on a motorway. Mercifully San Sebastián seemed free of cobbles, and soon enough I reached the bridge connecting the two waterfront parts of the city. I turned right and went to Playa Zurriola (also known as Gros) which is the newer part of town. I passed by some neat and tidy early twentieth century buildings, and through a smart pedestrianised area. The blocks were laid out in a grid and I quickly found my bearings and managed to locate the apartment that I was renting. I half-wheeled, half-dragged my case up the stairs and opened the door to my small, but neat, one-bedroom apartment. I opened the wooden doors on to the little balcony and looked out at the city. Finally, having offloaded my suitcase I could go back out and start enjoying myself.

I strolled down to the beach, which was only a few blocks away. San Sebastián is a well-to-do city, noticeably upmarket and trendy. I passed some bars, pintxos were lined up on display. San Sebastián is famous for its food - both for the breadth and quality of pintxos, but even more so for fine dining. A city of only 200,000 people, San Sebastián reputedly boasts more Michelin stars for its restaurants per capita than anywhere else on earth. Perhaps it's the coastal location, the excellent seafood, the city's position on the edge of Spain, nestling up to France, or perhaps Michelin starred chefs just like to surf, as that is San Sebastián's other claim to fame. Consistently rated as one of the top ten surfing spots in Europe, the waterfront was peppered with surf shops, offering lessons and rentals. I eyed one up and wandered in. I browsed the surfwear and the huge rack of impressive boards. I'd only ever surfed once before; my main memory was of repeatedly falling off. That and the taste of salt water. Yet I used to skateboard as a teenager, and I'd always liked the idea of surfing. So when a shop assistant came over and asked me if I was considering a surfing lesson, for some reason I blurted out yes. A few minutes later I had signed up for a 2-hour surfing lesson the following morning. It seemed like a good time to retreat, before I found myself walking out in a brand new wetsuit, and surfboard under my arm.

I meandered along the seafront and stopped for a few minutes on the stone wall to watch the surfers a few hundred metres out to sea. They bobbed about, riding the small swells, waiting for the onrush of a big wave. All of a sudden, several started paddling furiously, like inmates receiving the cue to make a desperate bid for freedom. A couple caught the crest, riding it majestically through its surging approach to shore. It was mesmerising to watch. Dozens of people lined the stone wall looking out to sea, spectating. I sat for a while, tuning in to the ebb, flow and swell of the sea. Eventually I decided to continue my walk towards the old town.

I left the beach behind and got to the bridge that crossed the river. Several grand buildings lined the other side. San Sebastián had been flattened by Napoleon's invading armies in the early 19th century, but this allowed the town to build again from scratch, and fortunately this was during a period of attractive architecture. I lived for a while in Coventry in the UK, a city of such unremitting ugliness you would think it would have a great personality (it doesn't). Coventry was unlucky enough to be bombed to smithereens in the Second World War and to compound its misfortune, its rebuilding period took place during the 1950s and 1960s. The architecture of the time was as uninspired and insipid as any in history. Boxy concrete buildings, multi-storey car parks, and assorted offences to visual sensibility make up the bulk of Coventry now. Yet San Sebastián had been rebuilt in the 19th century in the classical European style. Everywhere I looked were beautiful Art Nouveau and classical buildings (although to be fair, it might be easier to find parking in Coventry).

I passed over the bridge and admired the Hotel Maria Cristina, a huge belle epoque hotel which opened in 1912. Throughout the second half of the 19th century San Sebastián experienced a renaissance. The city became a fashionable tourist destination for the well-heeled classes from Madrid who wanted to escape the fierce summer heat. They also wanted to take advantage of the newly advocated therapeutic practice of bathing in the sea. San Sebastián capitalised, moving its shipyards out of town and remodelling itself as a glamorous and upmarket destination. The impressive city hall, striking theatre and this hotel, named and then opened by the Spanish Queen of the time, were all built then.

I kept walking, but before long decided to head into a bar. I'd only had a snack for lunch and I could see an inviting array of *pintxos* through the window. I ordered a beer and a couple of *pintxos* which the barman heated up for me. I ate them in turn: a skewer of prawns, and then a little plate of tortilla, the wedge of omelette that is common all over Spain. While I ate, I flicked through my guidebook and saw a section detailing the best *pintxo* bars of the city. Most of them were in close proximity and the afternoon and evening laid itself open before me. Off I went: green *padrón* peppers here, cod in rich tomato sauce there, arancini rice balls, more prawns, little fried octopuses, plates of mushrooms, and beer, always a beer at each place. I couldn't exactly order food without a beer. I chatted to the barmen, read my guidebook, and ate and drank to my heart's content. By my sixth, seventh or eighth bar (I'd stopped counting) I was full to bursting and more than a little tipsy. It was the middle of the evening and with only a vague idea where my apartment was, I rose and headed back along the seafront and over the bridge.

***

My alarm went off. *Why did I put an alarm on? Oh yes. I had a surfing lesson. Why had I signed up for a morning surfing lesson? Don't know. Want to go back to sleep. Can't. Surfing lesson. Was I tricked in to this? Or was it just because I'd seen Point Break too many times when I was a kid?* I just about had my eyes open when the familiar feel of a hangover kicked in. That was the real question. *Why had I gone out boozing the night before a surf lesson?* There were no answers, only consequences. The chief consequence was that I would be surfing while hungover. I dragged myself out of bed, feeling ok and well enough to negotiate dry land at least, then slowly got ready.

I walked the five minutes to the surf shop, entered and approached the shop assistant behind the desk. She looked familiar. I recalled that she was the person who had tricked me into booking the lesson. My hangover surged up in my stomach.

"Hi, yes I'm here for a 10am surfing lesson." I said, in English. I didn't feel up to speaking Spanish.

"Well hello, good morning! Let me just check if it's on, because the sea is really pumping this morning!" her eyes opened wide, presumably to emphasise just how *pumping* the sea was. She turned to ask a colleague something in rapid Spanish. Presumably he would decide if the lesson should go ahead. All of a sudden the idea that it might be cancelled filled my mind. I felt the relief and my hangover start to lessen. Meanwhile another young man had arrived at the counter. He had a beard that was straying between "designer" and "farmer", and was wearing a pair of sunglasses, even though we were indoors. He introduced himself, he was Russ from England, and he told me that he was also in my surf lesson. I looked sceptical, and was about to share the news when the shop lady came back, "Yes the instructor says we can go ahead. The swells are big for beginners but if you two can handle it, it's ok."

I started to stutter, but Russ cut me off, "Sounds great! I think we can handle it," and he slapped me heartily on the back.

How did he know what I could handle? I'm hungover, I wanted to mewl. Instead I just mumbled, "Sure. Sounds good to me." *Stupid pride and stubbornness.* My mind welled up with an image of me swallowing a lot of seawater.

Twenty minutes of wrestling with a wetsuit and carrying a huge foam board barefoot over the road to the beach didn't do anything to improve my hangover, or my opinion of Russ. He was incredibly enthusiastic, and didn't seem concerned in the slightest about the considerable swells and waves rolling in. I wondered if he was a better surfer than our beginner class would suggest. Our instructor, Mateo, was the typical surfer type, long sun-weathered straggly blonde hair, skinny, laidback, full of vacant enthusiasm.

First, he ran us through some stretches on the beach. Then we lay down on our boards to practice paddling. Next, we learnt the three step move to standing up on the board and riding the wave. It wasn't so bad. I was even beginning to forget about the hangover. We did the stand-up routine a few more times. Paddle, paddle, speed up as the wave comes on, grab the sides of the board, bring one foot underneath and push into a crouch, then push the other leg back and assume cool surfer guy stance. Ride swell while waving at adoring surfer girls lining the beach. *Ok, got it Mateo.*

We attached our surfboards to our ankles with a long rubber cord and Velcro strap. Then Russ and I followed Mateo I into the sea. He slid on to his board smoothly, and made a quick paddling motion which scythed him through the breakers until I saw him join a bobbing group of surfers a few hundred metres out. I had barely stepped into the water. It was freezing on my exposed feet. True, it was late March, but I *was* in Spain. Yet the water felt Antarctic. I walked into the sea tentatively. Russ had gone out a lot faster, rushing to keep up with Mateo. I watched him as I walked: he started paddling, and the swell of a wave immediately knocked him off and dunked him, his board exploding vertically upwards. I immediately saw how useful the rubber cord was. Inevitably, I would fall off soon, and not having to chase my board would be one small crumb of comfort. I kept plodding out to sea, like a man walking to his execution, the water up to my waist now, and the board floating next to me. Meanwhile Russ had jumped straight back on his board and was gamely paddling towards Mateo, like a mad dog, excited to be out playing.

After a couple of minutes of wading, swimming, and just about clinging on to the board as the swells rolled through I made it to Mateo. He was pushing Russ to help him catch a wave. I watched Russ make it through two steps of the standing up process, before wiping out.

"Great job, Russ," yelled Mateo. He turned to me, "Right Rich, now your turn," I nodded in resigned defeat. Maybe it was the swell of the waves, but I wasn't feeling good. It didn't matter - Mateo was looking at me expectantly, and he began helping me up onto the board. He held it steady while I clambered up, until I was lying on the board in position. I felt like a sealion trying to get comfortable on some rocks. Once aboard he shouted, "Ok Rich, you wait for the signal. When I say go, you paddle hard - four, five seconds, then you stand up! That's all there is to it man!" He sounded genuinely confident. I had no idea why.

A moment passed and then he gave me the signal. I felt the hefty shove from Mateo and paddled hard. I started to surge forward as the power of the wave caught me. I knew it was time to jump up, although deep down I could sense I was about to ruin a good thing. Nevertheless, I started to go through the routine. I stopped paddling, brought my hands on to the sides of the board smoothly and then beneath me. I moved into step two, pushing myself up and bringing one foot underneath me. Suddenly I felt the nose of the board dip down and the next thing I knew I was being dunked, the board flying up and away from me. I was underwater and then back up again. I took a gasp of air as I came up. *Well, now I've woken up,* I thought. *Albeit in the most horrible way possible.* I flailed around, managed to grab the board, and bobbed for a moment. Then I began slowly swimming back to Mateo.

I repeated the process a couple of times. Once I managed to stand up, and cruised the wave towards the shore, until it petered out and I was in about two feet of water. I hopped off. I wasn't sure if it was an achievement or whether I was a wally. If surfing to the beach *was* the objective, then it was strange that no one else had managed it. I began the long walk, wade, swim, paddle to get back to Mateo. He set me up again and off I went, this time just as I stood up, an idiot took my wave and headed straight for me. I had no option but to jump off to avoid a collision, and ended up dunking myself. I was furious. *Who was it? Russ? This was exactly the type of thing he would do,* I thought. I spun around in the water, but no, it was some other douchebag. For what it was worth, he appeared almost identical to Russ. I paddled away scowling, although almost immediately the effort of paddling made me forget about scowling.

I reached Mateo, and he set me up once more. He held me in place for a moment, treading water while he waited for the right wave. Suddenly a look of a surprise crossed his face, "Off!" he shouted. It was the code word to jump off and roll under the board because a big wave was coming. But the complicated manoeuvre was completely beyond me, so instead I froze, lying on the board helplessly, as my teacher disappeared under the water. A split second of calm - and then from nowhere a wall of water fell directly on my head. Suddenly I was off the board, upside down, and being sucked under. Down I went, rolling over and over. Unexpectedly, I hit the surface, broke through, and then was pulled under again. I could feel the swell and pull of the energy of the sea. I was at its mercy. I tumbled around, and came back out, gasping for air, but swallowed too soon, getting half a mouthful of salt water. Whatever love I had for surfing was gone, and was replaced in an instant by a doubling of my hangover. I bobbed around for a moment, trying to get my bearings, before I realised I'd been swept a fair distance from Mateo and Russ. I reeled the board in with the cord and looked back. I swear I could see Russ grinning inanely from here. I began to make my way over towards them. I couldn't do this anymore. I felt terrible. *Was I sea sick? Could you be sea sick on a surfboard?*

I finally paddled up to Mateo, *"Mi última vez,"* (my last time), I croaked.

He smiled widely, *"¿Cómo te sientes?"* (You feel ok?)

"Me siento cómo una mierda," (I feel like shit), I replied sincerely. He laughed. *Why was he laughing?* Mateo didn't strike me as a kindly man.

I lay on my board and let Mateo angle it into position. I was like Kate Winslet in *Titanic* – lying on a plank in the ocean, feeling that I might die at any moment. A moment later Mateo gave me the shove, and the wave took me. "Paddle, paddle," Mateo shouted, and I started paddling to catch the speed of the wave. Then, "Up, up!" I could hear his fading voice say, and a voice inside said, *No, just lie down.* So I stayed down, and let my head rest on the board. I could feel the wave carry me in towards the beach as I sailed onwards – I probably looked like a whale gleefully beaching, but it felt good. I didn't move, lying prostate on the board, as if it was a big foam bed. Gently the wave broke, but continued to propel me forwards until the water was no more than knee height. I washed up on the beach, like a man on an ironing board, but I didn't care. I rolled off the board and dragged it a few metres up the beach. I was done. I flopped down in the sand, happy to have the certainty of the solid ground beneath me.

I lay for a while, knowing that my expensive surfing lesson was taking place without me. *Screw it. Russ could fill his boots,* I thought. I continued to lay on the beach, listening to the wave, just relieved that my ordeal was over. Twenty minutes later Russ and Mateo came out of the sea. The lesson had finished.

"Are you ok?" Mateo asked.

I was still lying down. Clearly I didn't look ok, and I didn't raise myself from my horizontal position, "Yep. Good. Just taking stock." I was certain he wouldn't understand that expression, but it didn't seem important. We all knew what was going on.

"It was gnarly!" Russ said. I could imagine that Russ had never used the word *gnarly* before, but since I was lying down smacking him was out of the question.

"Good job guys!" Mateo said mildly. It was hard to argue that I'd done a good job on any level, but I *had* survived. Somehow. I felt like I had been through a washing machine. Like a piece of forgotten tissue, buried in the pocket of some jeans, that never should have gone in, and was now barely holding together. I slowly picked myself up and Mateo led us off the beach. I could still taste the saltwater.

Chapter 8 – Prime time

I did little for the rest of the day, nursing my hangover and recovering from the trauma of the surfing. I stayed in my little apartment and tried to watch some Spanish television, even though it was mostly beyond me. The news presenters seemed to have too much to say and were trying to squeeze it into the time allotted. Nothing else could really explain their rapid-fire rapping style delivery. I caught the odd word, and made some sense from the pictures, but it was tiring. I flicked over and a *Telenovela* was starting. *Telenovelas* (literally television novels) are produced in Latin America, and are the most popular genre of programmes there. It's estimated that over half of Latinos watch them, and they are also popular in Spain too. *Telenovelas* are broadly equivalent to soap operas, but the chief difference is that they end after six months to a year, rather than running indefinitely. Consequently, they have a very defined story arc and are characterised by high drama, such as star-crossed lovers, betrayal, a man on a quest for vengeance or twins separated at birth.

This *Telenovela* was a Mexican one called *Teresa.* From the title sequence alone I could tell the main character, Teresa, was bad, and not just because the lyrics were *"Esa hembra es mala. Es Mala. Mala. Mala."* (That woman is bad. She's bad. Bad. Bad.) But also because she was twirling around, wrapping herself in silks while sneering at anyone else who entered the titles – no mean feat. From what I could make out (and a little searching on the internet) our heroine, Teresa, grew up in grinding poverty (a common theme in telenovelas, given the unequal nature of Latin American society and the fact that poor women make up the majority of viewers). Due to a series of tragedies and humiliations, Teresa vows to do whatever it takes to be rich, essentially becoming, *mala, mala, mala,* as the song suggests. In the couple of episodes I watched, I saw betrayal, cheating, kidnapping, wicked stepmothers and more. High drama indeed. I particularly liked the way the villains self-identified by sporting comedy moustaches, sneering and smirking. They also had a rather reckless tendency of talking to the camera to reveal their evil plan the moment they were alone. Sometimes they barely waited until their unsuspecting victim had left the room. It was almost Shakespearean.

Telenovelas are big business. As well as commanding huge audiences in domestic Latin American markets they do well overseas, including the US, Eastern Europe, Italy, Spain, and even Russia. One Brazilian Telenovela was sold to 87 countries, while other shows, such as "Ugly Betty" were remade for the English-language market.

In Spain the Telenovelas are called *"culebrones"* (literally long snakes) due to their winding, twisting plots. This is perhaps unsurprising, since the programme makers will shoot only around 20 episodes (i.e. four weeks) ahead. This allows them to react to viewers tastes, or end or extend the show according to its popularity. One article described it this way, "Drastic measures are often used to increase ratings: one of Brazil's most famous screenwriters once killed off 35 of a 40-strong cast in an earthquake….

Perhaps more than any other drama genre, telenovelas are reactive to viewers' tastes. Baddies can become goodies and vice versa. In the dialogue between programme-maker and punter, one network receives 250,000 emails and 30,000 calls a month from viewers, and spends millions on research." But even with the massive popularity of Telenovelas in the Hispanic world, the allure of Hollywood is still tempting for the most famous actors. Notable breakout successes include the Mexicans: Salma Hayek and Gael Garcia Bernal, and the Colombian actress, Sofia Vergara. However, watching *Teresa* and seeing the heavily moustachioed villain shark his way across the screen again, I didn't get the sense I was watching a future star.

The following day I was determined to be more active, so I went back to the seafront and rented a bicycle. I walked the few blocks to the beach, past the surf shop, resisted a shudder, and came to the bicycle shop. I selected a trusty steed: shopping basket on the front – tick, bell for warning of impending collisions – tick, gears – three of them, all present and correct. I rode towards the old town, past the aquarium and round the headland to come to the second of San Sebastián's beaches, the impressive *La Concha* beach. I'd rarely seen such a perfect curving bay, encircled by nearly 270 degrees of sand with a mouth out to the ocean, and an island in the middle. I could see immediately why it was named *La Concha* – the shell. The sweeping bay almost seem to hold its water like a lake. The sea was calm and reflected the weak spring sunshine. It was obvious why San Sebastián had become such a popular seaside destination, and also why the surfers chose the other beach. The glassy water would have been perfect for me though, I thought ruefully.

I pedalled on, continuing to admire the beach as I made my way to the far side of the bay. I was heading for a funicular train, which made its way up *Monte Igueldo,* the mountain that towered over the western side of the bay. I parked my bike and paid the €3.20 fee which I thought was quite a lot, given the ride was only about 90 seconds long. Then I reasoned that the train was going both forwards and upwards which is twice as much movement as you get from the average train, so perhaps it was justified. I climbed aboard and the old wooden train set off, proceeding diagonally up the mountain. A moment later we bumped to a halt at the station at the top. I exited and found myself in a *"parque de atracciones"* at the summit of the mountain. It was neither a theme park (it had no theme) nor a fun fair (there didn't look to be any fun on offer). I was hoping for a "so bad, it's good" vibe, but quickly realised it was simply "so bad, it's just really bad". I wandered past the log flume which was almost completely flat, and featured none of the characteristic drops you might expect. It simply skirted around the edge of the park; it looked like an open drainage system as much as anything else. I stopped for a moment at the sad looking dodgems with no one on them. I considered having a go and just ramming the stationary cars, but figured that would be fun for two hits at most, and even that might be stretching it.

I wandered on and saw the looming, gaping open mouth of King Kong set into a wall. It was the entrance to the *"Casa del terror"* (house of horrors). With nothing else to do, I decided to take a quick peek inside. A bored-looking young man sat in the ticket kiosk reading a book. Clearly the ring of terror didn't extend to the reception area. I asked for a ticket and he looked a little surprised. He regarded me sceptically for a moment, as if I'd said, "Hello, I'm a fool and I would like to turn this 5 euro note into a sense of disappointment and displeasure. Could you help me do that as quickly as possible?" However he interpreted it, my fate was sealed and he handed over one adult ticket to the *Casa del terror*.

I stepped through the curtain of beads (surely the scariest of all curtains) and entered the gloom. I tried to make sense of the display in front of me. It was an old stone cottage with a bare wooden table, a few farming tools and stuffed birds on the wall. A pile of sticks were dimly alight, not flickering as such. Instead they cast a steady glow, as if they were switched on. I looked at the stuffed birds again. *Were they the scary part?* I glanced between them. *That owl looks shifty,* I thought. I waited a moment in case any of them sprang to life. They didn't, and I shuffled into the next room.

The next room featured two plastic skeletons playing chess. I looked at the display for a while. Nobody and nothing moved. Chess is a slow game at the best of times. Even more so when the participants are dead. I shuffled on to the next room. A small plastic stegosaurus eyed me from the corner. The only way to describe it was petite, it was no bigger than a spaniel. Maybe it was a baby stegosaurus. I was bemused. Surely something would have to happen soon? I wondered if the ticket guy might spring up from his book, don some sort of cape, scurry round through a secret entrance and jump out to scare me. I looked around the dark room and my eyes fell once more on the plastic dinosaur and I understood that none of that would happen. I was glad really, I'm sure it would have been more awkward than scary, just me and him – me, knowing I'd disturbed him from his book, him, wondering if I would ask for a refund. It all gave me an idea for a fun fair attraction, "The house of awkward encounters." I thought for a moment how that would work, and then realised that it absolutely, definitely wouldn't, and that I had been staring at the stegosaurus for some time.

I moved to the final room – a woodland scene. Out of nowhere (well, the left side of the display) a small wild boar leapt out. *Leapt* is perhaps strong, but it moved forwards on its rails from behind a piece of foliage towards the centre of the display rather quickly. A shrieking noise accompanied its appearance, and it paused for a moment, in all its glory. Then just as abruptly it reversed and retreated behind the foliage. *Now that was excitement.* I realised it was motion-sensor activated, so I moved to the entrance to trigger it again. *I'd get my money's worth,* I thought, and lo the wild beast attacked once more. I looked at its face, it looked quite cheery really. I watched it retreat once more, acknowledging that while I hadn't been terrified at any point, I was at least surprised. I would never have guessed that the *piece de resistance* of the *Casa del terror* would be a small wild boar on rails. Less than ten minutes after I'd walked in I emerged back in to the lobby. The bored-looking teenager was still reading his book. He didn't, or wouldn't, look up, and I exited into the spring daylight.

While the funfair was a disappointment, the views from the top certainly weren't. I went over to the viewpoint looking back down on San Sebastián. It was a fine vista, and *La Concha* beach looked even more amazing from the bird's eye position I now enjoyed. I could see along the coast, with headland after headland jutting out, like the edge of lacework. A single white sailboat nodded and dipped outside the mouth of the bay. I could see the endless ocean one way and beyond San Sebastián the hills of the Basque Country in the other. It was a commanding vantage point, and it was no surprise to learn that a lighthouse had originally been situated up here. I took some photos and then stopped for a drink in the café, pleased to take my time and just enjoy the fine view. Before long though I had to get going, as there was a football game I wanted to go to.

***

I walked along the river out of town and past the bus station. The stadium of Real Sociedad, San Sebastián's team, was a good half hour walk from the old town. I'd already seen a match in Barcelona: watching possibly the world's most famous football club perform one of their regular trouncings of whichever poor unfortunates happened to roll up at the *Nou Camp* that day. Barcelona won 5-0 and extended their unbeaten home run to about 784 games, a run which I believe stretched back to

Napoleonic times. I jest, but the inequality of Spain's *La Liga* is something to behold. Barcelona's all-time unbeaten record at home is an incredible 67 consecutive games! They only play 20 home games a season, and *there are only three possible results* in a football game – win, lose or draw, so that goes to show their dominance in the Spanish league. Apart from games against the very top teams Barcelona's matches often aren't very competitive. A lot of the time it's like putting a pub team up against, well, Barcelona. Throughout the history of the Spanish league, Barcelona and Real Madrid have completely dominated. Barcelona have won the title 24 times, and Real Madrid 33. All other teams put together have only won the title 29 times. In fact only nine different clubs have ever won the title in Spain. Compare that to England where 24 different teams have won the league.

Then again, perhaps this concentration of success is to be expected. While the English Premier League divides up their lucrative TV money more or less equally, that's not the case in Spain. In 2015 Barcelona received 12 times as much TV revenue as the most poorly paid club. However, realising the inherent unfairness of the situation (and the fact that they could all make more money by selling TV rights together) *La Liga* has decided to move to a collective model. Now the money will be distributed *more* evenly, so that the richest clubs will receive no more than four times that of the poorest. I don't think Karl Marx would quite describe that as a fair system, but then again he believed in the abolition of all property and the concept of ownership itself, so I doubt there's much about the multimillion dollar world of modern football that would be up his street.

Before long I was approaching the stadium and I could see clusters of people in the blue and white stripes of Real Sociedad. Real Sociedad (Royal Society in English) have a long and proud history, being one of the nine clubs that have won the Spanish league. They trace their origins to 1904 when workers returning from Britain brought the game of football back with them and formed a club in the city. Real Sociedad are also known, along with the other top flight Basque team Athletic Bilbao, for their Basque-only players rule. This recruitment policy originally meant that only players from the Basque Country could play for either team and was explained by the motto, *"Con cantera y afición, no hace falta importación"* (With home-grown teams and supporters, there is no need for imports). While Real Sociedad abandoned the policy in 1989 with the signing of Liverpool striker John Aldridge, they still make great efforts to nurture as many home-grown players as possible.

Incredibly though, Athletic Bilbao still have a Basque-only players policy (although this has now been relaxed to include familial links through parents and grandparents). This is in stark contrast to the trend of globalisation amongst most top clubs in recent years. In 2005 Arsenal became the first club in England's Premier League to field a side of 11 players that did not feature a single Englishman. In 2009 the first game to feature no English player in either line-up in the English Premier League took place, although 15 other nationalities were represented. That Athletic Bilbao - one of the top clubs in *La Liga* – are able to have a full squad limited to players from one small part of Spain is mind-boggling.

The policy is a controversial one – on the one hand it is praised as a symbol of localised football succeeding on a national and European stage, while also being a positive way to express Basque nationalism. However, whether it's positive or negative it's clearly discriminatory, and it's unsurprising to find that Atletic Bilbao were the last club in *La Liga* to field a black player (that ended in 2011 when they fielded a player born to an Angolan father and Basque mother). Nevertheless, football-wise the policy seems to be working for them. Bilbao are one of only three clubs never to have been relegated from *La Liga* and consistently finish near the top of the table.

I arrived at the stadium and wandered around. It was a modern concrete affair – a 32,000 capacity arena built in the 1990s. I went to the ticket office, mentally running through the question I needed to ask. I'd realised that most of the problems I had during my interactions in Spain were because I wasn't ready for the answers after I asked the question. As a lot of learners will know, it's all very well asking *"¿Donde está el baño?"* (Where is the bathroom?), but if you're not ready, or unable, to understand the answer, then you still won't know where the damn bathroom is, and you'll be crossing your legs.

I'd had this problem in a variety of scenarios, with all manner of questions: what the specials were, how much something cost or where something was. I simply wasn't ready for the response. I would carefully craft my question, and then sit back as if my work was done. But this time I would be ready, I had two questions, both of which I'd designed to produce a limited set of responses.

I reached the front of the queue and sized up my opponent – a young-ish lady sitting behind the glass window of the ticket desk. The first question was, *"¿Quedan entradas disponibles?"* (Are there tickets available?) A classic yes/no question. There either were or weren't.

She went with *"Sí"* (yes). Exactly as I'd planned. She was playing right into my hands.

Now I needed to find out the different tickets available. A potential minefield, but I planned to control the variables and get her playing on my turf. *"¿Qué precios tienen?"* (What prices are they?) Beautiful. She would have to respond with numbers, and I would simply pick the price I wanted. Unfortunately, as the famous war saying goes "No plan survives first contact with the enemy."

Mistaking my carefully constructed questions for a general ability to speak Spanish, she started rattling off the different sections and their features, I caught the odd word *"balcón"* (balcony), *"gol"* (goal), and a couple of random numbers, but it was a mash of mostly unintelligible words.

Having done this dance a few times, I did at least have a contingency plan: a sentence that was completely unbreakable, *"La más barata, por favor,"* (the cheapest, please). And that is how I found myself sitting smack-bang in the middle of the hardcore Real Sociedad supporters.

Of course, as I approached, I had no idea that my new chums would resemble the crowd in a prison recreation yard. My first inkling came as I took my seat and a man strode along, two rows in front, brandishing a megaphone. Soon megaphone man was joined by a man with a huge drum. He began warming up, striking the drum firmly, loudly, and repeatedly. Now I like a good beat as much as the next guy, but not when it's 50 centimetres from my face, so I decided to move to a spare seat in the next block. Happily, nobody came along and tried to force me back in with the ultras, and the match started. Immediately the hardcore supporters started singing and bouncing up and down. Megaphone man appeared to be their leader, marshalling them at will, and incredibly never once turned to face the pitch. It was very strange how excited he seemed by the goings on, yet how uninterested he seemed in the football itself. I wondered if he thought his ticket was good value.

To give them their dues the whole block of hardcore supporters next to me and those situated in the block directly above never once stopped with their drumming, singing and chanting. It provided a real heartbeat of atmosphere for the stadium. Often during exciting moments of the match their chants were taken up by large sections of the stadium. Given their limited repertoire I was even clapping along to some of their chants by the end of the match. While some of it was necessarily aggressive it was never directed at anybody, and it was good to see some passion (in contrast to the somewhat lifeless atmosphere in Barcelona). The Basque nationalism was in evidence too, with the characteristic Basque "national" flag - a red background with a white and green cross on it being worn and displayed by lots of the hardcore group.

The game was a decent affair, Real Sociedad went 3-0 up and turned it on for the crowd, before cruising in the second half. I wandered out with the jubilant supporters and on my way home made a mental note to learn a longer sentence the next time I went to a football match, *"La más barata, pero no con los ultras, por favor"* (the cheapest ticket, but not with the hardcore fans, please).

Casa dels ossos in Barcelona, designed by Gaudí in 1904.

A bench at Gaudí's *Park Güell* in Barcelona.

Artistic looking pinchos at a bar in San Sebastián

The Concha Bay in San Sebastián

Chapter 9 – Art attack

The following day I took the bus from San Sebastián towards the biggest city in the Basque Country, Bilbao. It was an easy one-and-a-half-hour journey tracking the coast westwards. The motorway gently wound its way along, hemmed in by the mountains inland to our right and the Bay of Biscay visible to our left. Towns and villages nestled in clefts and valleys, the ruffles and foothills of the mountains stretching almost to the sea itself. The bus swayed as it rounded the curves and we pressed on towards Bilbao. With a population of just under a million people, it is one of the biggest cities in Spain. It grew in prominence in the nineteenth century as an industrial and banking centre, despite being linked to a series of small civil wars called "the Carlist wars". These wars were each led by a different Carlos (Carlos the V, VI and VII to be precise). Each Carlos started a war in an effort to seize the throne from various other monarchs (who fortunately for clarity's sake weren't called Carlos).

Interestingly all Spanish monarchs appear to have a nickname, an appendage similar to "Alexander the Great", or "Richard the Lionheart". Most of these are fairly complimentary: "Philip the spirited" or "Alfonso the peacemaker", some are *a touch* obvious, "Isabella the Catholic" *(pretty sure they were all Catholic, weren't they? May as well call her Isabella the woman)*, some were much more subjective, "Philip the handsome" or Philip the prudent" *(according to who?)*, others seem blatantly contradictory, "Ferdinand the desired, and the Felon King" *(desired by who – the police?)* while a couple were just harsh, "Juana the mad", and "Isabel the one with the sad destinies" *(it's not just one sad destiny, it's plural).*

Most people agree that the Spanish Civil War (1936-1939) was the final Carlist war. The heir to the Carlists (none of whom had managed to take the throne during the previous three wars) was an 82-year old Carlos - Alfonso Carlos this time. The octogenarian had spent his most of his life kicking around in Austria in his private castle. His principal occupation was campaigning for an end to duelling. Who knew it was such a hot button topic? He'd found a niche though, writing articles and even a book on the subject and encouraging the establishment of anti-duelling leagues throughout the German Empire. However, when the Spanish Civil War broke out, Alfonso Carlos decided to weigh in. It turned out that while he may have been against two guys fighting to the death, he wasn't so opposed to hundreds of thousands of people fighting to the death. And so he instructed his followers to support the Nationalists (under the command of General Francisco Franco) against the Socialist Republicans. Not that this move helped Carlos, because when Franco eventually won the war he didn't bother to install a king, reasoning he was more than capable of being the sole leader of the country.

The Basque Country played an important part in the Civil War (as it had in the previous Carlist wars). And as the bus rumbled on, cutting inland, I was passing the site of perhaps the most famous moment in the war. In the distance, between us and the sea lay the village of Guernica, a mere 30 kilometres from Bilbao. This was the place that Nazi bombers decimated on the afternoon of 26 April 1937. The Nazis were allied to Franco's Nationalists (who were fascists and therefore ideological brethren). As well providing troops, the newly bolstered Nazi Air Force (Luftwaffe) were also at Franco's disposal. And he chose to use them to devastating effect on Guernica. Despite being just a village (and not particularly involved in the Civil War) it was ostensibly targeted because it was a possible route of retreat for the Republicans, if Franco managed to take Bilbao. Franco called in an airstrike, and the Luftwaffe obliged by carpet bombing the village. Three quarters of the buildings were destroyed, scores of civilians were killed, yet interestingly the only factory in town was left completely unscathed. Initial reports suggested 1,600 of the 7,000 population were killed, leading to international outrage, although nowadays historians believe it was between 300 and 800. Nevertheless, it was a massively disproportionate bombing for a village that was only tangentially involved in the war.

Hermann Goering, Commander of the Luftwaffe, confessed at the Nuremberg trials that Germany had considered Guernica as a testing ground. "I urged Hitler to support Franco, firstly, in order to prevent the further spread of communism and, secondly, to test my young Luftwaffe at this opportunity." For Franco though it's likely Guernica had another significance, as the village is the spiritual centre of the Basque Country. It is the home of *Gernikako Arbola* (the tree of Guernica in Basque) an oak tree that symbolizes traditional freedoms for the Basque people. Over centuries the Lords and Kings of Biscay swore to respect their peoples' liberties under it. To this day the President of the autonomous community of the Basque Country swears his oath there. When Franco specifically targeted Guernica, and in such a ferocious way, it was seen as an attack on the whole Basque Country – revenge against an area which had sided against him.

Although international journalists reported on the atrocity, it was Pablo Picasso who really brought the world's attention to what was happening in Spain. Picasso, originally from Catalonia, but who had been living in France for three years, was commissioned in 1937 to produce a large painting for the World's Fair in Paris later that year. He had originally chosen the theme of the artist's studio, but when he heard the news from Guernica he was seized (for the first time) by the desire to do something political. His disturbing masterpiece, named simply "Guernica" raised eyebrows at the exhibition and as the painting toured Europe it slowly began to grab the world's attention. As history shows though, it did not sufficiently raise people's awareness of the Nazi war machine; just two years later Europe was taken by surprise when the terror that had been tested in the Basque Country was unleashed across the whole continent.

The bus pulled into the station in Bilbao, and I got out and collected my bag. It was a bright, sunny morning and like all cities, Bilbao looked all the better for it. It wasn't too far to the hostel I'd chosen so I began strolling, down and along the River Nervión which cut through the centre of the city. I crossed a bridge and climbed some steps, tiring myself a little by the time I arrived. I dumped my bag and left again. I had one destination in mind in Bilbao and I was keen to tick it off my list. It was the Guggenheim Museum. The flagship attraction of Bilbao is almost single-handedly credited with leading the urban regeneration of the city in the 1990s that turned it from a gritty, industrial metropolis to an emerging, fashionable, cultural (but still slightly gritty) metropolis.

I walked along the river front, admiring the bridges, and the modern-looking trams which glided by. A wooded hillside, with houses dotted here and there rose up behind the city on the opposite bank. It was certainly more *pleasant* than I was expecting. The wide river curved gently, shimmering and reflecting the cityscape. Twenty minutes further on the characteristic and frankly bizarre-looking Guggenheim building hove into view. A twisted mess of golden curves, curls and huge glass windows that looked like it had fallen together, was emerging in the distance. I continued to approach, admiring some of the statues dotted around the building. One was a huge spindly-legged golden metal spider, grotesque and beautiful at the same time. Tourists wandered in and out of the sculptures, interacting with the art, taking photos, selfies and simply pausing for the view. I walked round the side, between the museum and the river, admiring the way the building gleamed and shifted in the light. I clambered up the steps to the mezzanine plaza where more statues and a few street performers marked the way to the entrance.

Bilbao, with its port on the River Nervión, was historically the industrial base for the north of Spain.

Throughout the nineteenth and early twentieth century, it boasted plenty of heavy industry and shipbuilding, and was also a centre for banking. Particularly important for the city was the processing and exporting of iron, which was mined throughout the Basque Country. Demand surged during World War I and brought Bilbao huge wealth. However, following the damage wrought by the Civil War and the general deindustrialisation of Western Europe in the latter half of the twentieth century Bilbao entered a period of decline. The return of democracy (after Franco) in the late 70's gave a boost to the whole of Spain, but particularly those "separatist" regions (like the Basque Country) that Franco had marginalised by centralising power in Madrid.

In a similar vein to Barcelona's successful bid to host the Olympics in the 1980s, Bilbao also began to plan for its own regeneration. In 1991 the Basque government finalised a scheme to lure the Guggenheim Foundation to build its first museum in Europe. In a nice twist they proposed that the new museum be built in Bilbao's dilapidated port area - the original source of the city's prosperity. The Basque government agreed to pay the cost of construction, create an acquisitions fund, all on top of paying the Guggenheim Foundation a fee - a total cost of nearly 200 million US dollars. In exchange, the Foundation agreed to run the museum and provide the exhibits. The museum opened to near universal acclaim in 1997, and is widely judged to have been a resounding success. In 1995 Bilbao counted just 25,000 tourists a year, by 2009 it was over 600,000. This rapid growth (and turnaround of the city's image) has been called the *Guggenheim effect.* The regeneration that followed the opening of the museum included a new airport terminal, rapid transit system and tram line, conference centre and a lot more.

I entered the iconic building and stepped into the central atrium. A huge glass window looked out on the river and beyond, to the wooded hillsides rising above the far bank. The renowned architect of the museum, Frank Gehry, nicknamed the atrium *The Flower,* because of its characteristic shape. It was certainly impressive, the staircases spiralled upwards, glass columns twisted down. The space was, huge, light and airy, yet every aspect felt sculpted and shaped. When Gehry had been commissioned to design the building he had been instructed to be daring and innovative, and it certainly was that - inside and out. A critic in *The New Yorker,* described the building as "a fantastic dream ship of undulating form in a cloak of titanium," and it was easy to see why it is so often named as one of the finest buildings of the late 20th century.

I passed out of the atrium and into a huge warehouse-like gallery. Inside was a collection of massive steel structures. Ribbons of undulating metal, at least 6 metres tall were arranged in circles, while others stretched out down the huge gallery, like long snakes. I approached one of the tall circles, the huge flat side of steel curved upward, and bent away from me. Behind it was a second sheet of metal, paralleling the first, creating an entrance, almost a tunnel. I ventured in and began walking along the corridor that was formed from the two pieces of metal. I had entered the circle, but as I walked I realised that the curves of the walls of metal were changing. At first they bowed outwards, away from the centre of circle, but as I walked through the bend their slant started to shift and the walls began to lean into the centre of the circle, and into me. It was an almost imperceptible shift, yet my balance was completely off kilter. I reached out to touch the inside wall of steel. I felt like I was on a ship in heavy seas, clutching on to the side to catch myself. I advanced around the curve, on and on, spiralling in on myself. Finally I reached the centre of the circle, and I emerged into a wide open space. It felt like I'd reached the end of one of those garden mazes, yet I'd just followed the path of the circle. I stood there a moment, and then another person was disgorged into the centre, looking just as disoriented as I had. I watched them get their bearings again and paused for a moment more, then I left, back the way I came.

I walked out and back into the gallery space, and then along one of the ribbons of sheet metal. It wasn't quite the same experience as the shifting circle maze, but I still appreciated how I was interacting with the sculpture physically, following the curve, as it snaked along the floor. Occasionally I reached out to touch it. All around me other people were doing the same. It was art, but not really as I knew it. Who wanted to look at a painting of a bowl of fruit, when you could interact with art in a tactile way? And why *were* painters obsessed with bowls of fruit anyway? *Endless* bowls of oranges and apples. They could at least make it interesting. For creative people, these artists had very mundane tastes in fruit. Would a picture of a kumquat and a kiwi be too much to ask for, just once? Considering how much these art critics like to yabber on, it was a subject I had never heard discussed.

I wandered back into the main atrium and went into another gallery. This one contained individual video screens, each one trained on a different member of an orchestra, and each with a speaker underneath playing out their part. It was an unusual effect. I didn't really know what it was trying to show, but I liked it all the same. Next I ascended the stairs. Half a dozen very tall, very thin electronic displays, like bars, were planted in the floor and ran up to the ceiling behind the staircase. They must have been fifteen or twenty metres high. Messages scrolled down the bars, like news headlines, or stock prices. They cascaded down in red digital letters, one after the other. I stopped to read them, *"Hundo mi cabeza"* (I flee my mind), *"Mi madre lo sabe"* (My mother knows it), *"Olvido su nombre"* (I forget his/her name). I watched the messages flash by, translating most, but missing some. I was puzzled, *What did it all mean?* I was clueless, but then again so much of modern art involves either being puzzled, or pretending you know what's going on, even when you are just grasping at straws. Perhaps my feeling of puzzlement was right, perhaps I was really tuning into this "art". Another message scrolled by, *"Estoy perdiendo mi tiempo,"* (I am wasting my time). I took that as my cue to move on to the next exhibit.

In the upper galleries, there were some more standard paintings, which I was able to be confused about in a more traditional way. There was some Andy Warhol, Ai Weiwei, Rothko and lots of the big hitters. I appreciated them, but felt it was hard for them to compete with the experience of the exhibits and sculptures on the lower floors. It is rare to find a sense of playfulness in an art museum, and I had enjoyed myself thoroughly. I went back down the staircase and out through the atrium, noting again the wonderful, airy space I found myself in. I followed the usual route out through the giftshop, noting the customary postcards, pencils and erasers. I was slightly taken aback at the official Guggenheim beret. I mulled the idea for a moment, but decided to resist the temptation to purchase one and instead made my exit.

Chapter 10 – Snakes, Axes, Ducks and Terror

Outside the Guggenheim the sky was a vivid blue in the spring sunshine and I decided to walk back to the centre through one of the parks, instead of repeating my journey along the river. The park was an oasis of tranquillity, beautifully tended and with a view back towards Bilbao's downtown. A few modern, gleaming office blocks, probably belonging to one of the city's many banks, glinted in the sunlight. In addition to the industrial decline that Bilbao had suffered under Franco, the city also lived under the shadow of terrorism, because it was here that the terrorist group ETA formed. Responsible for more than 800 deaths during their 50 years of activity, it's easy to forget just how violent ETA were.

ETA stands for *Euskadi Ta Askatasuna* which means "Basque Homeland and Liberty" in Basque. It was founded in 1959 by a group of youthful students frustrated by the Basque National Party's rejection of armed struggle. Initially, when they broke away the organisation used the word *Aberri* instead of *Euskadi*, making the acronym ATA. However, in some Basque dialects, *ata* means duck, and that doesn't sound very fearsome at all. So they changed the name to ETA. Fair enough, although with the old name it would have been very easy to come up with a logo.

It's hard to find a ranking of just how deadly ETA was - and I've tried. It is however, possible to find a list of all terrorist groups in the world – at the University of Maryland's Global Terrorism Database. This claims to include every single terrorist group, even if they have only ever conducted one attack, and there are some very strange ones out there. How about the *Anticlerical Pro Sex Toys Group* (one attack in Spain in 2013, two small bombs hiding in vibrators were sent to the Bishop of Pamplona, one minor injury). Ever heard of the *Erotic Anti-authority Cells* group? (one attack in Greece in 2000, a bomb package sent to the offices of Viagra in Greece, no injuries). Ever come across *The Angry Brigade?* That seems like a perfect name for pretty much every terrorist group that's ever existed, from Al-Qaeda to ISIS. However, this particular Angry Brigade were especially annoyed about the Vietnam War and were responsible for multiple minor bombings in the UK in the 1970s. Recently, the founder of The Angry Brigade, one Melford Stevenson, said he realised that he "was the one who was angry, and the people [he] met were more like the Slightly Cross Brigade."

Back to ETA and their campaign of violence, which was considerably more serious than the novelty acts mentioned above. In fact, in post-war twentieth century Western Europe ETA was second only to the IRA in terms of its deadliness. ETA aimed to establish a separate country which would be formed from the area covered by the current autonomous Basque Community, Navarre and a section of Southwestern France. ETA actually held their first assembly in France - in Bayonne - in 1962. Over the years ETA built up weapons caches on the French side of the border and to some degree used the territory as a safe haven. The French state turned a blind eye to the activities of ETA, in the complicit agreement that the group focused the vast majority of its violent activity within Spain.

Despite being founded for the express purpose of armed struggle in 1959, it wasn't until 1968 that ETA recorded its first killing. Two ETA members were travelling in a car through Aduna, near San Sebastián when a Civil Guard stopped them. Fearing they would be arrested, they shot and killed the officer. The pair were chased and one of them was also killed. ETA wanted revenge and so planned to assassinate the chief of the secret police in San Sebastián. They had a grudge against him anyway as he had a habit of torturing detainees in his custody. Two months later ETA was waiting at the police chief's home and shot him seven times, and the spiral of violence began.

Over the decades, ETA's campaign of terror was particularly notable for how political it was. In addition to the cause of independence, the group aligned itself to Marxism-Leninism very early on, probably partly because the hated Madrid government of Franco was fascist. ETA was not afraid of operating outside the Basque Country and attacking the Madrid government directly. Its most famous (and successful) attack was the assassination of Admiral Luis Blanco, the Prime Minister, in 1973. *Operación Ogro* (Operation Ogre) was designed to hit General Franco since Blanco, as well as being PM, was the predicted successor to Franco (who himself was only two years away from death), so in completing the action successfully and taking Blanco out of the picture, ETA undoubtedly changed the course of Spanish history.

Early in 1973 ETA rented a basement flat in Madrid close to the road they knew Blanco drove down to attend mass every day. Over five months, they dug a tunnel from their flat under the street. To hide their true purpose of their plotting, they told the landlord that they were student sculptors. By the day of the attack in December they had put in place 80 kg of high explosive – all of which was stolen from a Government depot. When Blanco drove by, they hit the detonator and the blast sent Blanco and his car 20 metres into the air and over a five-storey building. The car landed on a second floor balcony. Blanco, the driver, and bodyguard all died at the scene or later on.

Blanco was the only man Franco completely trusted, probably because Blanco was a complete adherent. He once said, *"Politics for me consists of total loyalty to Franco."* But Blanco was not well liked, and in many circles (and amongst much of the Spanish populace) people were pleased to see the back of him. In fact his assassination gave rise to the sarcastic slogan *"Up Franco! Higher than Carrero Blanco!"* A month afterwards ETA publicly claimed the attack. Ironically, as successful as the attack was, in some ways it laid the seeds of ETA's demise. For one it hastened Spain's move towards democracy which began just two years later when Franco died in 1975 without a clear successor. This transition reduced some of the Basque people's antipathy towards the Spanish government. Yet even more importantly this demonstration of ETA's willingness to strike politicians so ruthlessly had the effect of increasing the government's desire to crush ETA.

Following the success of the killing of the Prime Minister ETA increased their violent activity: bombings, shootings and assassinations were their stock-in-trade for the next few years. In fact, 1978–80 was ETA's most deadly period, with 68, 76, and 98 fatalities respectively. But the group was also interested in politics. ETA's motto is *Bietan jarrai* ("Keep up on both"), which is embodied by the two images in the group's logo – a snake and an axe (there are no ducks anywhere to be seen). The snake signifies politics and it is wrapped around an axe, which represents armed struggle. ETA had a political wing – Batasuna - which made the case for Basque independence in elections. Batasuna painted itself as much more radical than the Basque Nationalist Party (which ETA had originally splintered off from in the fifties). ETA's political wing did increasingly well in the early eighties, gaining over 15% of the vote, but could never win anywhere near enough support to win a majority in the Basque parliament. Around this time ETA also developed strong ties with the IRA, another separatist group that also had political aims (and a political party). Allegedly there was significant contact between the two movements, including exchanges of weapons, explosives and expertise. Intriguingly several ETA and Batasuna activists, fleeing arrest and imprisonment in Spain, including the hunger striker Inaki de Juana Chaos, found refuge at times among republicans in Ireland. Allegedly both the IRA and ETA also found common cause with FARC, the Colombian rebels. While all three groups were responsible for formidable levels of violence between the 1970s and 1990s, all three have now long since announced permanent ceasefires.

The demise of ETA came about in the late 1990s. It was a long time coming, and caused by a few different factors. Firstly, under Franco, the Basque people (like the Catalans) *were* undoubtedly oppressed, but following the transition to democracy in the late 70s the Basque Country was granted a high degree of autonomy – and this nullified a lot of ETA's demands. *Basque* was granted the status of nationality within Spain, which seems like a contradiction in terms, but indicates just how much the Madrid government wanted to keep the Basques onside. The Basque government were also given a separate police force, control over health and education, and tax collection and spending. The Basque Country, like Catalonia, is among the wealthier regions of Spain. In fact, Basques have the highest per capita income in the country, so it's understandable why Madrid was (and still is) so keen to prevent the breakaway of either area.

The second reason for ETA's decline was that the Basque people themselves began to grow weary of the group's campaign of violence. In the 1990s people began to turn against the group. The defining moment was in July 1997, when politician Miguel Ángel Blanco was kidnapped in the Basque town of Ermua. ETA threatened to assassinate him unless the Spanish government brought all ETA captives to prisons in the Basque Country in 48 hours. This demand was not met by the Spanish government and three days later Miguel Ángel Blanco was found shot dead. More than six million people took to the streets across Spain, including the Basque Country, where people chanted "Assassins!" and "Basques yes, ETA no".

Arguably though the most important reason for ETA's demise has been the government and security crackdown. In the 90's cooperation between the French and Spanish police improved considerably, ETA had less room to operate, and allegedly the police began successfully infiltrating the group. In 1995 ETA attempted to assassinate José María Aznar, a conservative politician who was leader of the opposition *Partido Popular (PP)*. Fortunately for him, he was in an armoured car and survived. A year later Aznar was later elected President and it became clear that the assassination attempt hadn't made him particularly fond of ETA. Aznar made it a personal priority to ruthlessly crackdown on the group: he banned Batasuna, ETA's political wing in 2003 and ETA itself was forced into a series of truces and ceasefires. Eventually the group agreed to a permanent ceasefire in 2011. In 2017 ETA recorded a video announcement that they would be disarming later in the year. The three men in their balaclavas and berets (an unusual look) said that all their caches of weapons would be handed over. The Spanish government reacted cautiously saying that the group must dissolve itself completely. Nevertheless, ETA has not carried out a deadly attack since 2010, and for the most part the shadow of Basque terrorism has lifted from Spain.

***

The following day I wandered around again, through the old town and the plazas, stopping at various cafés. I'd bought a Spanish comic and a children's book to try and work on my language skills while I was travelling. The comic was about a child footballer who, inexplicably, was allowed to play for Barcelona. Seemingly he had incredible ball skills and ran rings around his opponents, despite the fact he was only 9 years old. Later in the comic I learnt his secret – he had magnets in his boots. The fact that there isn't a corresponding magnet in a football wasn't explained – or not sufficiently for my liking anyway. Nor did the child seemingly show any guilt or concern for the fact that he was perverting the course of the games. Let's just say there were a lot of unanswered questions.

My patchy Spanish wasn't too much of a problem with the comic since the pictures were self-explanatory, and the size of the speech bubbles prevented any character from saying anything longer than twelve words. After the comic I tackled a book about the adventures of a mischievous child, entitled *"Los calzoncillos de Pablo Diablo"* (The underpants of Pablo the devil). It was aimed at children 7+ (and hopefully also language learners in their early 30's). As the title suggests, it was a much more serious piece of literature. The 94-page tome also featured other stories, including *Pablo Diablo se pone enfermo* (Pablo gets sick) and *Pablo Diablo come verdura* (Pablo eats vegetables).

Surprisingly I found it really difficult. It wasn't just the lack of pictures (always the sign of a serious book), but the grammar was actually very complex. There were all sorts of tenses that I wasn't familiar with – the subjunctive (a special verb tense for when a situation is hypothetical), the future tense and all three types of past tense (yes, three!). True, in language learning you must always push yourself to the next level, and I did need to know these tenses. Sooner or later I had to stop speaking in the present tense if I was to have proper conversations.

Recently I had been trying to use the past tense while speaking, but it was an effort, and in the case of the book I was overwhelmed by just how many different verb endings were used. Pablo Diablo, the little blighter, was always using the future tense, because he was forever plotting or scheming something or other. Besides the verbs, the range of vocabulary was also somewhat unfamiliar. The opinions of the eponymous Pablo Diablo tended towards the extreme. In the memorable story about Pablo's heroic fight to avoid eating vegetables, words such as *"asqueroso"* (disgusting), *"una arcada"* (a retch), *"gimío"* (he whined) were all new to me. At least I was learning, although I wondered what would happen to my vocabulary if I kept reading these books.

I returned to the hostel and went into the lounge. A Hollywood movie was showing on the TV and I sat down to watch it. A few minutes later, somebody walked through the door. It was at the edge of my peripheral vision, but I shivered - I knew who it was already. I turned and my suspicions were confirmed. It was none-other-than Russ, my erstwhile companion from the surfing lesson. As usual he was wearing his sunglasses, although once he realised how dim the TV room was he removed them. I greeted him, he peered at me and then raised his chin, in a reverse head nod acknowledgement. I wondered if he'd learnt that from The Fonz on *Happy Days*. He came over and sat next to me.

"Hey, how's it going Richie?" he asked. I'd never introduced myself to him, or anyone else, as Richie but I couldn't be bothered to correct him.

"Yeah, good I've had a nice couple of days here in Bilbao. I went to the Guggenheim, that was excellent. What about you?" I asked.

"The Goog? Yeah, I went there. Loved it. Art and all that stuff. Love it."

"Oh yeah? What was your favourite bit?"

"Hmmm, those huge ribbons and circles of steel. Really amazing," he replied. *Damn. That was my favourite bit too.* He paused and stroked his hipster beard, "What are you doing tonight Richie?" And before I knew it, and against my better judgement, I was heading out on the town with Russ.

We headed into the old town and hit a couple of bars. Like San Sebastián each bar had dozens of pinchos on plates laid out along the bar for customers to pick at. Surprisingly, Russ was a vegetarian, and a militant one at that.

"Barbarism, isn't it? Plain and simple," he said, explaining his views on meat.

"Well, there's a case to be made," I said. I was eyeing up a juicy piece of *jamón iberico* and wondered when we would change topic.

"A case to be made? Richie, open your eyes! The whole system is dystopian!" he said.

"Dystopian?" That seemed a bit strong. I decided not to tell him about my months-long trip around the USA, eating every food going, from ribs, to burgers, to hotdogs, pepperoni pizzas and so on. I thought for a moment, had I eaten anything but meat on that trip? Yes, cheese. There *had* been a lot of cheese.

"Yep, I think so." He paused, "I've been vegetarian for five years now. In fact, I'm verging on vegan."

"Really? Why's that?"

"Because of the animals." He rolled his eyes, "You. Are. Responsible. We all are." He pointed at my chest, "You vote with your dollars Richie. The almighty greenback. That's what it's all about."

"What if I'm spending euros?" He didn't laugh, and there was an awkward pause. I was anxious to fill it, "And I guess being vegetarian is good for your health?" *Was it?* I had no idea.

"Oh yeah, of course. In fact, I'm trying to lose weight." I looked at him, he was thin already. "Yeah, I'm at like 6 percent bodyfat right now. I want to get to zero percent."

"Zero percent? Is that even possible? Wouldn't that make you seriously ill?" I asked sceptically.

"Who knows? It's the dream anyway," he replied, and took a gulp of his drink.

We moved on out of the bar, and wandered away from the old town, back in the vague direction of the hostel. We crossed a bridge, back to the other side of the river. We passed a bar that looked lively, even though it was a mid-week night. We debated whether we should enter. Russ was in favour, so we made to go in, but the bouncer stopped us and asked us for five euros. I asked him if there was a band on.

"No toca ningún grupo, es otro tipo de espectáculo," (There's no band, there's a different type of show), he replied.

"¿Qué tipo?" (What type?), I asked.

The bouncer, half-winced, in a look that implied, how do I explain this? *"Es una comedia,"* (It's a comedy). He said, and garbled something else, which I missed.

"¿Es buena?" (Is it good?) I asked. As soon as I said it I realised how redundant a question it was. I've often asked that question in a restaurant before, and the answer from the waiter is always – *excellent.* But that answer is understandable. I mean they're never going to tell you that it tastes like a pile of pig's intestines. Which, if you're dining in France, they might well be.

He nodded, *"Muy buena – típica española,"* (It's very good, typically Spanish).

I looked at Russ, gave him the gist and he nodded, so we paid and entered. The room was dark and long. First we passed the bar, running along the left wall. We could see a crowd gathered at the far end, and two performers on stage. The show had started already. We approached the back of the crowd, who were laughing uproariously.

133

The audience was all men, but the two performers on the stage were women. Well, they were drag queens. So they were men too.

So this was the typically Spanish comedy we'd paid for, I thought. Both performers were wearing stilettos, very short dresses, massive wigs, and had done their make-up in a style they must have learnt in clown college. Russ looked unimpressed.

"Why didn't you tell me that it was a gay bar, and a drag queen show?" he asked accusingly.

"Because I obviously don't know the Spanish for drag queen, do I?

"Well, you should have told me," he said nonsensically.

"Why, is it a problem for you?" I decided to play the liberal card, and see if I could snooker him by getting him to admit or deny his prejudices.

His eyes narrowed, "No, I like it."

We turned and watched the show. I understood very little. Comedy is particularly hard to understand in a foreign language. Often comedy relies on cultural knowledge, switching your expectations at the last moment, or wordplay, with two or more meanings interchanged. For someone who was struggling to understand the language at its most straightforward it was too much. And I got the sense these two guys were relying heavily on *double entendres*. Those, and some very crude vocabulary which I just didn't possess.

The drag queens asked the audience if there were any foreigners in, and I considered volunteering Russ, but I glanced at him, and thought he might not take the joke too well. Fortunately, there was another foreigner present, and they dragged him on stage. They played a game of mystery boxes "deal or no deal" style with their onstage guest. Most of the boxes seemed to contain something that the two drag queens could throw at, or douse their guest with. Luckily he looked amused, but I knew I'd made the right decision with Russ. He didn't look like someone who wanted to be doused onstage.

The two drag queens began singing, which quickly turned into screeching and caterwauling. I looked over at Russ, he grimaced. I felt the same way. They began dancing suggestively, which brought the crowd out in hysterics. He jerked his head towards the door to suggest a quick exit and I nodded.

We passed the bouncer on the way out, *"¿Buena?"* (Good?) he asked.

And I answered like every customer, in every restaurant, when asked that question by the waiter, *"Sí, muy buena,"* (Yes, very good).

Chapter 11 - Tapas and pinchos

It was my last morning in the Basque Country. I was heading south, as I wanted to see some traditional Spanish culture: flamenco, bullfighting, Spanish guitars, tapas. Hopefully I would see a man fighting a bull and dancing flamenco at the same time. In an ideal world he would also be playing a Spanish guitar and chomping on some tapas, although I knew in my heart this was a long shot. If I stood any chance of seeing such a performance (or more likely the individual elements), I needed to go to Andalucía, the very southernmost region of Spain. Yet, despite being at nearly the halfway point in my three-month journey I was still in the very most northern region of Spain, so I really needed to get a move on. I debated heading straight to Madrid, in the very centre of the country, but I realised that I would be passing straight through La Rioja, the famous wine-producing region. The idea of touring a vineyard, or at the very least drinking Rioja in its birthplace seemed too tempting to miss. Also, La Rioja didn't seem like the type of place where I would accidentally pay for a drag queen show. So, it had that going for it.

I left my hotel, walked to the bus station and boarded a bus bound for Logroño, the capital of La Rioja. Very soon after leaving Bilbao we crossed the Cantabrian Mountains, a range of ridges and peaks which run parallel to the Northern coast of Spain. I watched the scenery pass by and thoughts of my imminent wedding speech loomed in my mind. While I had given a good deal of thought, time and energy to the language element (too much by any reasonable measurement), I hadn't really thought about the actual content of the speech. There was a lot of pressure - it had to be funny, suitable for all ages, it had to work in Spanish... and it was due in six weeks. A mild feeling of anxiety came over me and I toyed with the idea of doing some work on the speech. Instead I reached almost instinctively for my iPhone – I flicked through the menu, and saw the podcast app. *I could listen to a Spanish podcast*, I thought. I'd downloaded several and not got around to listening to one yet... *yes, I could listen to one of those, that would be like working on the speech. In a way.*

I played one of the podcasts which was described as intermediate. It was a real Spanish conversation about tapas. I couldn't believe how hard it was, it was a different beast altogether from the courses I had done thus far where I heard single sentences said clearly, slowly and in isolation. There was just so much Spanish. I missed words, half sentences, eventually whole sentences – I pressed pause and looked down to see how far through the conversation I'd got – 48 secs – *hmmmmm*. The vocabulary was challenging too, particularly where it varied from the standard word I knew. I kept having to look up what the words meant – and was frustrated when they were *similar but not the same* as a word I knew. For instance, they used the word *"platito"* which sounded similar to *plato* (plate), I was unsure, *did they just mean plate?* I rewound and listened again. "Plate" made sense in context, but the woman was demonstrably saying a slightly different word. I paused the audio, looked the word up, and saw it meant *little plate.* I went through something similar about thirty times. Clearly this wouldn't be a practical way for me to hold a conversation with anyone. They would need the patience of a saint.

In the case of the plate/little plate scenario - I later learnt that adding *-ito* was a common way of modifying a noun to mean small. The whole thing was frustrating, it turns out people don't speak in neat, ordered sentences like they teach in language courses. This is the way you're often taught a conversation will go:

You: *"Hello."*

Person in restaurant: *"Hello. How are you?"*

You: *"I am very well. I would like a table. Do you have a table?"*

Person in restaurant: *"Yes we have a table available in the restaurant. How many people would you like a table for?"*

You: *"I would like a table for four people. Can I see the menu please?"*

No, apparently, that is a completely unrealistic scenario (thank goodness), and people actually talk in rather indirect, occasionally repetitive and rather rambling ways. I tried to let the audio of the podcast conversation flow, but I couldn't. As soon as I got even slightly lost I struggled to pick up the thread and had to rewind and start the section again. But I persevered, taking an hour to get through the ten-minute conversation.

I looked up and saw we were crossing the Ebro River and entering La Rioja which is the second smallest autonomous community in Spain by size (only the Balearic Islands are smaller) and the smallest by population – with only 320,000 residents. The diminutive size of the province is down to a strange quirk of history. This area was the furthest north the Moors reached following their invasion of the Iberian Peninsula in the year 711. It took two hundred years before they were pushed back south by the neighbouring feudal king - King Sancho of Navarra. With the Moors in retreat he took the area of La Rioja in an attempt to add it to his existing territory. However, he wasn't the only feudal king on the block, and by 1067 no fewer than three different Kings, all called Sancho, were fighting over the region. In the appropriately named "War of the Three Sanchos" the kings of Navarra, Castile and Aragon fought for supremacy and control (and for bragging rights about who was the best Sancho).

At that time, following the withdrawal of the Moors and their Caliphate, Christian pilgrims had started traversing through the area on their way west to Santiago. This trade (and the Ebro River) gave the area some strategic significance, and a reason for neighbouring kingdoms to hold on to it. A bridge was built over the Ebro River in the 11th century and the city of Logroño was born. However, the territory of Rioja remained divided amongst other kingdoms. It remained this way until the early 19th century when the area was taken by the invading Napoleonic army during the Peninsular War. Yet Napoleon's occupation of the area did not deter Spain's national assembly from declaring La Rioja a province in 1812. The Spanish national assembly themselves were sheltering from the French General's forces in the far south of the country in Cadiz, and Napoleon's brother sat on the throne in Madrid, so it seemed like a strange time to be redrawing the map of Spain, but I guess they had to keep themselves busy while they were hiding out.

Unlike most autonomous communities (e.g. Catalonia, Navarra, Basque Country) Rioja was never really an independent kingdom. It's not big enough, and it doesn't contain a city of any great significance. La Rioja is much more of an artificial construct. Supposedly it was created as a buffer zone against the separatist area of the Basque Country to the north. The Spanish government reasoned that if they gave the people in La Rioja their own defined identity, they would be much less likely to be absorbed into the wider Basque cause. Since that move in the early 19th century La Rioja *has* managed to forge its own identity, and it is mostly based on what I could see all around me along the sides of the road: vineyards - rows and rows of neat vines, the white-green grapes in little bunches, clearly visible in the sunshine. In every direction they seemed to go on as far as I could see. La Rioja had made its economy, reputation and arguably even its identity, out of wine.

Soon enough we approached the outskirts of Logroño. Very quickly we passed into the city and pulled up at the bus station. I walked through the streets of the old town. It seemed calm and quiet, despite being the capital of the province. I passed along a pedestrianised street; two old men sat at a café in the sunshine, drinking small glasses of wine, watching the world go by. They looked rather companionable, even though they weren't speaking. I could imagine them coming out every afternoon just to watch the people walk by. I could see why older people in the UK move abroad to sunnier climes. It's far better to sun yourself in some exotic locale, instead of putting up with another grey day in the UK, stuck inside watching *Countdown* or *Deal or No Deal*, with the rain pattering on the window. These two old gents looked like they were enjoying themselves a lot more, although to be fair the wine was probably helping. That said if you had enough Rioja you could probably also have a good time watching *Deal or No Deal* on a rainy weekday afternoon, but it sounds like a slippery path.

I checked into my hotel and came back out for a wander around. After a while I came across the cathedral, known as *Santa María de la Redonda* (Saint Mary of the Round) – no she wasn't famous for always getting her round of drinks in first - the cathedral is actually named for its round floor (in reality it's octagonal, but let's not split hairs.) I stood out the front and took a picture. It had a fine, double-fronted aspect and was built in golden sandstone which caught the sunlight. Inside there were plenty of paintings, statues and other works of art. I walked slowly around, perusing the paintings of the familiar religious scenes. I also noticed a few modern-day pilgrims wandering around too, reminding me why this cathedral, and even the city of Logroño itself, had come into being. Pilgrims had been walking through this region for over a thousand years on the Camino de Santiago pilgrimage and so a settlement grew up and became Logroño. The city's other historical claim to fame was the Basque witch trials in the early 17th century. These were Spain's most famous witch trials and thousands were accused of witchcraft. Given the fame of the witch trials in the early Americas (i.e. the one in Salem) it's easy to forget these "trials" were also happening across Europe.

In the early 17th century there was a suspicion of a widespread witch cult in the Basque Country, and in 1609 the Spanish Inquisition came to investigate. Despite being on the very edge of the Basque Country, the investigation was handled from Logroño. The investigators urged anyone who was a witch or knew someone who was guilty to confess immediately. If anyone was accused and then charged, they were presumed guilty. It was a straightforward, if inflexible policy. Just for good measure the use of torture was also permitted during the trial.

The initial phase of the investigation culminated in 1610. 31 people were found guilty, and 12 burned to death. The lead investigator then toured the Basque Country and the denunciations poured in. 2,000 people provided "confessions", although most of these were children between the ages of seven and fourteen. Altogether the accusers implicated a further 5,000 named individuals. However, as the investigation went on, and with time to consider the severity of their accusations, all but six people retracted their confessions. This was typical of the mass hysteria associated with these investigations. The Bishop of Pamplona protested to the Inquisition, claiming the witch hunt was based on lies and delusions. He said there had been little knowledge of witchcraft in the region before the outset of the trials. As time went by, and the numbers of the accused escalated, one of the key judges became sceptical of the outlandish claims. He was willing to stand up against the prevailing madness and said this:

> *the judges should not pass sentence on anyone unless the case can be proven with external and objective evidence sufficient to convince everyone who hears it. And who can accept the following: that a person can frequently fly through the air and travel a hundred leagues in an hour; that a woman can get through a space not big enough for a fly; that a person can make himself invisible ... and that a witch can turn herself into any shape she fancies, be it housefly or raven? Indeed, these claims go beyond all human reason and may even pass the limits permitted by the Devil.*

In response two of his fellow judges accused the sceptical judge of being "in league with the Devil". They may even have added, *So there!* But the scepticism and concerns won over the Inquisitor General in Madrid. He had sanctioned the initial burnings with some reluctance, partly in order to quell the panic in Logroño, but in 1614 he dismissed all the outstanding trials in the city. Maybe he was in league with the Devil too. The trials had a significant effect on Spain and the Central office of the Inquisition issued stricter rules, demanding a higher burden of proof for witchcraft. This essentially brought witch-burning to an end in Spain – even while it continued in parts of Protestant Northern Europe. In fact, the Salem witch trials in North America took place over 80 years later in 1692.

In the evening I headed out to *Calle del Laurel,* the famous tapas/pinchos street of Logroño. There seemed to be an equal amount of both tapas (small plates of food) and pinchos (the tapas with a stick that are popular in the Basque Country). Perhaps this reflected La Rioja's borderland status between the Basque Country and the rest of Spain. However they were defined, there was certainly a lot of them. In fact, almost every place on the street was a tapas bar. Logroño, despite being completely untouristy, certainly boasted a lively and thriving food scene. I went inside one place and had a look along the offerings displayed on the bar. I was surprised how arty and well-crafted they looked. In San Sebastián, each bar had hundreds of tapas laid out, but here, the selection was much smaller. Yet seemingly all the effort had been put into the detail: little pieces of bread with a half-moon of goats' cheese, topped with chutney and pineapple, bowls of delicate octopus rings sprinkled with paprika, or trios of skewered croquette balls, encircled by a drizzle of cream sauce. It was art. I hesitated, they all looked so good, chose a couple and ordered a glass of rioja. The whole thing was such a success that on leaving the bar I immediately entered another and repeated the whole process two more times.

The following day I decided to head to a winery to learn about the drink that had made the region so famous. On the banks of the river was *Franco Españolas,* one of

Logroño's most famous Bodegas (which means wine cellar or winery). Each bodega is the branded company that sells the wine of one, or several, vineyards. We started the tour and immediately moved into a cellar area, where rows of huge wooden barrels filled up the massive warehouse space. Each barrel looked big enough that you could swim in.

The guide explained that wine had been grown in the region since the time of the Romans, primarily using the indigenous Tempranillo (red) grape. This is still the most common grape in Rioja, and it is so dominant that more than 85% of Rioja wine is red. As was typical across medieval Europe it was the monks who were the chief growers (and advocates) of wine. They often used the lands of the monasteries for cultivation of vineyards. In the 17th century the region became particularly known for the quality of its wines. In 1635 the mayor of Logroño reputedly passed a law prohibiting carts from passing by wine cellars, in case the vibrations of the rickety carts should affect the quality of the precious beverage.

As we walked between the ancient wooden barrels in the depths of the winery the guide told us that Rioja's wines only really took off with the arrival of the French in the late 19th century. While the Spanish had made a decent fist of winemaking, they'd never harnessed their potential, neither producing it on the scale, or at the quality, that they had in France. However, in the late 19th century France suffered a great misfortune. France's loss though was Spain's gain. In the 1870s an insect pest phylloxera began spreading throughout the vineyards of France. The pests attacked the vines themselves and caused a widespread blight. Crops were decimated and the French wine industry collapsed. Short of options many winemakers headed over the Pyrenees into Spain, bringing their knowhow, techniques and advanced production with them. This particular winery *Franco Españolas* (literally French Spanish wineries) had been founded by a man from Bordeaux in 1890. He, along with many others, found the growing conditions of the Rioja valley and the indigenous Tempranillo grape to be perfect, and Spanish wine was launched onto the world scene.

The Spanish were lucky that by the time the phylloxera pest arrived in Spain (in Rioja in 1901) the cure had already been found - it required grafting affected vines to American roots to create a hybrid vine. Practically all vineyards in the world now rely on these hybrid vines since a cure to phylloxera has never been found.

The tasting at the end of the tour was predictably enjoyable. Slices of jamón ibérico and cubes of manchego cheese were laid out for the group as we made our way through the range of wines that the bodega produced. As the group dissipated I hung around trying to make conversation with the guide in Spanish. He humoured me, even though his English was far superior. Nevertheless, I was pleased I'd given it a go. With the wine finished I made my way back over the bridge and into the city, strolling happily in the sunshine.

The next morning as I walked out of town and back towards the bus stop, I thought again about just what a fine little city Logroño was. It was neat, attractive and orderly - so much better than the last city I'd been to that was so strongly associated with the alcoholic drinks industry - Glasgow. Although Glasgow's connection is more about the consumption of it, rather than the production of it.

A few minutes later I arrived at the bus station ready to head to Madrid. I found the ticket office and nailed my request in Spanish. Just for good measure I even asked some questions to which I already knew the answer, just for some extra practice. I listened to the responses carefully – *the journey would take four hours, yes there was a toilet aboard, yes I had an assigned seat* etc etc. I think I almost preferred Spanish this way. It was a lot easier when I knew exactly what they would say, before they said it. I took my ticket, asked which bay the bus would leave from (which I already knew) and proceeded over to my ride for the journey to the capital.

Chapter 12 - La Crisis

The bus rolled in to the city. The journey had not been exciting, passing over plains and flatland, steadily drawing nearer the capital. I was now smack bang in the centre of the country, and even though I hadn't noticed, we had been climbing steadily. At around 700 metres above sea level, Madrid is the highest capital in all of Europe. It is also huge – its population of 3.2 million makes it the third largest city in the European Union (after London and Berlin). That said, it didn't seem to sprawl too far, and the efficient ring road and wide dual carriageway allowed us to glide into the centre of the city.

My hostel was near Gran Via (a main road cutting through the centre of the city) and I decided to orient myself with a leisurely stroll. I walked out of the hostel and down a pedestrianised street towards the main plaza. Almost immediately I realised I was in the red-light district. In amongst the shoppers and people going about their business I could see a fair few "ladies of the night". The only thing was - it wasn't actually the night – it was barely even mid-afternoon. Surely it wasn't a prime time for this trade? It would be like trying sell kebabs first thing in the morning, or porridge at midnight. There are certain times and places for things, and this didn't seem to be the time or the place for *that*. I looked over at the ladies, easily identifiable by their 7-inch platform stiletto shoes. I was curious to see if they were doing any business, but didn't want to look with such curiosity that they would think I wanted their business. To my surprise, a man in a suit seemed to be in the middle of a negotiation with one of the ladies. Well, I guess that was one reason to leave work early.

I wandered down the street, spotting various salesmen as I went. They each wore a fluorescent bib that said *"Compro Oro"* (I buy gold). I didn't have any gold and I wondered just *who was* wandering around with spare gold, happy to do a quick deal on the street with a man wearing a fluorescent bib. Presumably it happened. I realised the presence of these guys was probably indicative of *"La Crisis"* (the economic crisis). Even though the great crash had happened more than five years ago, Spain was still recovering. It had been hit harder than most; even now the unemployment rate was over 20%, and the youth unemployment rate over 40%. Spain had boomed during the good times, money was lent freely, roads and buildings were going up all over the place, and then the whole thing came to a crashing halt.

When the money ran out, suddenly all these projects – many of which should have never been started in the first place – were stopped, many not even finished. One airport – built for the city of Ciudad Real, a couple of hours north of Madrid, and named the "Don Quixote" airport - was completed in 2010, but abandoned less than two years later. It cost over 10 billion euros to construct, only ever served a handful of commercial flights, and was eventually purchased by a Chinese investment group for just 10 thousand euros (that's 0.000001% of what it cost to build). The truth is it should never have been built in the first place. It was a vanity project for the local authority, and wasn't based on demand. No one wanted to fly to that city – I mean, you've probably never heard of it - and it was served adequately enough by Madrid's airport. Nevertheless, so much cash was sloshing around in the Spanish system that people were willing to back these types of projects. There are lots of housing estates – particularly in the Spanish interior – for which there were no buyers. Now they just sit empty. One town, Ciudad Valdeluz, built for 30,000, has fewer than 1,000 residents. They're modern day ghost towns. The Spanish government believe that over 750,000 homes built in the boom years sit empty.

It reminded me of my only previous visit to Madrid. It was 2006, a couple of years before the world's economy fell off a cliff. I was working in London as a financial journalist, right in the heart of the city. That makes it sound glamorous. It really wasn't – both my first and second interviews for the job were held in a pub across the road from the office. I remember arriving for my first interview, suited up, clutching some copies of the university magazine where I had been music editor. The office building was sleek and modern, the receptionist cold, clipped and professional, but my prospective new boss was anything but. He barrelled through the door into the reception area, looking harried and dishevelled. I regarded him for a moment: gruff, bearded and rather scruffy, and he was the editor! I'd never felt overdressed for an interview before, but there was a first for everything I suppose.

We walked through the offices and he told me how he had been editor of this particular financial magazine for ten years and counting. Unfortunately, ten years of experience didn't help him when it came to gaining entrance into any of the meeting rooms. He had tried three already – the first one and then the rooms on either side. He had another go at the door of the original room, but it still refused to unlock.

"Doesn't seem to want to open," he said, rather obviously. "Wait here, and I'll see if I can find a different key."

I did as I was told, too nervous to notice the lack of organisation and planning that was to characterise the company as a whole. After all, I was hoping this would be my first proper job. My previous work had been restricted to tearing tickets at a theatre (after I while I had been given extra responsibilities – selling programs and ice creams), later I worked for a mystery shopping company, sending the mystery shoppers to various unsuspecting car dealerships. No, this was a proper job. I'd trained for a year to be a journalist and here I was. Sure, it was an industry publication, not something you'd find on the newsstands, but nevertheless, I was getting a foot on the ladder.

The editor shambled back into view, "Right, I've got another key," he said, brandishing the new key. He tried the lock. It still didn't work. "Shit," he muttered. "I don't think this is actually the right key either," he declared. There wasn't anything for me to say. He looked up at me, as if appraising me for the first time, unsure whether to proceed. *Fuck it,* his eyes seemed to say, "Do you mind if we do this down the pub? It's not far from here."

"Sure, sure. Not a problem," I stuttered. It was 11.30am.

We wandered over to the pub. It was an old East End boozer, named the "The Pig and Sparrow" or "The Cockfight" or something similar. The interview went well enough, and my editor-to-be only managed two whisky and lemonades during the course of it, so I didn't see any cause for concern. The next day I received an email asking me if I'd like to come to a second interview, this time with the commercial Director as well. The email finished with, "May as well just go straight to the pub this time. I think it's easier that way." And so began my not-so-illustrious career as a financial journalist.

***

As I left the mini-Red light district, the pedestrianised street smartened up and eventually I emerged into the *Puerta del Sol* (Gate of the Sun). It's Madrid's main square, although it's more like a semi-circle with roads radiating off in each direction. The centre of the Puerta del Sol is the centre point of the Spanish road network i.e. distances measured to Madrid start here at 0km. Madrid hasn't always been the capital or most important city in Spain (as say London and Paris have been in England and France respectively). Up until the 16th century it was a backwater. Unlike some capitals it's not situated on the key river in the country, and it doesn't command a prime coastal location. In the medieval period it was only a small town. In fact, the main city in the central plains region of Spain was Toledo. However, Madrid's luck turned in the 14th century when it was used as one of many seats for the royal court of the Kingdom of Castile. Nevertheless, it remained small and poor. One 15th century visitor wrote 'in Madrid there is nothing except what you bring with you'.

One thing Madrid did have going for it was its central location. As the Spanish kingdoms began to unify into what we think of as modern-day Spain, Madrid was well-positioned, but it was still far from favourite to assume the mantle of capital. However, Philip II who had risen to the throne in 1556 made the surprise choice to move the capital from Valladolid to Madrid in 1561. Allegedly it's because his wife preferred it there, but the true reason behind the move has been lost in history.

Once capital status was bestowed upon Madrid it began to expand. The Puerta Del Sol had originally been a gate in the city walls. It was on an eastern orientation, so it welcomed the sun in the morning - hence the name *Gate of the Sun*. But very soon, Madrid grew beyond its old city walls and the Puerta Del Sol was absorbed into the city itself.

I looked around at the people milling about in the sunshine, and the street performers plying their trade to tourists (that trade being standing still for the most part). It was a convivial scene. People sat on the low wall surrounding the fountain eating ice cream, with the water rippling behind them. They were framed by the tall, historic buildings that ringed the plaza, like walls of a grand arena.

I was on the lookout for a famous statue – *the* famous statue of Madrid. My guidebook had described it as "must see", yet as soon as I saw it I wondered why. It was *La Estatua del Oso y el Madroño* (The Statue of the Bear and the Strawberry Tree) – pretty descriptive as far as statue names go. Michelangelo didn't even bother to give his statue its last name, even though the bloke David must have had one. (*"Which Dave is this? Do I know him?"* I can imagine early visitors in Florence saying.)

The Bear and the Strawberry Tree is actually the symbol of Madrid. It's emblazoned on their crest, taxis, government buildings and so on. I scoured the centre of the plaza looking for the statue. I imagined some kind of Nelson's column, huge, towering into the sky, but I was sorely disappointed. I couldn't see it at all. Eventually I asked a policeman. I didn't know the word for strawberry tree (fair enough) or statue (obvious in retrospect – *estatua*), so I simply asked *"¿Dónde está el oso?"* (Where is the bear?). He paused for a moment. I had one extra word in my vocabulary which I had debated using the first time round. I decided to throw it in for good measure, *"el oso famoso,"* (the famous bear). I sounded conspiratorial, but he nodded in comprehension. I really didn't think adding "the famous bear" would have been that helpful. After all, it seemed unlikely there would be more than one bear in this plaza. And if there *was* another bear running around here amongst all these tourists, it wouldn't be long before it too was famous, particularly if it was a real bear.

Nevertheless he pointed me in the direction of the corner of the plaza, and there hidden away behind a gaggle of tourists was the statue. It was in heavy bronze, a bear leaning with his paws on the trunk of the tree, but it was disappointingly small, barely four metres high. People waited in turn to take their photo in front of it. I watched for a moment. I couldn't decide if I wanted my photo in front of it... It reminded me of visiting Brussels' *Manneken Pis*, the small statue of a boy weeing – continually. That statue is the symbol of Brussels *and* Belgium. It is suitably disappointing, although fitting, given the city it represents.

I ummed and ahhed and finally decided I *should* have my photo taken in front of the bear statue. After all, it was Madrid's most famous one. I did so, but as I walked away I immediately realised that that didn't make it *actually* famous. Madrid's most famous statue is a bit like Amsterdam's most famous fountain, or Sydney's most famous tree. *Not that famous.* Well, to be fair to the bear, it *is* famous in its own city. It reminded me of those endless "world famous" restaurants I came across when I drove across the USA. They weren't even famous in the next town, let alone around the world. Intriguingly though, Madrid does actually boast a world famous restaurant - *Botin Restaurant* – which the Guinness Book of World Records says is the oldest one in the world, having been open and serving since 1725. Unfortunately, while it may have been open for nearly three hundred years, it wasn't open at 4.30pm on a Tuesday afternoon, so instead I took a stroll down to the Museo Reina Sofia.

Madrid boasts some of the best art galleries in the world, and the first one I headed to was the Reina Sofia, which is Spain's national gallery for 20th century art. It's the most popular one in Madrid, attracting over 3 million visitors annually (which ranks it 12th most popular in the world –no.1 is in Beijing). While the Reine Sofia contains plenty of international artists, it majors on Spanish ones. However, there was one painting in particular I wanted to see, *Guernica*, by Spanish artist Pablo Picasso. I've already mentioned Guernica – the small village bombed to smithereens by Franco's allies, the Nazis, during the Spanish civil war – for its importance to the Basque Country and in the Spanish Civil War itself. But the painting of the same name also made a huge cultural impact of its own.

I wandered past some Salvador Dali paintings, and paused at some Rothkos, which despite their simplicity, have always appealed to me. After a while I continued to the room where *Guernica* was on display – and it did indeed have its own room – not least because it was mural-sized. It took up a whole wall, dark and brooding, different images interlinked, all speaking to the horror of war. I'd seen a copy of it before, but seeing it in the flesh was a different matter. It's identifiably a Picasso painting in the sense that each image, the people, the animals, the strange disembodied limbs, all have a cubist, surrealist quality. But there's something particularly arresting about this image. Ghostly figures surge forward, screams are captured escaping from people animals alike, violence and pain are almost tangible on the canvas.

I took a moment to take it all in. A bull watches over a woman clutching her dead child, while a horse rears up in pain, as if injured. There are no bombs in the painting (unlike the actual events in Guernica, but nevertheless the symbolic violence of war is there). Critics have endlessly debated what the different figures mean. Clearly the bull and the horse, so closely associated with Spain, represent the country itself, and the pain of the individuals represents the suffering of war, but beyond that it's up for debate. Picasso said so himself in a fine riposte to the type of windbag critics who insist on some great meaning behind every brushstroke. Picasso said this:

> "...this bull is a bull and this horse is a horse... If you give a meaning to certain things in my paintings it may be very true, but it is not my idea to give this meaning. What ideas and conclusions you have got I obtained too, but instinctively, unconsciously. I make the painting for the painting. I paint the objects for what they are."

So there you go, the bull was just a bull all along. Next time you're in a gallery, looking at a Picasso, listening to an audioguide describing the hidden meaning of this or that, you can simply fast forward. What Picasso did intend to do though was bring attention to the suffering of the Spanish people (and the barbarity of Franco). The painting was completed in black-and-white, using as matte a paint as possible, to bring to mind a news photograph, and the title was intended to draw attention to what Picasso considered a war crime. He hoped that he could raise awareness amongst the international community.

The painting didn't make waves though, and only slowly accumulated its fame. After being exhibited in 1937 at the World's Fair in Paris, it was on exhibition throughout Europe, and then the USA, before coming to reside in New York's Museum of Modern Art. However, during the Vietnam War in the late 60's and 70s' *Guernica* became a gathering point for anti-war vigils, and it became known as anti-war symbol. Following Spain's transition to democracy, the painting eventually came to Madrid. However, a version of *Guernica* remains in New York. A tapestry of the image hangs on the wall of the United Nations building as a salutary reminder of the horrors of war.

Chapter 13 – Royal blood

The following day was sunny and I wandered over to the *Parque del buen retiro* (Park of the pleasant retreat). Madrid's most famous park lies on the eastern side of the city centre, but was easily walkable from my hostel. I passed the girls working the morning shift and nodded, heading for my breakfast of *café con leche y bollo* (pastry). Twenty minutes later I arrived at the entrance of the park and I strolled up a wide, open path. It was almost boulevard-esque and led straight into the centre of the park. People rollerbladed, cycled, skateboarded and jogged by in the morning sunshine. Further in, a forest of exercise frames and jungle gym equipment lined the side of the path. A group of human gorillas swung from the bars, preening, admiring themselves and each other. I observed them for a moment, trying to understand their primitive behaviour. They had established a pecking order - certain alpha males maintained possession of the scarce resources (the popular equipment) while the adolescents were forced to the outer edges of the pack. Many of them made do with no equipment at all, performing press-ups or sit-ups in ones and twos. They grunted away in what I assumed was a primeval form of communication. I noted too that clothes were also scarce; very few of them had progressed to wearing t-shirts.

I strolled on, making my way to the impressive lake in the middle of the park. Technically it is a pond, but that seems to be rather underselling it. A pond brings to mind a back garden, a few fish, and perhaps a gnome. This "pond" (*estanque*) has a surface area of 37,000 square metres, and was filled with people boating across it. And there were no gnomes anywhere to be seen. Instead there was a big monument. A series of huge columns in a wide curve with a massive statue in the middle rose up imposingly on the opposite side of the lake. The colonnade was the Monument to Alfonso XII.

Alfonso XII – who was king between 1874 and 1885 - was one of the unluckiest monarchs Spain ever had. When he was a child his family were deposed in one of the Carlist wars, and they were forced to flee to Vienna. Years later, following a military coup, Alfonso was allowed to return to Spain to take the throne. At first things went very well – Spain's overseas territories including Puerto Rico and Cuba thrived, the economy was on the up and Alfonso had his pick of all the women in the land. Surprisingly, he chose to marry his cousin, but that was the fashion at the time. Regrettably she promptly had a miscarriage, then died from typhoid – all less than six months into the marriage. Alfonso married again the following year, although on his honeymoon, the luckless King was greeted by a would-be assassin, who attempted to dispatch him and his new wife. Fortunately they both survived, but, just five years later the unfortunate Alfonso died from tuberculosis and dysentery at the tender age of 28.

Alfonso was succeeded on the throne by his yet-to-be born son (which is a lot of pressure to put on a foetus). Presumably very few decisions were made during that period. Some years after his death Alfonso's widow commissioned the very monument I was looking at now. It was impressive and gave the scene a very regal air. In the late-19th century though the whole park was still the private reserve and gardens of the monarchy, hence its name as the Park of the Pleasant Retreat. However, it wasn't long before the park was passed into public ownership and was opened for the enjoyment of all the citizens of Madrid.

I decided to carry on my royal themed tour by taking a walk over to the Royal Palace *(Palacio Real)*. The huge white building is in the centre of the city and I approached through a manicured garden and fountain. I passed a few street artists and made my way to the back of the considerable queue of tourists snaking out of the ticket office. While the Palace is the official residence of the royal family, they don't actually live there. I don't blame them, I wouldn't want to encounter a horde of visitors armed with selfie sticks on a daily basis either. The family instead choose to live in a more modest palace on the outskirts of Madrid. It seemed a shame that they rarely used the Palace though, since it was such a grand and impressive building. Perhaps it *was* the selfie sticks that had driven them out, perhaps it was simply for privacy. More seriously, I wondered whether it was a calculated decision to distance themselves from the opulent lifestyle and wealth of the monarchs of the past. After all, from what I had gleaned thus far on the trip, the Spanish royal family weren't popular.

The subject of the British royal family had come up in conversations a couple of times during my travels. It's not unusual; as a Brit abroad I often find myself asked for my opinion on the royals. Like most Britons I don't have a problem with our royal family (they're not really a factor in daily life, and contrary to some people's opinions, they don't really wield much power). However, the Spanish royals seemed much less popular than their British counterparts.

More than one Spaniard had told me they believed that the King and his political cronies (specifically the right-of-centre *Partido Popular* (PP)) were responsible for robbing the country and siphoning off a lot of its wealth. I gathered that the resentment of politicians and the royal family was partly because Spain was still experiencing the after effects of *La Crisis* (the worldwide economic crash). General anger over high unemployment, and the fact that the economy was in the toilet, mixed with a residual distrust and dislike for the monarchy and government. Unlike in the UK I hadn't detected any great affinity to the royal family amongst anyone I spoke to in Spain.

One incident I heard mentioned repeatedly was the scandal of an infamous hunting trip in 2012. Several people used the scandal to illustrate the supposedly high-handed and out of touch attitude of the King. In the middle of the depression brought about by *La Crisis,* King Juan Carlos undertook a secret hunting trip to Botswana. There he was pictured having shot and killed an elephant. When the picture leaked - that of a ridiculous aristocrat on an exotic safari, with a majestic creature slumped dead in the background, all paid for by a country that was experiencing 25% unemployment - let's just say the reaction wasn't one of happiness and delight. The public turned on the King and the Spanish newspapers, who had long kept the King's mistress a secret, revealed that she too had accompanied him on the trip. The King's popularity took a nose-dive.

Despite the scandal some Spaniards retained a vaguely positive view of King Juan Carlos. Decades before, following Franco's death, he was nominated as head of state and successor to the dictator. Yet, instead, Juan Carlos chose to usher in democratic reforms, and elections swiftly followed. But that was a long time ago and the hunting incident seemed to be the proof many people were looking for; in their minds the royal family were out of touch and an unnecessary burden. The following year, a public poll suggested approval of the royal family had fallen to an all-time low of 3.7 out of 10. Seeing the writing on the wall, Juan Carlos decided to abdicate in 2014, and made way for his son, Felipe. (This was actually the second job he lost as a result of the hunting debacle. Incredibly, Juan Carlos *had* been President of *World Wildlife Fund Spain*, until the pictures were released and his penchant for killing exotic creatures was revealed. He was about as appropriate as using Pavarotti to front a *Weightwatchers* advert).

The young King Felipe has proved to be more in touch than his father. In 2015, he announced that he would cut his annual salary by 20% due to the continuing recession. The royal family's popularity has recovered a little, although I still got the sense that they were on thin ice, which may explain their continued residence in an out of the way palace on the outskirts of Madrid, rather than the iconic building in front of me.

I proceeded inside and was immediately struck by how big it was. It's the largest palace in Western Europe, nearly 1.5 million square foot of space, and over 3,000 rooms. It was hard to get my head around the scale of it. Imagine if you lived there and you couldn't find your car keys. What a nightmare.

I passed through a succession of grand rooms, each adorned with tapestries and artworks. Big solemn portraits looked down from the walls - old paintings of old men – typically. I browsed the wide array of furniture, silverware and other artefacts. The sheer amount of stuff was somewhat overwhelming. These royals really weren't down with the trend for minimalism. I passed into the throne room, which was incredible. A huge red and gold space stretched in front of me, a fresco adorned the ceiling, and dual thrones sat in the centre of the room. I could imagine the ceremonies that would have taken place there. I looked too in the royal library, royal pharmacy and armoury. The palace had it all. It was like an ancient shopping mall. The armoury was particularly impressive. Several full replicas of suits of armour for horses and their riders were set up as if in motion. Some of them were tournament pieces for jousting contests. They looked incredibly heavy and it was a wonder that a horse could run wearing such a thing.

I wandered through a gallery and saw more paintings of old men, each wearing one of three expressions: serious, dour or serious and dour at the same time. Then I exited the buildings into a grand courtyard. It was huge and surrounded on three sides by the white palace buildings gleaming in the sunshine. A series of archways ran along two sides, forming open-air style corridors. Out here it was easy to see the similarities with the Louvre buildings in Paris. Columns, sculptures and detailing gave it a very French look. Supposedly, the design of the palace was inspired by sketches made by Bernini for the construction of the Louvre in Paris. I wandered around, taking in the size and scope of it all. On the far side the courtyard looked out over one side of Madrid. I hadn't realised that we were on a hill, and the city, which was surprisingly low-rise, spread out into the distance. Although there were a lot of buildings, there was a pleasing amount of greenery too, most of it belonging to the huge *Casa de Campo* park, the largest in the city, and formerly a royal hunting reserve. In the far distance I could see the mountains that surround Madrid, the *Sierra de Guadarrama* range.

That evening I decided to go to a bar. Madrid has literally thousands of bars. They all seem to feature a similar sort of set-up. Lots of men hanging out around the bar, a TV with football on, a giant leg of ham hanging up or set up for slicing and Mahou and Estrella Damm beer on draft. I passed through the *Puerta del Sol* and on to one of the many streets radiating off it. I kept walking, passing a few bars, and stopped once I figured I was far enough away from the touristy central plaza. The bar looked similar to many of the others - a narrow entrance led to a room which reached far back off the street. It looked as good as any other and I entered. I took a stool right at the bar. The large and friendly barman, turned to me and lifted his head to ask what I would like.

"*¿Qué quiere tomar?*" (What do you want to have?)

"*¿Me pone una caña?*" (Can you give me a small draft beer?)

I used an authentic sounding Spanish phrase to order my beer. I'd learnt it the previous day, and it literally means "put me a small beer", which sounds strange, but it seemed to work just fine as the man returned with a glass of beer. He also placed a tapa on the bar too, a small dish of potato, tomato and meat mixed together. I was accustomed to receiving tapas with a drink, but typically it was just crisps or olives. This was much more substantial, and very tasty. Better yet, it was free and the beer itself cost less than two euros. I reasoned this could well be the most cost-effective way to eat and drink I had found yet. I decide to settle in. I looked past the leg of ham placed on the counter top and saw Real Madrid were playing on the TV. Everything was as it should be, Real Madrid were already 2-0 up and the camera was showing a close-up of Cristiano Ronaldo pouting about some decision that had not gone his way. This was a truly authentic Madrid experience.

I ordered another beer – the Spanish like to serve the beers in rather small sizes – the *caña* is the most common draft size (it's not quite half a pint), and the *botellin* is the most common bottle size (which is a little smaller than a regular bottle of beer). The Spanish supposedly favour these small sizes because of the heat. It makes sense - smaller beers are finished more quickly so won't get warm. It would never work in England though – I mean, how is one meant to get completely and utterly bladdered if the beer comes in such tiny vessels?! It doesn't make any sense.

Strangely, despite the huge number of bars there were in Spain, I was yet to see anyone certifiably drunk in my whole time in the country. This was despite the fact I *always* saw people drinking wine at lunch, and yet by mid-afternoon I never saw a single drunk. I had come to the shocking revelation that these Spaniards were stopping after one drink, a concept I found completely unfamiliar.

Right now though, it was the evening and I would not be stopping after one drink. After all, the match was still on and Cristiano Ronaldo was on screen alternately flouncing about, scowling at the referee, the opposition, and occasionally even his own team mates. The night was young. I ordered another beer. The barman placed it in front of me. I was worried that the tapas tap might have run dry, but I needn't have been concerned. Another plate duly arrived - this time some freshly cut ham - and I tucked in.

All of a sudden, the bar erupted in clapping and cheering. Real Madrid had scored. I hadn't realised that so many people had been watching. Even the barman, who I honestly thought hadn't been paying the slightest attention to the screen, was getting in on the act. He picked up a big silver metal lid from a hot tray of food and banged it up and down with a huge clattering noise. The whooping and racket continued while the replay showed the Madrid striker calmly slotting the ball home. In the melee I noticed that on a smaller screen in the back they were showing Atlético Madrid's match (Madrid's second team).

After the noise had died down, I spoke to the barman, *"Oye, ¿Siempre ponéis Atlético en la pantalla más pequeña?"* (Excuse me, do you always show Atletico on the smaller screen).

He nodded, *"Sí, pero sólo cuando coinciden el Madrid y el Atlético en el mismo horario. El Atlético es casi de segunda."* (Yes. Well, whenever both Madrid teams are playing at the same time. They are less popular).

I nodded, *"Y el Barça?"* (And Barcelona?) I wanted to know what happened if Spain's other big team, Barcelona, were playing at the same time, and whether they were shown in the bar.

He laughed, and spoke up, so that some of the other patrons could hear. *"Si quieres ver el Barça, mejor que vetes a Barcelona."* (If you want to watch Barcelona, you should go to Barcelona). He and a couple of the others in the bar laughed. I wasn't sure if I was partaking in some banter, or if I was the subject of it, but either way it was another little achievement, and I laughed along with them.

The match continued, as did the beers and tapas. By the fourth round I was confident enough to request the particular tapa that I wanted. I chatted intermittently to the barman. It was a convivial atmosphere, and one I was sure was being repeated all over the city. The bar is an important part of Spanish culture. One study suggests Spain has a bar for every 140 inhabitants, and therefore ranks second in Europe in this regard (after Cyprus). The same study revealed that two thirds of Spaniards claim to know the name of the waiter in their favourite bar, while nearly a third say that they would trust the waiter enough to give them their house keys. I presume that those who would hand over the house keys are the same who already know the name of the waiter. That wasn't specified though, and we can't rule out if some Spanish people are just incredibly trusting with their house keys.

The match had finished but the bar was no quieter than when I had entered. It was nearly 11pm and people were still arriving. They certainly do go out late in Spain. On a previous trip I'd been to a nightclub, sometime between midnight and 1am. My friend and I ventured downstairs and found a completely empty room. We asked the bouncer where everyone was and he told us that most people arrived around 2am. I was shocked, but perhaps I shouldn't have been, since a lot of Spaniards will start eating their evening meal at 10pm. Almost everything seems to happen a couple of hours later here. For me though it was time to go. After my fifth small beer and plate of tapas, I asked for the bill. I gave the barman a ten euro note and incredibly I was still able to tell him to keep the change. I rose from my stool and left into the warm night.

The following day was my final one in the city, and I took a walk north. I wanted to do a tour of the Bernabéu, the stadium of Real Madrid. It was an hour-long walk, but I figured it was fine in the cool of the morning. As I walked out of the historic centre, and up the grand *Paseo de Recoletos* I started to recognise some of the skyscrapers from my previous trip to Madrid, back when I was a financial journalist. It came towards the end of my rather unnoteworthy tenure at the magazine. It was a strange time. I worked in an office with a bunch of staff writers for other financial publications owned by the same company.

Most of the other people in the office were sales people. They were led by a high energy, low empathy, sales director, who had a rather cutthroat attitude to sales and his staff. I remember speaking to one shell-shocked new recruit who, when they had asked for some training in their first week was told, "It's sink or swim, no point training you if you're not going to be here next week. If you're still here next month, come and talk to me then." Let's just say staff development was not his strong point.

It was not much better on the journalistic side. My managing editor (who had interviewed me in the pub) only came to the office once a week. I was left without supervision, colleagues, or really much of an idea of how to go about writing stories on complex loans and financial instruments. Typically, my editor would call me about 11am every day to ask me what I was working on. Usually he sounded as if he had just woken, or at the very least hungover. Sometimes I wondered if he was still in bed.

I took his morning call to effectively signal the start of my working day. Effectively this meant that I surfed the web until about 10.45am, at which point I panicked and had a look around to see what other people were reporting on, and what press releases were available. In his sleepy and confused state it was easy to come up with something to pacify him. Every Thursday he would come to the office. He would arrive about 10.30am looking flustered and dishevelled. He would bustle in, sit for an hour or so, before inevitably turning to me and asking if I needed to learn about the finer points of French PFI contracts, or the biggest banks in Greece, or something else suitably arcane. I would answer in the affirmative, and every time he would say, "Excellent, better if we do it down the pub don't you think?" and off we would head to "The Three-legged Mare" or "The Bareknuckle Fox" or whatever it was called.

To be fair to my editor, those pub sessions, while first and foremost a chance for him to drink several whiskey and lemonades at lunchtime, were nevertheless illuminating. I learnt about the rapid expansions in loans, the falling cost of financing them, and the increasingly unlikely projects that were getting funded. Intriguingly, countries like Greece, Spain and Portugal were funding an incredible number of infrastructure projects, such as new roads, bridges and airports. Money was easy to come by and was being shuttled around at levels never seen before. Unfortunately I didn't have the wherewithal or acuity to realise that it was all a house of cards and was about to fall down imminently. All I could see was a lot of people (principally bankers) getting very rich.

As part of my beat I occasionally travelled to Europe and interviewed bankers about the various loans and deals they'd been cutting. In 2006 I travelled to Madrid, where a lot of action was taking place (remember the story about the newly built, now abandoned airport, that never welcomed more than a fraction of flights that were planned? That was one such project). When I arrived in Madrid, I remember being ushered into various plush offices at the top of gleaming glass buildings. A besuited, slick young banker would enter, and eye me with a mix of suspicion and braggadocio while I tried to prize out details about the loan tranches, interest rates, guaranteed payments and who knows what else, on the various deals they had been making. I didn't like it, not only because it bored me, but because I knew that these guys were earning in a week what I earned in a year. Something about the whole thing felt off, and lo and behold a year or so later the whole world knew it.

Chapter 14 – Learn the lingo, gringo!

I was leaving Madrid, en route south. It was the middle of April and I only had another five weeks in the country, six before the wedding. My Spanish still left a lot to be desired and I realised that being a tourist wasn't doing much for it. I needed to base myself in another city for a few weeks, take some more lessons, and keep talking to people. As a tourist, it was surprisingly easy to get by with just English. I stayed in hotels where people tried to check me in in English, restaurants where people tried to take my order in English, and visited museums and attractions where the Spanish was almost always translated into English just underneath.

People like to think us English speakers are lazy, that we simply can't be bothered to learn languages. Well, yes, that is often largely true, but largely true is not the same as completely true! I think we English speakers face a few unique problems that dissuade us from learning another language. In a way, it's just *too easy* to speak English, but the flipside of that same coin is that it's often too difficult to learn another language. I don't mean that it's just difficult to learn another language (it is, but that's not the point). I mean that as an English speaker abroad you are often presented with an opportunity to speak, read or listen in English, and therefore it is difficult to use the language you are learning. And for those who say we're just being lazy, look at it this way, if you need to get somewhere and you have both a bicycle and a car, how often do you actually take the bicycle? No, you make life easy for yourself. But in some ways, it is even worse than that.

The following example is typical of my experiences in restaurants and bars.

"¡Hola!", I say as the waiter approaches.

"Hola, buenos días," (Hello, good morning), the waiter replies.

"Buenos días, ¿Qué tal?" (Good morning, how are you?) I say, in an effort to have a little conversation. Immediately I can see his face change. He realises I'm foreign, probably an English speaker.

"I'm good, thanks. What do you want?", says the waiter (changing to English).

"¿Me pone una coca-cola?" (I'll have a coke please), I say, sticking with Spanish.

"Ok, a Coca-Cola, and do you want anything to eat?" Waiter says, sticking with English.

(I hesitate, wondering if I should continue this absurd battle. I decide to continue*), "Sí, me da un bocadillo de queso, por favor,"* (Yes, give me a cheese sandwich).

"Sure, anything else?" The waiter says.

At this point, I realise that both of us are locked into this strange contest, whereby we both insist on speaking our non-native, weaker, language. I concede defeat. "No, that's all, thank you."

It wasn't an isolated incident. It happened all the time. At first, I didn't understand why they would respond in English. Slowly I realised a couple of things. Firstly, they thought they were doing me a favour. After all, most English people would prefer to speak English, and for some reason they weren't clocking that I *was* trying to (and managing to) communicate in Spanish. Secondly, I realised that a lot of them *wanted* to speak English. It made sense. Presumably they had gone to a lot of trouble to learn the language and this was their opportunity to exercise it. Sometimes this even applied when the other person didn't even know much English. Occasionally I would conduct a conversation like the above completely in Spanish, but when I asked for the bill, the waiter or barman would say the amount I owed in English, ignoring the fact that we had conversed without problem in Spanish.

It was even more frustrating when I spoke to people in conversation. A lot of people speak English, and it is even more common among young people. Often, despite my efforts, the other person would switch our conversation to English, even though we were in Spain and I was making the effort to speak their language. The truth is that the language spoken between two people generally defaults to whichever language one of you has the higher ability in. It's like the bicycle/car example above, you'll speak in whichever language it's more efficient and easier to speak in. This means that you either need to reach a good enough level so that *you* are the one with the higher ability, *or* you need to find people who don't speak any of your language. In which case, you'll always get the chance to practise their language. This is why it is a particular problem for English speakers, since so many people speak English, and many speak it to a high level. I wondered if it would be just easier to pretend I was Bulgarian. I could pretend I only spoke Bulgarian and Spanish, and lo and behold, they would have no choice but to speak Spanish to me.

The more international and cosmopolitan the place, the more people will speak your language, and the more expats and foreigners there will be. I think for this reason people often choose to go to out of the way places to immerse themselves in the language and culture of a country. I had already found in Barcelona (at the school) that it was very easy to surround myself with a lot of English-speaking friends.

In Spain I had noted a generational divide – very few Spaniards above 40 seemed to speak English well, whereas amongst younger people it was more common, although not universal, like in some European countries. I wondered how an English speaker would ever learn Swedish or Dutch, for instance. Pretty much every Dutch and Swedish person seems to speak English (often to a better level than English people). Not many people will humour you and allow you to stumble along in their language (a necessary part of learning) when they can speak your language fluently. As English becomes more universal, perhaps it will become even harder for English speakers to learn another language. Most young people around the world want to speak English, it's just a useful skill, like driving or computer skills. It's a pre-requisite for many jobs in other countries. Whereas for English speakers, what language do you even choose to learn? Spanish, French, Portuguese, Chinese? There's certainly no obvious candidate, in the way that English is to the rest of the world.

The fact that English is *so* universal is the other factor that gives other nationalities an advantage. Switch on the radio abroad and at least half the songs are in English, switch on the TV and the slogans for companies like Nike and McDonalds tend to be the same the world over. English words are creeping into other languages at a surprising rate: "parking", "jetlag" and "meeting" are just some of the words used frequently in Spanish (albeit said with a heavy Spanish accent). The point being is that even if you don't want to learn it, the modern world forces English on everyone. This just doesn't happen in the UK and USA. With the honourable exceptions of the odd crossover song e.g. "Despacito", "La Macarena" or "La Bamba" (that should just about cover you, no matter your age) we don't tend to hear foreign language songs. Spanish people find it surprising to hear that British or American radio plays about 95%+ English language songs. It's the same with other media; while every young French or Spanish person is watching *Game of Thrones*, in contrast foreign language movies and TV in the UK or US is regarded as "arty" and "intellectual".

It's not that English speakers don't want to learn other languages, I think most people do. Many people say they really want to learn French/Spanish/Italian – and people really do have good intentions. However, for all the reasons above (and the fact we don't start teaching children languages until 8, 9 or 10) learning languages, particularly reaching a high level, will probably always be a niche pursuit amongst English speakers. It's a shame because it's an enriching, challenging, satisfying and useful pursuit. That said, many English speakers do still make the effort to learn, and whatever level they reach, it's always a good thing to be learning and making the effort. That all being said, if only they made something as good as *Game of Thrones* in foreign, then that would be a start.

***

I was on the high-speed train rocketing at 180 miles per hour towards Seville. The journey, despite covering half the country, only took two and a half hours. When I arrived, I emerged into the rather grand Seville train station. The station was light and airy, but the air itself felt warmer here. Seville (*Sevilla* in Spanish) is in the middle of Andalusia, way down in the south of Spain. I was now close to the southern fringes of Europe itself. Seville is on the same latitude as Algiers and Tunis in North Africa, and unsurprisingly the climate is noticeably warmer than elsewhere in Spain. Even now, in the middle of April, the temperature was in the high twenties (celsius).

I'd chosen Seville, the fourth-largest city in Spain (after Madrid, Barcelona and Valencia), as the place to spend a few weeks and really work on my Spanish. For many people Andalusia (*Andalucía* in Spanish) was the heart of Spain. When people think of typically Spanish things, odds are it comes from Andalusia: Flamenco dancing, bullfighting, tapas, olive oil, gypsy dresses, dancing horses, Spanish guitar and many more. No other region in Spain seems to be as filled with culture, and I was looking forward to exploring it.

I took a taxi to my accommodation, intrigued, excited, and just a touch fearful about what I'd find. I'd chosen to attend more lessons at a Spanish school, like in Barcelona, and this meant living with a Spanish host family again. Who knows what type of host I would have? This time around I hoped my Spanish would be good enough to make conversation. The taxi driver dropped me on the main road, and gestured down a narrow alley. My flat was inaccessible by car and I had to walk. Reluctantly I grabbed my bag and set out in the direction he indicated. Within a few steps the narrow alleyway widened to a much brighter passageway. The pathway turned to cobbles and high whitewashed walls opened up on every side. I was in the historic Santa Cruz neighbourhood, the former Jewish quarter of the medieval city. I looked at the map and saw I was not far from my flat, so I navigated a couple of tight turns through the labyrinth of streets.

I arrived at the correct building and peered through the tall gate. It was a two-story whitewashed building set around a courtyard. I pressed the intercom and a moment later the gate buzzed open. At the top of the stairs my landlady greeted me at the door to the apartment. She reminded me of Luisa, my landlady back in Barcelona. True, there was less hot pink lipstick, but the apron was there, the dyed hair was present and correct, and once again I understood almost nothing she said to me. I caught, *"¡Qué calor!"* (It's so hot), and then almost nothing else.

We proceeded inside and she continued her monologue. It was like a radio broadcast that was too crackly to make out. I could tell words were being spoken, but I couldn't grasp them for the life of me. I tried to catch the gist, and then just the odd word, but I got almost nothing. She was speaking in a way I couldn't follow at all. Just then, something sprang into my mind. It was a fragment of conversation with a Spaniard I'd had a few weeks before, *"...but the worst accent? The worst are the Andalusians".* I thought about it a moment longer and the same fragment floated across my mind once more, like a flashback in a movie. It reminded me of the type of scene where the hero is cursed by a witch at the beginning of the film, but he dismisses it and forgets all about it, because, like, what do witches know anyway? Later the main character remembers the curse as he sees each of his family members perish one-by-one. Exactly as the witch said. Normally it takes until about the third family member until the hero clocks it and thinks, *"Wait a minute! The witch!"* I always wondered why a curse wouldn't stick in his mind. Seems notable to me, and yet here I was in my own witch-curse situation – and I *had* forgotten. Except my problem was just that I couldn't understand my landlady and her impenetrable accent, which by curse standards is on the low-end.

I unpacked. It was another modest room. A simple single bed and writing desk, with a wardrobe and a window to an inner courtyard. I came back out for dinner, and discovered I had two roommates. Two young Italian guys were living together in another bedroom; they spoke no English, and no Spanish either, so it was a challenge to communicate. They were about 19 years old and from Sicily. Much more than that would remain a mystery to me throughout my stay. That first day I tried to engage them in conversation regardless. One of them gamefully tried to speak to me in Italian (a completely pointless endeavour, but one I took as a sign of friendliness), while the other said nothing at all. Yet it was amazing how much we could communicate, even with no common language whatsoever. We talked about football, which teams we supported (mainly just naming teams until someone gave the thumbs up), and we discussed the controversial Italian footballer, Mario Bottelli (three sets of thumbs down).

I also recounted a recent road trip I'd taken around Sicily with my wife Robyn. I tried to tell them that I thought the driving in Sicily was surprisingly reckless, but they didn't seem to understand what I was indicating, which was fitting, since drivers in Sicily didn't seem to understand indicating either. I named some places I had visited, and they named some places, and we nodded and shook our heads. At one point we may have even discussed the mafia (general thumbs down again for those guys). I don't think we used a single adjective or verb, just proper nouns. So, who knows, maybe learning languages is for mugs. Not knowing any vocabulary certainly keeps conversations to the point, I'll say that much.

The following day I went for a walk around the historical centre of Seville. I was surprised by just how big it was. The warren of streets wound around and stretched on and on (maybe I was just walking in circles) but it certainly felt large. Narrow streets, whitewashed walls, gave way to small alleys, hemmed in by buildings four stories high on each side. Plazas and churches appeared regularly. Eventually I emerged into the central square. It's not really a square, more of an uneven open space which links three of Seville's most important historic buildings: the Cathedral, the Archive of the Indies and the Alcázar (palace). I was here for a few weeks, so I knew I'd get round them all, but I thought I would start with the most historic of the lot, the Alcázar.

I've mentioned previously that the Moors - Muslims from North Africa - had at one point controlled nearly the whole the Iberian Peninsula (modern-day Spain and Portugal). However, their grip over the northern half of the territory was much more short-lived and less influential than their control over the South. It was here in Andalusia that the Moors had their powerbase, where their rule lasted longest, and where their influence can still be seen today.

The Moors invaded from North Africa in 711AD, quickly conquering the majority of the Iberian Peninsula, including a small part of southern France. The Moors were Arabs and Berbers, a semi-nomadic people, from modern day Morocco, Algeria and Libya. Their territory in Europe, which they called Al-Andalus (it's easy to see where Andalusia gets its name from), was only one province of their empire, which they called a "Caliphate" – ruled by a Caliph (leader). When modern day crackpot terrorist murderers the Islamic State/Daesh talk about "restoring" an Islamic Caliphate they include all of the Iberian Peninsula, in reference to the territory once held by the Moors.

The problem for the Moors was that faced by all empires. Their capital was in Marrakesh, in modern day Morocco, and the Spanish territory was always the furthest northern reaches – the frontier so to speak. They fought periodically with the Christian kings of Northern Spain, France and Northern Portugal who (when they weren't fighting each other) would band together to fight the Moors. Occasionally the Pope would call for a crusade and they would be bolstered by other knights from across Christendom. But it was far from a time of continual warfare and strife. There were periods of peace and, Al-Andalus itself was a positive beacon in the dark ages of medieval Europe. In the tenth and eleventh centuries, public libraries in Europe were non-existent, while Moorish Spain boasted seventy. Scientific progress in Astronomy, Chemistry, Physics, Mathematics, Geography and Philosophy flourished in the territory.

Writers use the word 'Moors' as if they were one homogenous group, but they weren't. For one, they weren't a self-defined group (like say the Romans or the Ancient Greeks), instead 'Moors' included Berbers, Arabs and even European-born Muslims. It's a catch-all term because those groups defy easy categorisation (so I'll keep using it). More importantly for the Moors themselves they had rival dynasties and families pulling the strings at different points (and continually trying to kill each other).

Like many empires this plotting and internal warfare ultimately weakened the kingdom itself. Al-Andalus had been ruled from Córdoba, but following a dispute over succession and a revolt the Caliphate fractured in 1031. When the next dynasty of Moors took over they chose to move their capital to Seville.

Under pressure from the Christian Kings in the north the Moors' territory was reduced from the high watermark they had reached in about the year 1000AD. The border between the two moved back and forth, but in the early 1200s the Christian Kings launched a concerted attack known as the *Reconquista* (Reconquest). The Moors eventually lost most of their power base – Andalusia - around 1250. They managed to cling on in places and did not lose their last city-state (Granada) until 1492, nearly 800 years after they had arrived.

A lot of the architecture of Seville still has Moorish and Islamic influences. The Cathedral, originally built as a mosque in 1172, is easily identified as such by its distinctive tower. It still looks like a minaret. Today though I decided to join the shorter queue outside the Alcázar. Even from the outside it was impressive, with its huge stone walls topped by crocodile teeth-like battlements. The original building was started in 914 when the Caliph ordered government premises to be built in the growing city of Seville. With this new palace and fortress built so close to the city's Guadalquivir river the Moors made the first step towards Seville's emergence as a great port city. And this would come to define Seville's fortunes in the centuries to come.

I entered the building and it immediately felt palatial. There was an air of elegance about it. The term 'Alcázar' comes from a Hispano-Arabic word 'Alqáşr' which means 'Royal House' or 'Room of the Prince'. In fact, it is the oldest royal palace still in use in Europe. The upper levels are still used by the royal family as their official residence in Seville. I wandered round the palace (unfortunately only the lower levels), marvelling at the décor and design. It felt very Islamic, reminding me of buildings I'd seen in Morocco.

I wandered into the "courtyard of the maidens", supposedly named because the Moors demanded a tribute of 100 virgins every year from Christian kingdoms in Iberia. In the centre was a large, rectangular reflecting pool with sunken gardens on either side. A series of arches and pillars ran round each side. Each arch was immaculately detailed, and the walls above them were full of ornate circles set within geometric diamonds. The lower walls were covered in colourful mosaics made from ceramic tiles.

A lot of the palace had been remodeled over the years, but much of it was preserved too. Many of these "modifications" are centuries old themselves. Various additions made use of the *mudéjar* style, which was developed after the end of the Moors' rule, but was the trademark of the craftsmen who remained behind in Spain. The resulting style is architecture and decoration that is distinctively Islamic.

The rooms branching off the courtyard were just as regal and ornate. The ceilings and walls in particular were sumptuously decorated. The use of arches through to the courtyard meant there was plenty of light, unlike the dark historical buildings of England that I was used to. Perhaps most impressive was the Hall of Ambassadors, arguably the centrepiece of the palace. It featured a huge golden dome in the centre of the ceiling. The dome was rebuilt in 1427 and is made from gilded wood, although it looks like pure gold as you stand underneath it. It was like looking up at a starry night sky. The huge doors, extensive plasterwork decoration and tiling of the walls were all original and constructed in 1366. Any visiting ambassador lucky enough to visit the palace would have left impressed.

Even more remarkable than the Alcázar building itself are the extensive gardens. An oasis of seven hectares: neat hedgerows, palm trees and fountains were lined up in geometric shapes. I climbed up a series of stone steps which led to a viewing gallery. I strolled along, looking out at the vast gardens beneath me. The palace and gardens have been used as the set of several really famous films and TV shows, including *Game of Thrones, Lawrence of Arabia* and Ridley Scott's *Kingdom of Heaven.* Admittedly that last one was pretty forgettable, so much so that I wonder if Ridley Scott even remembers it.

It was easy to see why the Alcázar is so beloved of flimmakers - the whole complex obviously looks like something from a different era altogether, but it also looks alive. It didn't seem like some ruined old relic. And the garden was a huge part of that – it was vibrant and flourishing. All the palaces of Al-Andalus featured sizeable gardens which contained fruit tree orchards, vegetable plots and an assortment of beautiful flowers. Water was a significant aspect too with irrigation channels, fountains, ponds and pools. The Alcázar has a huge pool called the Mercury Pond which is full of fish. The gardens fulfilled the dual purpose of supplying food and being a relaxing place for retreat and pleasure. I certainly had enjoyed my time exploring, although now I felt like something different and I couldn't shake it. I just really fancied watching some *Game of Thrones.*

Chapter 15 – Hot hot heat

It was lunchtime during my first week in the city, and I was back home eating at Mercedes' table. The TV was on and she was busying around the kitchen, apron on, hair pinned up.

"¡Qué calor más insoportable!" (What unbearable heat!), she exclaimed.

I was pleased she was talking about the heat. While my ability to understand her was still low, it was nevertheless growing, and this was a favourite and therefore familiar topic of hers.

"Sí, ¡Qué calor!" (It's so hot) I said, in sympathetic union. Repeating some, or all, of what had been said directly back in reply was something I'd taken to doing recently. True, I did sound a little like a simpleton, but at least I knew I was always grammatically correct. As a method for learning to speak as Spaniards spoke, as opposed to a clunking, word-for-word translation from English, it was very effective. And more often than not, the other person seamlessly moved the conversation on, allowing me to participate and converse more easily.

Mercedes turned to me, resting her back against the countertop for a moment, *"Aquí hace mucho calor. ¡Sobre todo en primavera! A mi no me gusta."* (It's so hot, especially for Spring. I don't like it).

"A mi tampoco," (I don't like it either). I was getting better at stock phrases too, which sound much more natural. Although we think of languages as individual

words, most of the time we're using little blocks which always fit together and sound good to the ear. In English it's easy to think of pairs like "salt and pepper", "ladies and gentlemen", "rain or shine", but it goes much further than that. We tend to talk in stock phrases or "idioms", which is a way of speaking that is natural to native speakers of the language. Think of: "at the end of the day", "to be honest with you", "I can't be bothered," or "when all's said and done".

A non-native speaker of a language may say something that makes sense, but nevertheless sounds clunky. We use idioms so frequently, that if you don't use them, you sound unnatural. Take for example "I can't be bothered," (typical in the UK) or "I don't feel like it" (typical in the US). Instead of using either of those idioms a foreigner might say, "I do not want to pass my time doing that." Grammatically and logically it's correct, but it sounds unnatural, even a little unpleasant to the ear.

Sometimes idioms are much more abstract or metaphorical like, "you're barking up the wrong tree," or "you've let the cat out of the bag." Of course, they have just as many of these metaphorical idioms in Spanish too, but I think these should be used sparingly. As a non-native speaker overusing them could make you seem like a comedy character. It also sounds completely incongruous if you're making extremely basic grammatical errors and then suddenly coming out with a canned phrase like "He's as fit as a fiddle!" (The Spanish version of which is *"Está más sano que una pera."* in case you wanted to know. It literally means "he's healthier than a pear").

I think, in general, normal idioms like, "I don't feel like it," should be used at every opportunity. Not only do they sound natural, but they're also guaranteed to be grammatically correct (unlike the sentences you create in your head). I was also finding that they were significantly improving my speaking flow. I had a few favourites that I tried to drop into conversation often. They were *"Eso si que es"* (That's correct, or That really is... e.g. that really is bad, good, beautiful or whatever) – it's a good one because it's pronounced S O C K S, so it's easy to remember. I was also dropping in *"Espero que sí"* or *"Espero que no"* (I hope so or I hope not) and *"Claro que sí"* or *"Claro que no"* (clearly or clearly not) which were great immediate responses to keep a conversation flowing.

Picking up on these idioms was also helping me understand the almost indecipherable Seville accent. Halfway through class every day we stopped for a break and went to the coffee shop outside. I would order a coffee and occasionally a croissant or toast. After I ordered my drink the barman would say either:

"¿Algo más?" (Anything else?) except with his Andalusian accent he would say it without the 's' – making it, *"¿Algo má'?"*

Worse was when he asked, *"¿Na' má'?"*

It took me several occasions to figure out he was asking. In this case, he was unhelpfully leaving out about half the syllables, and *"¿Na' má'?"* was actually, *"¿Nada más?"* (Nothing else?).

Once I figured it out, I never had to think about it ever again. It goes to show the importance of learning idioms. It is also one reason why it's so much harder to understand a foreign language than your own. When you listen to a foreign language you try to catch every word in order to make sense of it. In your own language the phrases and idioms are so familiar that you can often finish the other person's sentence just from hearing the first part of it.

Seville was proving a particularly difficult place because of the distinctive accent. In centuries gone by there was a lot of emigration from Andalusia to South America, and consequently the South American accent has a lot of similarity to the Andalusian one. For example, across most of Spain they pronounce any C's before I's and E's as "th" – think of *'Gracias'* – pronounced *'Grathias'*, or *'Cerveza'* - pronounced *'Cervetha'*. In Andalusia (and South America) that C is pronounced as an "S", e.g. *"Grasias"* or *"Cervesa"*. That difference is fine once you know it though, no issues there. The real problems come with the way that Andalusians miss out letters altogether, so *"pescado"* (fish) is pronounced without a D and becomes *"pescao"*. The S is often missed out altogether, so *"esta"* (this) is pronounced *"eta"*. In academic-speak, the missing S is called an "aspirated S", perhaps because they only have the aspiration to say it, and they never actually do.

This tendency to miss out more consonants and vowels than the starting board of *Wheel of Fortune* was why my waiter friend pronounced *"Nada más?"* (Nothing else?) as the almost unintelligible *"Na' má'?"*. So, no, it wasn't that he was a lazy oaf after all, although the speed he got my coffee suggested he might be. It was just his accent. Well, his and everyone else's.

I had essentially landed myself in the equivalent of Glasgow in the UK, or Mississippi in the US - places with accents so strong that even native speakers find it a struggle. Still, if I could make it here, I could make it anywhere.

Fortunately, back in the kitchen Mercedes was still talking about the heat. She kept on talking too fast, and I lost her for a while. Eventually she trotted out one of her old tropes, something she always said sooner or later, *"Pero no es un gran problema, de hecho no me importa."* (But for me, it's no big deal, it doesn't bother me).

Despite saying that the heat didn't concern her, it seemed to be pretty much *all* that concerned her. It was a varied subject though: the heat in various seasons, weather in other countries, how hot is too hot, how unfortunate people with overheated houses stayed cool. Oh, her opinions on the heat were numerous, wide-ranging and continuous. And it wasn't even summer yet.

I couldn't really think of anything more to say about the heat, so I gestured towards the TV, and simply asked, *"¿Qué es esto?"*

"¿Este programa?" (This programme?") she asked, and I nodded. It seemed to be on every lunch time and from what I could tell it was a kind of *Jerry Springer / Jeremy Kyle* chat show affair. The only difference was that

everyone on this show looked great: perfect hair, well-dressed, immaculate shiny TV smiles, as opposed to looking like they'd been interrupted halfway through a KFC bargain bucket.

The show was almost impossible for me to follow though, they spoke rapidly and most of the time they spoke over each other too. The excitable audience continually whooped and hollered and made it even harder to understand. The only clues I had were the guests' over-exaggerated facial expressions, lots of finger-pointing and a good dose of finger-wagging.

"Este programa", Mercedes continued, *"se llama Mujeres, hombres y viceversa. Es una tontería.* (This programme is called Women and men and vice-versa. It's nonsense).

I'd known that really. After all, it was on every single day, but I wanted to talk about it. Anything but the heat. *"¿Te gusta?"* (Do you like it?) I asked.

"¿Este? ¡No! Es absurdo." (This? No! It's absurd).

How strange, because we seem to watch it every single day, I thought.

Mercedes had turned back to the sink and was washing up. I watched the TV for a minute or two but was a bit confused. As far as I could tell yesterday's guest seemed to be presenting today's show. Yesterday, the man, a rather flamboyant young gay guy with a quiff that reached for the ceiling, a spray tan, and very tight trousers, had seemingly surprised his (presumably) straight friend with a declaration of love. At one point I swore I heard him say, "*¿A que no sabes qué?... ¡Te quiero!*" (Guess what? I love you). The second man, who looked very happy with himself when he came on stage, looked rather less so when the first man sat him down and told him the news. Fortunately, a moment later the pair hugged, the young gay guy wiped away a tear, and the crowd whooped.

Today the pair had returned but the situation had changed dramatically. This time it looked like the gay guy was helping the straight guy find a date from an array of women parading around the studio. For a guy who had had his heart broken the previous day, the gay guy looked remarkably chipper. Maybe he just liked being on TV. I didn't really understand it, but I think I understood enough to agree that Mercedes' summation of it as "absurd" was bang on. I finished my lunch, thanked Mercedes and left the flat.

***

I was still acquainting myself with the city and decided to go for a wander. The sun was shining, and I was out in flip-flops and shorts. It *was* hot. Surprisingly hot. Perhaps Mercedes was right after all. I walked out of my *barrio* (neighbourhood), through its narrow streets and whitewashed walls and into the much wider, open *Avenida de Menéndez Pelayo.* I turned right into a shaded path lined by trees, and set away from the road. The path ran along the long wall at the bottom of the gardens of the Alcázar that I had visited a few days previously. On the other side of the path there was an open space, with borders of neat plants, plenty of trees and benches every so often. I took a seat on one of the benches and took in the scene. There were plenty of palm trees, and shorter trees too in fragrant, colourful blooms, but what caught my eye were the orange trees. Seville is famous for its oranges, and they were everywhere: in the trees, on the ground, and the smell of them hung heavy in the air.

Seville's oranges – despite their fame – are not that suitable for eating. They're a fairly big, bitter-tasting orange. Introduced to Spain by the Moors in the 10th century, they were used as herbal medicine, as a flavouring and for their oil. However, six or seven hundred years later they began to be used in the production of marmalade. Legend has it that around 1700 a storm-damaged Spanish ship, carrying Seville oranges, took refuge in Dundee harbour in Scotland. The cargo was sold cheaply to a local merchant whose wife turned it into a preserve.

The other crucial ingredient for marmalade is sugar, and around this time the British Empire had access to lots of it through the colonies in the Caribbean. Britain started to develop a taste for marmalade and Seville oranges were imported in large numbers for the mass production of the stuff. Even today the most famous marmalade is made in Dundee, and the vast majority of Seville's oranges are exported to the UK, not eaten in Spain. This explained why there were so many unwanted oranges on the floor, and also why the man across from me who'd just bitten into one was screwing his face up like he was sucking on a lemon.

I carried on walking along the pathway, parallel to the wall of the gardens of the Alcázar. I turned at the corner of the wall and continued along a pedestrianised street. People walked and biked by in their shorts and sunglasses. People really do look happier in the sunshine. If someone is walking along in the sunshine grinning it looks perfectly in keeping, and totally understandable. Yet someone walking along in the rain beaming from ear to ear would look nothing short of psychopathic. There's nothing amusing about the rain. It's certainly nothing to laugh about, much less sing about (Gene Kelly, I'm looking at you). Yet out here in the sunshine the people eating at café tables looked happy. Sure, for all I knew, they could have been sitting there complaining about the heat to each other, like Mercedes, but they *looked* happy.

I continued, past a huge fountain and emerged at the river. I saw my destination immediately, the *Torre del Oro* (the Tower of Gold). Unfortunately, it wasn't actually a tower made of gold. Instead, the name comes from the fact that the stone reflects a golden light onto the river. The tall, dodecagonal structure (12-sided – yes, I had to look it up too) was a military watchtower. Imposing, but standing starkly on its own by the side of the river, it was built by the Moors around 1220 to protect the Alcázar.

There used to be a second, corresponding tower on the other side of the river. This enabled the Moors to link them with a chain and block any ships from sailing up the river and attacking the city. It sounds like a nice plan, but it failed to protect Seville during the *Reconquista*, when the city was besieged by a group of Christian kings.

In 1247 Seville was the biggest city still under Moorish control and in the line of sight of Ferdinand III of Castile. That summer Ferdinand gathered his armies outside the city and surrounded it. The following year, he attacked and sailed a fleet up the Guadalquivir river. The ships broke through the protective chain and attacked from the water while the troops besieged the city from their position on the outskirts. Ferdinand's fearsome armies were equipped with cannon, making it the earliest recorded use of gunpowder in the West. Not long later, Seville surrendered. That left Granada as the only major city still under the control of the Moors.

I went inside the tower and had a look at the displays. Most of them were focused on maritime history. And it's true that Seville is one of the proudest maritime cities in Europe, despite not being on the coast. It has a port on the river Guadalquivir though, and the Guadalquivir is wide, navigable, and flows to the Mediterranean Sea.

I looked at the various paintings and displays of old sailing paraphernalia. I continued round the cabinets and was quite quickly back at the start, as is the way of things when you're looking round the inside of a circular tower.

I climbed up and out onto the open turret area. It was a fine view. I could see all along the river, and over to the other side – to Triana, the poorer, more working-class part of the city. On my side of the river, towards the centre of Seville I could see the bullring and the *giralda* – the tower of the cathedral that looked like a minaret. Taking in the view wasn't a particularly time-consuming activity and before I knew it I had taken a look from each of the twelve (subtly) different sides.

I made my way back down the stairs and out into the sunshine once more. There was still plenty of time left in the afternoon and I was intrigued by the images of Seville's maritime history. So, on the spur of the moment I decided to head to the central square to visit another of Seville's famous attractions, the Archive of the Indies.

In the late 1400s there was a lot of change afoot in Spain. The marriage of Isabelle I of Castile and Ferdinand II of Aragon in 1469 unified those two kingdoms and was the foundation for modern day Spain. This signified a move away from inter-kingdom fighting within Spain and a desire for Spain to start to project power outwards. After all, other European powers were building their empires. Isabelle and Ferdinand started out by conquering the Canary Islands, and then they kicked the last of the Moors out of Spain in 1492. They also funded Italian explorer Christopher Columbus to sail to "the Indies" in that same year.

Columbus had been travelling around the royal courts of Europe for several years trying to drum up interest and find a backer for his voyage. Eventually, in January 1492, he received an audience with Queen Isabelle in the Alcázar. She was initially sceptical of Columbus's idea of reaching Japan by going West instead of East, but she decided to sponsor him anyway. It was a spectacularly successful investment. Columbus set sail from Andalusia that summer, and as we all know, he ended up 'discovering' the Americas. Interestingly, during his four voyages, he visited several Caribbean Islands, Central America and South America, but he never once landed in what is now the modern-day USA. Perhaps even more intriguingly, over his four voyages, Columbus never admitted that the lands he had discovered were not part of the Indies. To the end of his life, despite mounting evidence, like any good man, he never admitted that he had been lost. Even 15 years later! Some say that Columbus's refusal to acknowledge that he'd found a new continent was why the Americas were not named after him, but instead after the Italian explorer Amerigo Vespucci, who came a few years later.

Columbus's journey to the "Indies" was the making of Seville. As colonisation and trade began in earnest in the early 1500s, Seville won the exclusive rights to handle all goods heading to or from the Spanish Americas. This monopoly led to a golden age for Seville as the riches of the colonies passed through the city for distribution throughout Spain. Seville became one of the biggest ports in the world and a huge centre for trade. Its population grew to more than 100,000, and it was for a time the fourth biggest city in Europe.

I approached the Archives, which is in the old merchants' exchange, originally built in 1572. It was an impressive renaissance building: square, elegant, somewhat understated. I entered and was struck by how quiet it was compared to the other tourist attractions. Only a few people walked along the marble corridors, between the shelves containing thousands of documents. Supposedly every transaction carried out before 1785 by the Spanish in their dealings with their empire is contained in the 80 million pages that live here. Unlike the Dutch and English, who allowed companies to run the trade to their colonies (think of the Dutch East Indies company for example) the Spanish crown maintained a much tighter grip. In 1503 they established the *Casa de Contratación* (House of Trade) in Seville to collect all colonial taxes and duties, and control all voyages of exploration and trade. Supposedly, no Spaniard could sail anywhere without the approval of the House of Trade, although this was frequently flouted.

Trading with the colonies was good business for the crown and for Seville. A 20 per cent tax, known as the *quinto real* (royal fifth) was imposed by the House of Trade on all precious metals entering Spain, mostly silver which was being mined in great quantities in Mexico, Peru and Bolivia.

I wandered around, looking at old maps – many were the "Here be monsters!" type with landmasses only vaguely sketched in. Europe and Africa were well defined, but where the Americas should be was just a vague outline of the US East Coast and the top of South America. They were a fascinating insight to a time when much of the world was still a mystery to Europeans.

I carried on perusing, finding a dictionary of the indigenous Quechua (Peruvian) language into Spanish and various bills of lading. I reached the end of the corridor and went up a grand marble staircase. Back beneath me were shelf after shelf of the old documents.

It was an interesting slice of history, but like everything it came to an end. In the late 16th century Cádiz was authorised as another port of trade and Seville's monopoly was over. Worse still, by the late 17th century the Spanish empire itself was creaking from overreach. Bureaucratic incompetence and continuous war meant Spain was in debt and in trouble. Ships arriving with riches from the Americas or the Philippines were routinely handed straight over to Spain's creditors as soon as they docked.

Spain's empire fell apart in the War of Spanish Succession in 1713. Her possessions were carved up by other European powers, although she managed to hold on to the colonies in the Americas. Seville suffered a final blow when the new Spanish King decided to designate Cádiz as the sole port for trade with the Americas. Seville's golden age was over.

***

That evening I had agreed to go out for a drink with a guy I had met in the school. I'd suggested we meet in a bar near my place. It was fast becoming my local. I went there every day after school for an early afternoon coffee, although it seemed to be open whenever I happened to walk past. It was an unpretentious place, with an affiliation to Real Betis, one of Seville's two professional football clubs. Unfortunately, Real Betis played in green and white stripes, giving the interior a rather ghastly colour scheme. For this reason (along with the heat) I preferred to sit at one of the tables outside.

My acquaintance from school arrived. Nick was English too, but very northern, a little older than me, in his mid-thirties. Dark-haired, bluff and from the city of Manchester he was like a friendly Liam Gallagher. He sat down at the table and gave me a firm handshake. I already had a beer and within a minute the waiter arrived to take Nick's order.

¿Que desea? (What would you like?) said the waiter, using the formal style of address.

"¿Kay teepos de ser-vaysa tee-en-es?" asked Nick. It was Spanish, but no type of Spanish I'd ever heard before. The waiter looked at him quizzically, and Nick rolled his eyes, as if this happened all the time. He repeated the question, exactly as before.

"*¿Cerveza?*" (Beer?) the waiter said tentatively.

"¿See, kay teepos?" affirmed Nick, and the waiter, began to list the various types they had. I finally understood what had happened. Nick was speaking a very rare form of Mancunian-Spanish i.e. Spanish with a thick Manchester accent. He wasn't making any allowances for pronunciation whatsoever. It felt as if Liam Gallagher himself was ordering a *cerveza*.

Nick chose a type of beer and the waiter left to fetch it. I asked Nick how long he had been studying Spanish. "Oooh, a couple of years," he replied.

"And have you had much speaking practice?" I asked.

"Not really. I mainly just learned the grammar, you know, the verbs and all that."

It was evident when he spoke. His grammar was good. It was just his pronunciation that left a lot, or actually everything, to be desired. "Don't take this the wrong way, but in the spirit of helping each other learn, I reckon you could do a bit more on your accent."

"What do you mean?" he said, on the verge of taking it the wrong way.

"Just, I don't know, you could sound *a bit* more Spanish. It sounds very... English. I think it might sound a bit better if you put a bit of an accent on."

He scoffed, "An accent? Don't be daft. They can understand me. The words are right. What difference does it make?"

"Well, I see what you're saying, but the accent is part of speaking. I think they'd understand better if you made it sound a bit more... Spanish."

It was something I'd noticed a lot of English speakers having trouble with, or more specifically, being resistant to. A lot of people have a natural block to using an accent, as though it's too difficult or maybe faintly embarrassing. In many ways though, cultivating a natural(ish) sounding accent is part of mastering the language.

Nick considered my argument for a moment, "No, I don't think it's so. The French don't put an accent on when they speak English do they? You can tell they're French a mile off. *And* you can still understand them."

It was a fair point.

We chatted about a range of topics including Nick's football club Manchester City, (not doing well), Nick's investment in a company speculatively drilling for oil in Ireland, (not doing well) and my preparations for my wedding speech (not doing well).

"It's more difficult than you think, I've tried to start writing it half a dozen times," I said.

"It's not difficult. I've been a best man, just take the mick out of the groom, compliment the bride, compliment the venue and catering, old anecdote of the two of you together, preferably something that embarrasses him and then a toast. Easy," he said, breezily.

"Yeah, but half of it needs to be in Spanish. To Spanish people. In Spain!"

"Oh, it'll be a piece of piss."

"You can talk! Well, actually you can't," I said laughing, and fortunately he laughed too.

Chapter 16 – Sugar, sugar

It was early afternoon and I was sitting at the Real Betis bar enjoying a coffee. I was pleased for a whole host of reasons. For one, as soon as I sat down my regular waiter had greeted me and asked if I wanted my usual order. I had never had a waiter know my usual order before. It's the type of service you only get by visiting a shop or café every single day, and most of us don't have the time to do that in our normal lives. I'd been in Seville a couple of weeks now though, and had made a habit of coming to this particular bar/café around the same time every day. With the exception of its ghastly interior colour scheme, it had a lot going for it. I liked the fact its clientele were locals, that it was cheap (even for Seville), and that they hadn't translated their menu into English, but the main thing I liked about it was the sugar.

Every day when I was served my coffee I was given a packet of sugar, and on each of these packets was a different saying e.g. *"Hoy es un buen día para tener un gran día"* (Today is a good day to have a great day).

I liked everything about these sayings: from their cheesy, schmaltzy upbeat tone, to the way it enabled me to integrate a little Spanish learning into my daily routine. Sometimes they were quite challenging, *"Si el plan no funciona, cambia el plan, pero no cambies la meta"* (If the plan doesn't work, change the plan, but don't change the goal). It was an inspirational and honourable thing to read, even if my only plan that day was to have a siesta and maybe go for a couple of beers.

Deceptively simple, but also surprisingly complex, the sayings were a good opportunity to see some of the language concepts I'd been learning about in action. Take for example this particular packet, *"Educad a los niños, y no será necesario castigar a los hombres"* (Educate the children and it won't be necessary to punish the men). As well as being strikingly philosophical for a condiment, the sentence features both the future tense and an imperative verb (an instruction or an exhortation) i.e. *Educate them!*

I liked the wide variety of them too. I never knew whether I was going to get a banal greetings card-esque wish to have a nice day, or an incitement to pick up arms and join the revolution. I started taking pictures of them and, before I knew it, I was making a collection. I was even frustrated when I got a duplicate. It reminded me of collecting albums of football stickers when I was a kid. I realised it had become a bit of an obsession when I bought a second coffee, even though I didn't need one, just to see whether I'd get a new sugar packet. As I say, my days weren't *that* busy.

That particular afternoon I was messaging a guy I'd met on a language exchange website. The idea of these websites is to pair up language learners who are interested in speaking the other's language, so that they can do an exchange (*intercambio* in Spanish). You meet up (or talk online) and speak or write half the time in each language. It gives both people a chance to improve and is much cheaper than taking classes. In my attempts to radically improve my Spanish I felt it was the best route to progress and I was keen to start having some real conversations.

Federico, had messaged me first, asking if I wanted to meet up. I had been keen, but that was a couple of days ago, and now he was proving hard to pin down. The previous day I had suggested we get a beer. He'd agreed and then cancelled a couple of hours before. *Was he playing hard to get?* Maybe this was more like internet dating than I cared to admit. Another message arrived.

"The problem is I not accustomed to speaking English with someone. Is hard for me," Federico said.

Well, that could be a problem, I thought. I paused for a moment, then began to type slowly. "Don't worry, it'll be fun! I'm also very patient (smiley face emoji)." *Don't want to scare the horses here,* I thought.

A minute passed and he replied, "Or other idea is you play football with me. I play every week on Wednesday. I pick you up."

Now that was unexpected. Maybe he wasn't playing hard to get after all. Could I trust him? Maybe this was all a ruse for an elaborate kidnap attempt. Since when was meeting strange men off the internet so difficult?

Naturally I was wary about the idea of him picking me up in his car, but on the other hand I enjoyed playing football, and I hadn't been exercising enough during my time in Spain. I asked him more questions about the football, trying to suss out whether there really was a football match or whether he was planning to take me captive. I told him I'd think about it and put my phone down.

It was a shame Federico had backed out of our language meet-up, even if I was interested by his offer of a football match. However, I couldn't imagine it would provide that much in the way of language learning, other than shouting, "Pass!" or "Man on!" to my teammates.

I really needed someone I could have a proper conversation with, so I decided to send out a couple of opening messages on the language exchange website. I still felt like it was my best option, especially after my experience the previous evening. Nick had suggested we go along to a language meet-up and I had agreed. It was a regular event held in a bar: anybody could turn up, locals wanting to learn a foreign language, and foreigners who wanted to learn Spanish.

If the language exchange site was like a dating site, with users creating profiles, advertising their wares, and browsing to see who likes the look of who, then a meet-up event was more like speed-dating. Nick and I entered the bar. It was a quiet Monday night and we were on the outskirts of the city centre. It was obvious who the language learners were. 20 or more people were sat around a long table in the centre of the large room. There were only a couple of other customers in, and they were at the bar.

Nick turned to me in his usual straightforward style, "Right Rich, time to dive in."

We grabbed a couple of spare seats, taking our chances with who we landed next to. I turned to the girl to my left. She was Australian, but she insisted on talking to me in Spanish anyway. Her level was basic but she gabbled at a decent speed. After a moment I noticed that everything she said was in the present tense.

"I study in Seville three months more, I am here one month, before, I study one month Madrid. After I travel in Spain, I see places. I visit places. I'm going visit other places. Barcelona. Do you like it?"

It was like speaking to a malfunctioning robot, but it was undoubtedly Spanish. In a way, it was a lot easier to speak to her than an actual Spanish person, certainly than someone from Seville. I asked her how long she had been studying Spanish. She said it was less than two months, and she had started not knowing a single word. I was impressed. Admittedly, it was like listening to the garbled ramblings of a drunk (perhaps it didn't help that she *was* drunk), but she was able to express herself. I'd been learning on and off for a few years and it had taken me a long time to build up any kind of flow or ability to speak.

I asked what her secret was, and she told me she *only* spoke in Spanish, no matter who she spoke to, even with her classmates from the US, France or wherever. I had to admire her determination and the fact she had overcome her inhibitions. She didn't seem to care about making mistakes at all, although that could have been the beers.

On the other side was a Spanish person (which was an improvement), but he was, to use a non-technical description, completely crazy. I didn't learn his name, where he was from or indeed anything about him. What I did learn was that China was on a mission to take over the world. Supposedly China was using Spain as a gateway to buy up large parts of Latin America.

"I've never heard that before," I said, rather reasonably I hoped.

"Look at the map!" he said, as if it was obvious.

I didn't have a map so I couldn't, "Ok, I will do," I said, hoping that would satisfy him. It didn't.

"What is halfway between China and Latin America?" He asked, staring at me for emphasis.

"Europe?" I ventured.

"Spain! Just look at the map," he repeated. It wouldn't have surprised me if he'd whipped out a great scroll of an atlas and unrolled it on the table there and then.

He continued on about various conspiracy theories, and the shadowy forces behind *La Crisis,* and before long I wished I was talking to the drunk Australian girl again. Trapped, I stared longingly across the table, but the pair opposite me were engaged in deep conversation. The conspiracy man sensed an opportunity and started launching into a tirade against the Spanish monarchy. I stopped him in his tracks and excused myself to find Nick. I approached and could hear the tones of his Spanish, by way of Manchester, accent, but anything was preferable to more conspiracy theories.

***

I finished typing a message to another potential partner on the language exchange website and got up to leave. My language school was taking us on a walking tour and I was going to be late.

I walked out of the old town, down past the gardens of the Alcázar and into the Plaza de España, where we were meeting. I found my group and the teacher began her story. Seville had held a grand world's fair in 1929, known as the Ibero-American Exposition. A huge new park was developed – the Parque de María Luisa – which was the main site of the exposition and included the grand Plaza de España that I was looking at now. The exposition was 19 years in the planning and several zones in the city were rebuilt. In order to prepare for the crowds there was a modernisation plan for the whole of Seville which included building new hotels and widening the streets. It was a key event in the development of the city and we could still see the influence of the exposition even now.

The plaza itself was enormous, across one side of it was a huge semi-circle of one continuous light brown stone building. In the centre of it a pavilion extended out in both directions in a series of pillared alcoves, reaching two huge towers, one on either end. It was almost too much to take in. In fact, no matter how far back I stood, I couldn't capture it all in one photo. In front of the semi-circle was a canal. It looked like a reproduction of Venice, complete with mini-bridges and little boats. It was a stunning space, full of grandeur, but exquisite detail too.

Our teacher told us the style was "neo-mudéjar and renaissance", which sounded like a rap duo to me, but I am assured is a legitimate architecture style. Mudéjar was the style that evolved at the end of the age of the Moors in Spain. Much of the park was built in the style of a Moorish garden, with tiled fountains, walls, ponds, pavilions, and benches scattered throughout. The park was also filled with palm trees, orange trees, Mediterranean pines, and lots of flower beds. We strolled around the main pavilion building. In front, a series of alcoves were covered in ceramic tiles, each represented a different province in Spain. We looked back across the plaza, plastered in strong sunshine. It had been used as a filming location for *Lawrence of Arabia*, and even *Star Wars: Episode II – Attack of the Clones,* but that wasn't the plaza's fault.

We walked through the park, listening to more of the history of the exposition. In the early twentieth century Spain had recently lost the very last of its colonies (Cuba, Puerto Rico, Philippines and Guam in the Spanish-American war), and the Spanish civil war was still a few years away. The general of the army, Miguel Primo de Rivera, believed very strongly that politicians had ruined Spain and so he launched a military coup in 1923. He thought that governing without politicians was the way to bring the nation back to greatness (which was convenient for him, since he was a dictator). He was keen to show off Spain's prowess to the world and so pushed ahead with the great exposition in Seville in 1929 (and the world's fair in Barcelona which took place at a similar time).

The Seville exposition was known as the Ibero-American Exposition, and was specifically about promoting the relationship between Spain and the Americas, most of whom were its former colonies. I wonder if these were awkward calls to make, given almost all those countries had fought wars of independence *against* Spain in the previous century. *("Yes, we're having an exposition. And you're invited. What's the theme you say? Well, it's about us and all our formerly enslaved colonies. So we thought of you. Hello? Hello?")*

Most of the countries of the Americas did take part in the exposition and they built *pabellones* (pavilions) to house their exhibitions. These permanent buildings were intended as a legacy after the end of the exposition. Each was deliberately built in a different style: mududéjar, neo-barroque, Andalusian. Some were rather grand affairs, the Argentinian one resembled a theatrical palace and was now the home of the centre of Flamenco dancing. The Guatemalan one was much more modest: a small blue and white tiled building at the edge of the park. Unfortunately, it was more reminiscent of a public toilet than anything else.

Curiously, the exhibition was planned in the run up to, and then held in the year of the Wall Street Crash (1929). They didn't plan it like that, obviously. It just happened that way. The 1920s were a heady thriving time for the West. Capital was easy to come by and it seemed like the good times were never going to end. People thought boom and bust was a thing of the past (sound familiar?). Of course it didn't last, and the economy exploded spectacularly. This wasn't good for Spain or Seville which was left with millions in debt and lots of buildings without occupants. The situation was not dissimilar to the economic crash of 2007-8, when Spain went on an infrastructure spending spree. New roads, bridges, airports, sprouted up, all on borrowed money.

Spain finally seems to be coming out of *La Crisis* now, but the unemployment, abandoned buildings and working poverty (i.e. people barely earning a living wage) still exist. Spain will recover eventually though, just as it did from the 1929 crash. The pavilions are still here today, and used for a variety of purposes: museums, consulates, cultural centres. They are now just another beautiful part of the city. One day this crisis which has cast such a long shadow will also be forgotten and then the airports, bridges, roads and buildings won't seem like the legacy of a crash, but instead just a part of the landscape.

***

I was drinking again with Nick in the Betis bar, and asking him for more advice on my wedding speech.

Nick was in full flow, clearly he liked giving advice, "You've got to go for some gags. Embarrass him. Find a weakness and then mercilessly target it."

"Really? Sounds a bit savage. He's my friend, not my enemy."

"People will expect it. You've got to give the people what they want."

"But what if they don't do that at Spanish weddings?"

"Pfff, of course they do. It's universal," said Nick confidently.

We carried on drinking, and discussed our plans for the evening. We were both interested in seeing some flamenco, after all, Seville was famous for it. It was everywhere, lots of shows, both daytime and evening, were advertised throughout the city but they were typically aimed at tourists. According to the guidebook, the quality was generally good but the ticket prices were high and the atmosphere lacking. Most of the real flamenco clubs were in the outskirts of the city. However, I had read about one, La Carbonería, that was in the old town. Supposedly it was authentic, mostly filled with locals, and even better, free.

We set off, wandering the narrow streets. I'd read that the club was poorly marked, and it took us a while to find it. In fact, it didn't seem to be marked at all, but eventually I saw a large red door, and we stepped inside. It looked like a church or a grand cellar, with huge stone walls and wooden beams across the roof. We passed through a small bar and into the main bar area. It was filled with long wooden tables and the atmosphere was already lively. People were drinking bottles of beer and jugs of sangria. Nick and I went to the bar and ordered a jug of sangria to share, before settling down on one of the benches.

Not long after 10pm three people walked on to the stage at the far end of the room, and the audience fell quiet. The first man was the very stereotype of a Spaniard. Almost comically so. His gelled dark hair was slicked back into a semi-mullet. He had designer stubble, the type last seen on George Michael in a *Wham!* music video. He was dressed in a fancy black shirt with elaborate white trim, although I can only presume he had got distracted halfway through buttoning it up.

An older man came on stage and took a seat next to the first, who by now had picked up his guitar. Finally, a woman entered the stage. She was wearing a simple long, red dress, with a pink flower in her hair. Her outfit wasn't as showy as I was expecting, and that set the tone for the stripped-down performance.

The man began playing his guitar, slowly at first and then speeding up, but the woman stood there, allowing the music to build. The second man began singing and clapping and finally she broke into dancing. She whirled, stopping in one pose, then shifted suddenly. The movement flowed through her, twisting her body. She twirled again, threw out her arms, and began winding her hands out in a spiral. She tossed her head back, waited a beat and then pulled her gaze back to the audience. An intense fixed look was on her face, as if she was focusing on something intangible, something within the music. It was mesmerising in a serious, almost austere way. The only percussion was provided by her finger clicks, the man's hand claps and the occasional stomp of her feet.

I turned to Nick and he nodded appreciatively, "It's impressive," he said. And it was. We really were watching a performance. I'd read that flamenco dancers tend to be middle-aged as younger people are not considered to have the emotional maturity to truly evoke the soul of the music. Unlike other forms of dance which is tilted towards younger dancers, most flamenco dancers don't hit their peak until their thirties or forties. This woman was certainly a masterful dancer, intense and forceful. She conveyed something from within the music. It spoke through her. The guitarist started up again and she began to whirl once more.

Chapter 17 – Death in the afternoon

After class I decided to get out of my comfort zone and go to a different bar for lunch. My collection of sugar packets would have to wait for another day. I headed for *El Rinconcillo*, the oldest bar in Seville. It was founded in 1670 and has been an institution in the city ever since.

The sun was shining as usual and I strolled towards the centre. Before long I found the bar on the corner of two streets. *Rincón* means corner, so I realised the name must mean little corner. I was pleased with myself. I was like a language detective, and my secret weapon? My basic understanding of Spanish.

I entered the bar. It looked very traditional, even for a Spanish one. I'd got used to this type of place: ceramic tiles on the wall, a long wooden bar, and huge legs of ham hanging from the ceiling. Yet this one was particularly old-fashioned. It looked like it was from another age entirely: nothing at all like your typical British boozer, with a fruit machine in the corner, and salt and vinegar crisps and peanuts behind the bar. No, this bar had two small wooden barrels of wine, black and white photos, a chalkboard, and strangely, a huge calendar of the Virgin Mary. Why was she in the bar? I am not sure she'd approve of being in a bar. Unless I'm totally clueless and she loved a drink. Maybe she's actually the patron saint of drinkers.

Like most of the other patrons I chose to stand at the bar. I ordered a glass of white wine and took in the scene. The place oozed history. Ok, perhaps not the 17th century, the date it was founded, but certainly it had an old-time aura. From the wooden cabinets, containing all manner of historic looking bottles, to the ceramic tiling on every wall, everywhere I looked was some new eye-catching detail. Just as interesting were the staff and customers. The barmen were all dressed in black waistcoats and white shirts. I half wondered if they were going to offer me a Ferrero Rocher. Although judging from the dozens of legs of ham hanging from the ceiling, perhaps a platter of ham was more likely. The stuff was everywhere and there even appeared to be one man whose sole job was to continually cut and slice ham from the big legs. At one point I think I saw him slicing cheese, but I could have been mistaken.

A middle-aged man approached the bar. He ordered in pretty good Spanish and then began to text someone on his phone. His drink arrived and then a couple of plates of food. He took some pictures and sent them on. Classic tourist behaviour, but he appeared to be alone. Since he had a good level of Spanish, I thought it would be a good opportunity to practice. I really needed to get some conversations going, even if it was with other foreigners.

"¿Qué es esto?" (What is this?), I asked, pointing at one of his plates of food.

"Boquerones. Es un tipo de pescado. ¡Muy rico!" (A type of fish - anchovies. It's delicious!)

He seemed open to conversation, so I carried on, *"¿De dónde eres?"* (Where are you from?)

"De Madrid (From Madrid)*"*

I couldn't believe it. His Spanish was so clear, and so different to what I'd been hearing recently that I assumed he had to be a tourist fluent in Spanish. It was then that I truly understood how hard Andalusian Spanish was. Of course, the benefit was that if I could understand Spanish here, then I could understand it anywhere. Unfortunately, I *couldn't* understand it here.

I kept talking to my newfound friend. He was actually a tourist, here in Seville for a few days, which explained why he was taking pictures of food, and why he too had come to the oldest bar in the city. He asked me why I was studying Spanish and I told him I'd always liked the idea of learning another language, but he pressed me and eventually the whole story about the wedding and the best man speech came out.

I had been getting nervous about the speech over the past week, but here I was having a real conversation with a native speaker. I was pleased and a little bit surprised I could understand him, even if he did come from the place with the clearest Spanish of all.

Eventually he had to get going and we said our goodbyes.

"Bueno, buena suerte. ¡Hablas español muy bien!" (Ok, see you and good luck! You speak Spanish very well!)

My first compliment, I couldn't believe it, *"Gracias, me defiendo bastante bien"* (Thanks, I can handle myself ok.)

"Claro que sí. ¡Hasta luego!" (Yes, exactly. See you!)

All this time I had been trying to find a language partner online for a conversation, when I could have just headed to a bar and see who was there. Perhaps the old ways are still the best.

***

Over the next couple of days my attempts to arrange a language exchange finally paid off. I agreed to meet a guy called Francesco at a bar near the centre for a drink. I was a little bit nervous. Despite chatting via text message, we didn't know each other. Yes, we wanted to speak each other's language, but would we actually have anything to say?

Francesco arrived, and we shook hands. He was younger than me, in his early twenties. He was a little nervous too, which, rather strangely, set me at ease. In this type of situation, I remembered something my best friend, and groom-to-be, Jack, used to do. Whenever we visited a theme park, he would look around our group to see who was the most scared and then "joke around" with them. *"I heard they only service these rides once a year,"* he would say as we waited in line. Then, as the rollercoaster climbed towards the first big drop, he would yank on the belts and buckles. *"These safety harnesses feel pretty loose today,"* he would announce, delighting in the nervous looks and gulps of whoever was obviously petrified. One time, after we got off, I asked him why he did it, and he replied, *"Well, humour, obviously,"* he paused, *"but I guess, I can get a bit nervous up there, so if I see someone else more nervous than me, then it helps take my mind off it."* Which I guess had a certain logic to it.

Either way Francesco seemed a little anxious, so I led the conversation, suggesting we speak for half an hour in each language. He agreed, and we spoke Spanish first. I asked him how his day had been, and told him about mine. A teacher of mine had once told me to practice talking to myself in Spanish in odd moments, walking to work, or waiting for the bus. It was a good tip, apart from one time at the bus stop when a woman began looking at me strangely and started edging away. I realised I had been muttering to myself in barely formed sentences, like a madman crossed with a toddler.

The practice had certainly helped though. I found I could speak at a decent speed. I stumbled occasionally, and made a lot of grammatical mistakes, but Francesco was patient and forgiving. Rather than speaking, it was understanding Francesco that was the tougher test. I had to ask him to slow down several times, and he did, although he generally sped up again. One technique I'd learnt was to try and stay with the general gist of what was said, rather than understand every word. We're used to understanding everything in our own language, but listening to a foreign language is about focusing on what you do know, rather than getting completely lost in what you don't.

Francesco told me that he wanted to improve his English and German, and was considering living in the UK or Germany for a while. He was in IT, but thought the prospects in Spain were poor. In fact, several of his friends had already moved to the UK. Almost everyone I met seemed to have either lived in London or had a friend living there. Sometimes people here assumed I was learning Spanish for work, as learning English is a key skill for employment in Spain. It's understandable people want to make themselves more marketable since youth unemployment is so high and the economy so poor. Mercedes had recently said to me, *"Seville is like a Christmas card for the tourists, but underneath it's a totally a different picture."* Well I think she had said that. Given how much I understood her, she may have said, *"You absolutely must come back to Seville at Christmas! I should show you a picture!"*

Francesco and I switched to English. He wasn't especially confident. He had never spoken to anyone in English before, but watched a lot of English TV, so his comprehension was good. I tried to talk as clearly as possible, although occasionally he didn't understand because I used some slang or colloquial expression.

When our half an hour in English finished we called it a day, as we both had plans that evening. I felt happy that I had handled a conversation with a native speaker. Speaking half the time in each language had worked well. I wondered whether ordinary, conventional dates could borrow the idea? Allocating half the time to each person would put a stop to boorish jerks who dominated and spoke only about themselves. Then again introducing an element of clock management to a date might seem a *little bit* cold and calculating. Stopwatches don't really scream romance.

That evening I had decided to play football with my language partner that wasn't really a language partner, Federico. I judged it was unlikely he would try to kidnap me, and that he did just want extra players for his football match. Besides, I told Mercedes where I was going and left both mine and Federico's numbers, just to be on the safe side. She nodded and smiled, but I'm not sure she really understood me. I wondered if that vision of her smiling and waving me out the door would come back to haunt me when I was chained to a radiator in Federico's warehouse.

Ten minutes later I was waiting at a bus stop on the side of *Avenida de Menéndez Pelayo* with my football kit. I use a very loose definition of football kit. I had shorts and two different colour t-shirts, as instructed, but my shoes left a lot to be desired. When I was packing for Spain I hadn't anticipated being called up for any football teams, and so unsurprisingly I hadn't brought any football boots with me. I only had flip flops and deck shoes - so deck shoes it was. *It would be fine*. If you've got the skills, you've got the skills. Unfortunately, I had neither the appropriate footwear *nor* the skills.

After a minute or two I noticed another guy waiting near the same bus stop. He had a football shirt and shorts on, and I suspected that he too might be waiting for Federico. I asked him and it turned out that he was going to the same football match. My detective skills really were that strong. He was Swiss and had also met Federico on the language exchange website. I wondered whether Federico was trying to learn English, or if he was just looking for footballers.

Federico pulled up in a beaten-up old Ford Focus, a few minutes late. He was in his early twenties, and I noted *not* in a football kit.

He wound the window down, *"¡Hola chicos!* (Hi guys!)

¡Hola! We both replied.

"Subid al coche," (Get in the car), said Federico.

Well, at least he was direct. We did as we were told. There was already another passenger in the front seat and one in the back, so I was surprised to hear Federico announce we were going to pick up another person. We stopped a few minutes later, and another guy climbed in the back with us. It was a heck of a squeeze. Maybe Federico was kidnapping us for our organs; he now had eight kidneys on the back seat.

Fortunately, my worries were assuaged when we arrived at a sports complex five minutes later. The door opened and we emerged like clowns falling out of a mini. I shook myself off and did some stretches. I looked around, there was a collection of hard tennis courts and small astroturf football pitches. I looked at my deck shoes again and then at their soles. They had no grip whatsoever; they resembled the surface of a bowling ball. I looked around at some of the players already warming up. They passed the ball fluidly, occasionally chipping it to each other,

225

controlling it effortlessly. I looked down again at my desk shoes. *This wouldn't do at all.* It would be like turning up to a tennis match with a baseball bat. Not impossible to hit the ball, but seriously likely to hamper one's chances of winning. I went over to Federico and explained my situation. He looked at my shoes and agreed with my diagnosis. He shouted at the guys on the pitch and fortunately one of them had some spare boots. I tried them on. They were a little tight, but they would do.

We separated into two teams, whites against darks (the colour of our shirts, it wasn't some really racist way to pick teams). The Swiss guy was on the other side, so the other six players on my team were all Spanish. I was like the fancy foreign import, the flair player, brought in from overseas to dazzle and beguile with his silky skills. That's what I would have liked to have thought anyway, but it quickly became apparent most of the players were quite a bit better than me. I wasn't completely out of my depth though, and I persevered and got into the game.

The game was played at a high tempo. I quickly learnt some key phrases *"¡Estoy solo! ¡Pásamela!"* (I am free, pass to me!), and *¡Penal!* (Penalty!), but I was mainly running around and playing. A football match is not really the place for a deep and meaningful.

I've played a lot of football back in England, much of it 5-a-side, or 7-a-side, and I was struck by a few differences. Quality-wise there were some very good players, with excellent ball skills, but the key thing was the lack of shots. I've always been used to people shooting on sight of goal. Occasionally even without sight of goal. For some English players, if they've had the ball for more than a few seconds, shooting is almost an involuntary reaction. But here there was a lot more restraint. Shooting was carefully considered, and not done until there was a good chance of scoring. *What a revolutionary concept! These foreigners, with their fancy tactics.* I felt I would certainly benefit if I were to play with these guys regularly. Perhaps even the England football team could benefit from a game with Federico's friends.

The game was closely matched, but we lost narrowly. Or at least I think we did. The guy who announced the score had a thick Sevillano accent, so who knows. I was exhausted, and took a seat on the bench, taking a long gulp from my water bottle. Federico dumped himself next to me.

"*¿Te gustó?*" (Did you enjoy yourself?) he asked.

"*Si, me gustó. Fue duro, pero un buen partido.*" (Yes, I enjoyed it. It was hard, but a good match).

"*Bien, ¿Quieres que te lleve?*" (Good. Do you want a ride back?)

"*Sí, por favor*" (Yes, please) I responded, and we got up to walk towards his car. I realised at that moment that he hadn't said a single word in English, which was rather strange given I'd met him on the language exchange website. Not that it mattered. I'd learnt a few things that evening, both on and off the pitch.

***

My time in Seville was drawing to a close and there was one thing I was still deliberating about - bullfighting. No, not fighting a bull of course, I wasn't mad. I meant going to see a bullfight. It's a highly contentious topic, particularly amongst animal rights campaigners. They believe it's barbaric and outmoded, and want it banned. However, it's still very popular in Spain, and there are many who ardently defend it.

I was in two minds whether I should go, but when Nick invited me, I agreed to join him. It felt so culturally significant, so *Spanish,* that I decided to overcome my preconceptions, and see it for myself. It was an emotive topic though; Nick invited several of our classmates and some were adamantly against it. I'd already seen it on TV a couple of times (sometimes it was showing in bars), and I had to admit I didn't like the look of it. *Give anything a go once,* I thought. Except perhaps actual bullfighting. That would likely lead to a swift and fatal goring.

The Romans popularised fighting dangerous animals for sport more than two thousand years ago (if the movie *Gladiator* is as accurate as I assume). In the 12th century bullfighting began to catch on in Spain, although the matador fought on horseback. In 1726 in Andalusia the modern style of bullfighting emerged with the matador on foot, going toe-to-toe with the animal. Apparently, the added danger really drew the crowds.

The modern, colourful costumes that the matadors (also known as *toreros*) wear have their origins in Andalusia too. The costumes (known as *traje de luces* or suit of lights) are custom-made, and are inspired by traditional 18th century Andalusian clothing. Typically, they are a combination of reds, pinks, golds and blues, and embroidered with white, silver or golden thread.

Andalusia and the South is a stronghold of bullfighting in Spain. The sport's popularity varies significantly across the country. It's prevalent in central areas, the North-East and the South, but elsewhere (e.g. the North-West) there is no tradition of it. In Catalonia, it has become a political issue. The Catalan government banned bullfighting entirely in 2012. Ostensibly it was based on a concern for animal rights, but some accused the Catalan parliament of thinly-veiled nationalism, arguing it was an attempt to block an activity seen as culturally Spanish from the region.

Bullfighting remains alive and well in Seville though. The bullring, the *Maestranza,* is the second most visited in Spain (after Madrid), and has a capacity of 12,000. It's a beautiful building, down near the riverfront. Bright white, and magnificent in scale and appearance. Nick and I approached the entrance of the twin towers, with their arabesque detailing and tiled roofs. The late Spring sunshine drew a sharp contrast between the imposing white outer wall of the bullring and the thick orange-yellow outlines of the evenly-spaced entrances to the arena. We kept walking round until we found our door.

"It's bloody hot," said Nick. He was a pasty-white northerner and was already sweating.

"Did you bring any sun cream?" I asked.

"Sun cream? Don't be soft. It's not a day at the beach."

"I did tell you that we got sun seats though."

"Sun seats?"

"Yes, you remember, you told me to get the cheapest ones. So I got the ones in the sun."

He tutted, "Bloody ridiculous."

It was true, there were broadly three categories of seats in the bullring: *Sol* (Sun), *Sol y sombra* (Sun and shade) and *Sombra* (shade). Given the ferocious heat in Seville, it was unsurprising that the seats in the shade were the most expensive, while those that got shade as the afternoon drew on were next, and those in the full sun were cheapest. I did have some sun cream with me, but I thought I'd wait to see when Nick stopped thinking it was "soft", before I told him.

We made our way to our seats and looked down into the bullring. The wide circle of golden sand beneath us was ringed by a red wooden wall which separated the fighting area from the front row. The rows of seats, like an old Roman amphitheatre, were long continuous benches growing wider and wider in concentric circles. At the top level, a magnificent circle of white stone pillars and arches ran around the whole bullring. It provided some shade for the lucky people sitting underneath it. I'd visited the Colosseum in Rome some years before and it was remarkable how similar the design was to a building that was more than two thousand years old.

A trumpet sounded and out came our contestants. I was surprised to see not one, but six, matadors. It was clear this would not be a fair fight. A moment later, a gate opened and a huge bull shot into the ring. He came out like the clappers, charging to the far side before turning to look at who else was in the ring with him. To my surprise the matadors seemed nervy. They retreated to the outer edges of the arena and it was soon clear why.

The bull eyed the man nearest to him, looked away and then fixed on him again, breaking into a fast run. He didn't hang around. He scarpered the three steps to the wooden wall, and jumped it in one move, just before the bull clattered into it. That didn't seem fair. The bull wasn't allowed to leave the ring, so why should the fighters? I felt that the rule should be, *once in the ring, you stay in the ring*. We wouldn't stand for a boxing match where one fighter hopped out the ring every time his opponent approached, just because he didn't like the look of him.

This cat and mouse game proceeded for a while until another trumpet sounded. At the noise our cowardly fighters left the arena and two men on horseback appeared. They strode out confidently to the centre of the ring while the bull watched. They were armed with huge lances and the horses were covered head to toe in armour. *No wonder they were confident.*

They rode in a circle around the bull. It waited, looking alternately at the two riders, until, suddenly, it picked a target and charged. The rider turned his horse side on and the bull hit it with some force, twisting his head in and forcing it upwards. However, the armour prevented his formidable horns from gouging in. The bull lifted his head and butted the horse again, attempting to gore its side. As he did so the rider stabbed him repeatedly from above. He aimed the lance between the shoulder blades, piercing, withdrawing and stabbing again, until the bull freed himself and circled round, understandably pissed off.

"Surprisingly violent," I said to Nick.

"You're at a bullfight. I wouldn't call it surprising."

"Just *violent* then, I guess."

He nodded, "Yes, it's a strange sport."

"You know what Ernest Hemingway said about it?" I asked. I had read a bit about the author, prior to coming to the bullring. He famously loved Spain, bullfighting and booze, and not necessarily in that order. After watching the running of the bulls in Pamplona, he had become obsessed with bullfighting, writing about it in *The Sun Also Rises* and later, a whole book on the subject: *Death in the Afternoon.*

Nick shook his head, so I told him, "Hemingway said: *There are only three sports: bullfighting, motor racing, and mountaineering; all the rest are merely games.*"

Nick considered that, "Yeah, but he was around before Premier League football wasn't he?" and I could do nothing but nod.

The next stage of the bullfight began and three matadors came back out. They were each carrying two short barbed sticks. The bull wheeled around and looked at the new entrants. The blood flowed from its neck and on to its back where it had been lanced repeatedly. Slick and thick on its black coat, it glinted in the hot sun.

The matadors stayed close to the walls, but the tension was higher now. They would need to get close to stab the bull with their sticks. The bull watched impassively as the men edged closer. A minute later three other matadors with capes entered. The bull looked around with more urgency now, sizing up which man to go for.

Sensing the bull might charge, one of the fighters with barbed sticks made his move. He shouted, waving to the bull, spreading his arms wide, tempting him. The bull swung his head round and bolted for him. It was a good twenty metres away and was picking up speed. It lowered its head, and at the last moment, the man jumped to the left, and the bull weaker now, moved too late. In one fluid motion, the matador brought his sticks down between the shoulder blades of the bull. They stuck, the barbs digging into the flesh. The bull turned around, looking to charge again, but another matador shouted, swirling his cape, distracting the bull a crucial split second. The bull looked between the two men, undecided, stock still.

This was repeated twice more, until all six barbed sticks were planted in the bull's back. Red and blue, lurid and bright against the black coat, there was something deeply unpleasant about the way they hung there. The animal was waiting longer between its charges now, visibly panting from the effort. We were entering the final stage of the fight, the *Tercio de Muerte* (part of death). This is the most recognised part of bullfighting, where a single matador with a red cape and sword faces the bull alone.

The matador strode into the arena, facing down the bull. It looked exhausted, and had no doubt lost a lot of blood. He strode around the bull, flourishing his cape. It watched him, wary, exhausted, unwilling to charge until he took a step closer. He did so, waving the cape once more, tempting it to attack. It did so, putting its head down, sprinting a few steps and going through the cape. The crowd gave an appreciative, *"¡Olé!"* and the matador raised an arm in acknowledgement.

Although the bull looked fatigued, and could only charge a few metres now, this was still the most dangerous part of the fight. The sheer proximity of the matador in the repeated charges in this final section puts him at significant risk. Most matadors have been gored, and they do occasionally die – although pretty small numbers when compared to the death rate of the bulls (100%). Injuries are so common that there is speciality in surgery in Spain to treat *cornadas* (horn-wounds), and every bullring has an infirmary and medical staff on standby.

The matador encouraged the bull through a dozen or so more charges, presenting the cape each time. By the final time, it could no longer charge, merely attempting to twist and thrust its horns through the cape. It was getting uncomfortable to watch, but the crowd grew more appreciative, sensing the end was near and the danger for the matador greatest. The matador twirled around pointing at someone in the audience, dedicating the death of the bull. He turned to face the bull once more, and drew his long thin sword. He pulled his cape for a final time, shaking it, just beyond the reach of the exhausted animal. The bull bowed its head to charge and he plunged his sword in to its neck. The bull staggered, took a step towards him, and then fell, heavy, its resistance ended, and fate fulfilled.

Chapter 18 – Double entendre

My time in Seville was over and the wedding only
two weeks away. More importantly my speech only two
weeks away. *It was best not to think about it. What was
that saying? Cheer up, it might never happen… Yes,
perhaps the bride would get cold feet and call the whole
thing off. That would work! Sure, it would be hard for Jack,
but at least I wouldn't have to do the speech. I probably
shouldn't be hoping the groom gets jilted. Was there a way
for me to avoid doing the speech without a jilting? That
would be best for everybody.*

I snapped out of my feverish thinking and started
packing my bags. I had said goodbye to Nick the previous
night during a tour of the bars of Seville. I realised I'd
rather grown to like the city. It wasn't quite as unique and
interesting as Barcelona, but it was characterful, fun and
had a strong sense of its own identity. Early on in the warm
summer evening we sat outside sipping *tinto de verano*
(literally summer wine – a drink similar to sangria).
Periodically the sprinkler system attached to the terrace
awning let off a fine mist of water droplets. I'd never seen
them anywhere else but they were common in the city,
and cooled the customers down in the oppressive summer
heat.

Later on, we'd walked past the Cathedral and
down some of the narrow streets of the old town. I was
looking for a bar I'd heard about several times: *El Garlochi*.
It was dedicated to Seville's celebration of *Semana Santa*
(Holy Week). They love a parade in Seville; not the

tickertape, dancers and floats type, no, instead, rather formal, sombre, religious processions. A couple of times on the walk home from a night out, I'd heard the sound of drums echoing off the high, closed in walls of the old town buildings. Once, I had followed the noise until I came across a throng of people making their way through the narrow street. In the middle of their group they carried a huge golden effigy of the virgin Mary. She sat on a golden throne, with elaborate, ornate candles all around her. Behind the main statue a group of twenty drummers followed playing a march. A crowd lined the street, watching, even though it was nearly midnight, as the group passed.

I had asked Federico, my language exchange partner, and a Seville native, about it:

"Why do they parade around like that, and who are they anyway?"

"Is a big tradition in Seville. Each parade is done by one church. They organise where they want to parade and it is the members of the church who carry. The statue can be very heavy, so it's better to be in the marching band," he chuckled.

"Interesting, but where do the statues come from?"

"Each church has a Virgin or a Jesus and they live in the church most of the year. The people always parade the statue around during Holy Week, but sometimes they get them out at other times too. I don't know why."

237

"Maybe it's a bit like taking the dog out for a walk, or an outing with Grandma?"

Federico just nodded his head, unsure what to make of that, and I remembered that language exchanges were rarely a good place for surreal jokes.

In the bar with Nick, I looked around at this celebration of Holy Week. It was such a busy and strange sight that it was hard to take in. A huge crushed red velvet awning with elaborate gold trim hung above the bar. Golden statues, effigies and paintings took up every available square inch on the walls, while over-elaborate golden candelabra covered the bar. It was as if we'd wandered into the store room for the Holy Week parades. I don't think I'd ever seen more religious iconography in one place. I wasn't actually sure whether it was an ironic, pastiche of the parades and religion, or a heartfelt, sincere tribute. Nick and I ordered the house special – a strong cocktail called "The blood of Christ" and I still wasn't sure.

It had been a memorable and fitting final night, and Nick had given me a typically understated handshake to say goodbye ("None of this hugging nonsense" he'd said only half-jokingly). Now it was time to leave Seville itself. I closed my door and passed through the kitchen. Mercedes was waiting there, in her apron, with the television on as usual. I had grown rather fond of her, even if I hadn't grown to understand her. We said our goodbyes (or at least that's what I'm assuming she said) and I headed out.

I had decided to rent a car to see some of Andalusia and make the most of my last couple of weeks in

Spain. I negotiated the outskirts of Seville and set my course west towards Córdoba. After I had left the city behind the rolling landscape settled in. The sun was beating down; it was only early May, but the temperature had been rising in the last week and the display on the dashboard said 35 celsius. Endless groves of olives covered the hillsides. Occasionally I passed fields of small trees, sprouting citrus fruit, but mainly I saw only neat rows of olive trees on parched looking fields. The traffic was light, and my mind wandered, as it does on a long drive.

A couple of hours later I was approaching Córdoba. I left the motorway and entered the city. I pushed on towards the historic centre and the satnav treated me to a few laps of Córdoba's one-way system. Enjoyable as it was (it certainly wasn't) I eventually decided to disobey the satnav and turned away from its route. I ignored its hectoring to "make a u-turn as soon as possible" and decided to go by instinct alone. After squeezing down a road that was barely wider than the car itself, I finally found my hotel.

I was happy to spend the rest of my time in Córdoba on foot, so I dropped my bags off at the hotel and set out to explore. I found that I had landed in the city during their "patio festival". No, it wasn't a celebration of small sections of non-descript paving in back gardens, although maybe there would be a niche for that, if perhaps somewhere like Milton Keynes or Swindon needed a local festival. In this case, the patios referred to the internal courtyards of the historical buildings in the city. Many of these courtyards were adorned with beautiful flowers and intricate decorations. Ordinarily, they were private, since they were people's homes, but during the festival, anyone was free to wander in and have a look.

I dropped into the tourist information office where I found a leaflet explaining the history of the patio festival, and a list of the top houses to see. While the contest has been going since 1918, the history of the patios goes back much further than that. Córdoba has a particularly hot and dry climate and from the time of the Romans (and later the Moors) houses in Córdoba were built with a central internal courtyard. These provided a cool and shaded space and were often filled with plants and water features which helped keep the rest of the house cool. The decorating of patios became a tradition in Córdoba, and around 100 years ago the local City Hall realised they were too good to keep hidden.

In 2010 UNESCO added the patio festival of Córdoba on to their list of *Intangible Cultural Heritage of Humanity*. The festival joined such obvious candidates as Tango in Argentina, Yoga in India and less obvious candidates such as: Kırkpınar, the oil wrestling festival of Turkey and the *Lads dances* of Romania, a type of folk dance, not yobs dancing to Oasis.

I walked up the street, navigating my way to one of the houses listed in the guide. A few people stood in line, waiting at an iron gate, outside the white-washed wall of the building. I joined the queue, and a couple of minutes later the attendant let us in to the patio. There were flowers everywhere. Baskets of pink, red and white flowers were hung by the dozen up the high internal walls. In the middle of the courtyard was a lovely stone fountain; its never-ending stream of water flowing out of the centre, pushing the water in the upper basin down to the wider, lower basin. The whole scene was a delight: a hidden garden, and a celebration of colour. It looked like a wonderful place to relax in. Although probably only after the tourists who were sniffing about, posing for pictures and wielding selfie-sticks, had moved on.

I carried on to a second home, also recommended in the guide. It was a little further from the city centre and this time there were no people outside. I was ushered straight in, although rather strangely I had to walk through the hallway of the house. I couldn't imagine opening up my house this way. I can get a bit sick of guests, even when I actually know them and like them, let alone when they're strangers gawking, and poking about.

I passed into the courtyard, and it was another visual treat. There was a greater variety of flowers this time, but the main thing I noticed was the fragrant smell: jasmine, orange blossom and lavender mixed in the air. There weren't many other tourists and I paused to take a moment. It was a calm, relaxing space, and it seemed to invite me to stay a while. I sat on a bench and read the guide: it said that "much of the city's architecture still derived from the Islamic idea that family life should take place largely indoors, behind a blank exterior façade." It was an interesting point. From the outside most of these houses looked the same, yet hiding behind the gates and blank white walls were these little garden paradises.

I toured a few more patios before returning to the hotel. I had heard from tourist information that there would be flamenco performances in the old town as part of the festival. I tried to find the details on the web, but without any luck. It had been the same thing when I was trying to find a place to see flamenco in Seville; none of them had a website. Not even a static page with the address, the time of the show and the cost. *Nothing.* I don't know whether it was a Spanish thing, or something about flamenco, but in an era where everything is on the internet: every embarrassing photo ever taken of you, living on forever, stalking you as you vainly try to move towards middle aged respectability, these flamenco places were like ghosts. I had felt like Jason Bourne: confused, and in desperate need of some basic information.

It was inexplicable. The festival was aimed at tourists – who needed information. It was exactly the type of thing that needed a website. I remembered when I was a student there used to be a jacket potato van that worked the roundabout at the end of the local high street. It had a website *and that was 2003*. There wasn't any possible reason why it needed one. There was no extra information you could plausibly need about the van (it sold jacket potatoes, in the same place, every lunchtime), but it had one anyway.

I asked the hotel receptionist where the flamenco was, and she told me where she thought it might be. I walked through the city on the warm summer's evening, passing through squares edged with cafes, people sitting out at the tables, teenagers mingling and chatting in small groups. I entered the narrower streets of the old town, and before long got a little lost. The receptionist had told me that I had to walk south towards the river, through the old town, until I came to the large wall of the *Mezquita*, the famous Mosque-Cathedral. Since the old town was such a labyrinth, she said I wouldn't be able to see the wall of the *Mezquita* until I was upon it. Yet, seemingly no matter how far I walked, I couldn't find it.

Most frustratingly, I couldn't work out where I was from the map the hotel had given me. The map was completely covered with adverts and coupons: 10% off steak, a free souvenir with any purchase, €2 off at the torture museum. *What garbage.* Further complicating matters were the lines drawn from each advert on to the map itself, indicating where to collect my free souvenir, or eat my slightly discounted steak. All the criss-crossing lines made it impossible to read the street names, rendering the map about as useful as double-sided playing cards.

I decided to stop and ask someone if they knew where the flamenco was. I picked an older lady who looked like a local, rather than a tourist (i.e. she didn't have a camera around her neck or a Hawaiian shirt).

"Disculpe. ¿Sabe dónde hacen el flamenco esta noche?" (Excuse me, do you know where the flamenco is on tonight?)

"¿Cómo?" (What?), she replied. I tried my question again. She still looked puzzled, and asked, *"¿El flamenco?"* (The flamenco?)

Now she was asking me the questions.

This wasn't what I wanted! I hadn't stopped her to tell her about the flamenco. *That would have been weird.* I was tempted to cut and run, but I was in too deep, so I tried to explain: I knew there *was* flamenco on tonight, but I didn't know any of the details. She finally seemed to understand.

"¿Sabes dónde lo hacen?" (Do you know where it is?), she asked. *Hang on,* I thought, *wasn't that the very question I asked you at the start of our conversation?* Although to be fair to her, that did feel quite a long time ago now.

I responded, *"No lo sé. Está cerca de la Mezquita. Estoy buscando la pared."* (I don't know, it's near the mezquita. I am looking for the wall.)

"¿La pared? ¿Qué quieres decir?" (The wall? What do you mean?) she asked.

Another question! She was like a bridge troll. All she had was endless questions. I wanted to leave, so I excused myself. I guessed at the direction and started walking. I could understand why she didn't know about the flamenco (although her desire to chat about it, given her lack of knowledge on the subject, was surprising). What I couldn't understand was that she didn't know where the Mezquita was. It was the most famous building in all of Córdoba. I wonder if she even knew she was *in* Córdoba, or perhaps she just enjoyed confusing tourists.

After more wandering through the narrow streets I was finally spat out at the huge and imposing wall of the Mezquita. I walked along it, mixing with the groups of tourists, passing the Alcázar fortress. By then I could hear the music. I followed it and found the outdoor stage. Pleased to have made it, I sat down at one of the plastic tables, surrounded by families and groups drinking beer in the warm evening dusk.

Various performers took to the stage, one after another. First a traditional small group, formed of a guitarist and dancer, and then later a gaggle of small school girls, about seven or eight years old, all immaculately turned out in their colourful flamenco dresses. They were surprisingly good, and it was heartening to see children learning and taking forward their traditions. Clearly it's important for culture to connect with the younger generation, otherwise it withers away. Unfortunately, I can't imagine a group of English children learning and performing morris dancing on a Saturday night. It just doesn't seem to appeal to the youth of today, instead it's the preserve of very elderly men. In fact, I think the youngest morris dancer in England is 84.

I wandered back to the hotel. The same receptionist who had given me the vague directions at the start of the night was still on duty. She asked me if I'd found the flamenco. I considered simply saying yes and going to bed, but I couldn't help myself, so I related the story of the strange woman, who seemingly had no knowledge of the flamenco, or indeed the city of Córdoba. The receptionist looked perplexed, until a knowing look crossed her face, and I asked her to explain. It turned out that *I* had caused the lady's confusion (yes, I was surprised as you are). Apparently, I had used completely the wrong word for wall, and this would have completely thrown her. Confusingly, Spanish has three words for wall, when, English, as we know, only has one. I had been dimly aware of this fact, but not aware enough to know which wall word was for which wall.

In Spanish the three words are: *pared* (internal wall, and the word I used), *muro* (external wall or a stand-alone wall, like the Berlin Wall), and *muralla* (fortified wall or rampart). I didn't think it would matter, that they would be close enough, but in this case I really should have used *muralla*. And while *muralla* and *pared* are related, they are *conceptually* far apart. Let me give you an example in English. Imagine if a foreigner said they would arrive in a red bus. You would have a clear picture in your mind, and you wouldn't expect them to arrive in a red car. However, both are motor vehicles, with four wheels, that carry several people. If the foreigner didn't know the word for car, but they did know "bus", they might assume it would suffice, or that it was close enough not to matter.

Although you could argue buses and cars are similar things, in our mind they are completely different, completely separate entities, and a native speaker would never conflate or confuse the two. It is the language we use that helps structure those thoughts and concepts. We don't have a word that covers both bus and car (*automotive vehicle* perhaps, but it's not commonly used), so "car" and "bus" remain separate in our mind. Consider the opposite example though: "plane", which is actually a very general word. That could mean a 2-seat light aircraft, or it could mean a 700-seater double decker jumbo jet. Those two types of plane are really different in size, scale, capability, cost, features, yet they *feel* closer together – partly because of language. If someone says they are arriving in a plane, it could well be a small aircraft, or it could be a jet, and neither would be wrong if they had said plane.

This brings us back to where we started – walls. In English we have a general word, whereas Spanish has different words for different types of wall. The categories and concepts are separate. I didn't just use the wrong word with the woman, I used the wrong concept. I conjured up the image of an internal house wall in her mind, when I meant a fortified outer wall. No wonder she couldn't make the mental jump.

This cuts to the heart of a pretty nuanced issue, which is that no language directly maps across to another. As language learners we tend to want a one-for-one translation i.e. this English word means that Spanish word. It's understandable: it's easier when things are simpler. Yet to really get to grips with a language, you must understand it on a conceptual and a cultural level. We all remember the trivia about Eskimos having 50 words for snow, and that makes sense, because we can imagine that snow is much more important to them and their lives, than ours.

The person who discovered this fact was an anthropologist called Franz Boas. He was travelling amongst the Eskimos in Northern Canada in the 1880s and was fascinated by their language. He recorded the elaborate terms they used for their frozen landscape including *"aqilokoq"* meaning softly falling snow and *"piegnartoq"* meaning snow that is good for driving sleds on. Even here it's clear the culture is bound into the language. It's only *because* they use sleds so much that they need a word for the type of snow that is particularly good for sled-driving. (And if you thought the Eskimo/Snow thing was excessive, reputedly the Sami people of Northern Scandinavia and Russia have around 180 words for types of ice and 1,000 words for different types of reindeer).

Languages evolve to fit the ideas and needs of a culture, which is why its easiest to illustrate this concept by comparing our language with that of a very different culture. Yet even between similar European cultures, there are conceptual and cultural differences which are both reflected in, and perpetuated by, our language and vocabulary.

As a beginner learner, it's enough to just know some vocabulary and use it at (more-or-less) the correct time, but to master a language you need the nuance. The idea of having two words for one of ours is difficult to wrap your head around, but it's manageable for physical things – types of wall, or plane or whatever. What's harder is when this happens with a concept rather than a thing. The most famous example in Spanish is "to be" and this will be familiar to anyone who's ever studied Spanish (they are *ser* and *estar*). The problem is that they are used all the time, so you can't really avoid them. Any time you say "is" "am" "are" "we're" you have to know which type of *to be* to use - what a minefield! Anything from "I am annoyed" to "Where are you from?" is completely incorrect if you use the wrong verb. In this case the key to understanding the use of one form of *to be* from the other is around permanence - if you're talking about permanent characteristics e.g. tall/short/where someone is from, you use *ser,* and if it's a temporary state of being e.g. angry/sad you use *estar.* That's massively simplifying it, and there are loads of exceptions and peculiarities, but suffice to say Spanish language learners find this really tricky.

It's not one-way traffic though, there are examples where there are two or three words in English that translate into one catch-all word in Spanish. For instance, *esperar* means to wait, to hope and to expect. We might think that those are quite separate words and concepts, but not in Spanish. Whether you are waiting, hoping or expecting there's a sense of being on hold, in the anticipation that something is going to happen. You undoubtedly lose some nuance by only having one word instead of three, but you can still get your point across. And on the bright side it certainly makes things easier, as you only have one word to remember.

Today is a good day to have a great day, Coffee in Seville

Flamenco dancer in Córdoba

Horse and carriage at the Jerez Horse Fair

The Alhambra. Sometimes featuring the author in a hat.

Chapter 19 – The Inquisition

The following day I walked through the old town of Córdoba. I felt more confident during this, my second visit. I didn't need to confuse any more locals with questions about walls. Instead, I took in my surroundings as I walked. The old buildings were painted white and yellow; above little balconies with iron railings overhung the narrow street. All about me were the signs and rituals of daily life: washing hung out of windows, people walking by with their groceries, and plant pots full of colourful flowers standing either side of doorways. I spied through some of the uncurtained windows, glimpsing families eating, watching TV, and going about their business. It was strange to think people had lived in these very houses for centuries, generation after generation. Although, admittedly, with probably fewer tourists peering through their windows.

The vibe began to change as I got closer to the Mezquita and Alcázar, and I saw more tourists and souvenir shops. I kept walking until I found the first stop on my tour: the synagogue. In the middle ages Spain had a very large and vibrant Jewish population. Although southern Spain was under the control of the Muslim Moors, society was a mix of Muslims, Christians and Jews. While Islam had governmental and institutional preference, there was a high degree of tolerance of the other two religions. That all changed at the end of the *Reconquista* in 1492 when the Christians finally retook the last city that had been under control of the Moors. Religious tolerance in Spanish society was over, and almost immediately the reigning monarchs decided to forcibly convert or expel the country's Jews.

The persecution of the Jews started in earnest in Spain in the early 1200s. Encouraged by decrees from the Pope, King Ferdinand III of Castile declared that Spanish Jews should be forced to wear a yellow badge on their clothing in order to stop them mixing with Catholics. This was already enforced in France (so, no, Hitler wasn't the first to have that idea in the 1930s. It was a medieval practice – literally and metaphorically). Several other laws, including a ban on new synagogues being built, were also enacted.

Throughout the 1300s anti-Semitism increased, and the clergy continued to whip-up hatred of the Jews. In 1391, mob violence against the Jews broke out in Seville. It quickly spread to Córdoba, which experienced one of the worst massacres. The Jewish quarter of the city was burned down, and men, women and children were murdered. By the end of the rampage, more than 2,000 corpses were left on the streets.

In the immediate aftermath Jews began converting to Catholicism in large numbers. Scared of the violence and the growing hatred shown towards them by the population and the state, most felt they had no choice. At the same time increasingly harsh laws were passed in a deliberate attempt to drive Jews into humiliating poverty, and encourage them to convert to Catholicism.

During this period around 250,000 converted, and they were known as *conversos* (New Christians). However, there were persistent rumours that these former Jews were still secretly practising their old religion. In 1477 a prominent clergyman from Seville convinced Queen Isabella of the existence of this secret Judaism amongst Andalusian *conversos*. The proposed solution? The Spanish Inquisition. After all, what says church, God and love like setting loose a gang of secretive torturers who encouraged friends and neighbours to turn on each other?

Two titles I considered for this book were, "A very Spanish Inquisition" or "Tales from a modern Spanish Inquisition". It didn't take much reading about the real Spanish Inquisition to realise that this was a *terrible* idea. If I had used one of those titles you could be forgiven for thinking this was a very different, and possibly anti-Semitic, type of travel story. Happily, I didn't make that mistake, and chose a title that will only offend those who find puns themselves offensive – which admittedly, is still quite a lot of people. And if you think the title I did choose was bad, you should see some of the ones I rejected: *"Hola! Is it me you're looking for?"* and *"Tapas of the morning to you"*.

Back to the history, and back to medieval Spain. Just as the Catholic monarchy and clergy were putting Jews (and Muslims) under increasing pressure, they were also growing in military might. In 1492, the combined forces of Isabella I and Ferdinand II took Granada, the last enclave held by the Moors. In doing so they completed the Christian reconquest of Spain which had begun centuries earlier.

The fall of Granada set the scene for the Alhambra Decree. This established a new level of religious intolerance in Spain: while Muslims supposedly had their rights protected, all Jews were to convert to Christianity or leave the country within four months. After nearly three centuries of persecution there were fewer than 100,000 Jews left anyway, but those that remained were faced with a tough choice. Many emigrated to North Africa and Turkey, and many more converted. Within a year officially there were no Jews left in Spain.

In front of me was the only synagogue left in Andalusia (and one of only three in the whole of Spain.) It was built in 1315 and was seized by the authorities in 1492 and used as a hospital for people suffering from rabies. I was surprised by how small it was, but what struck me more was the intricacy of the decoration and plasterwork. Despite being a Jewish place of worship it was decorated in the Moorish Muslim *mudéjar* style. The arches and elaborate patterning on the wall reminded me of the Alcázar fortress in Seville. It was a reminder of how closely the Jewish, Moorish and Christian cultures had lived together and intermingled.

Unusually this synagogue had been preserved, even though almost all the others had been destroyed. This was down to a quirk of fate. After a century as a hospital it was taken over by a shoemakers' guild in the 16th century. They chose to plaster over the original decoration, but make only minor modifications to the building itself.

When the plasterwork started to fall off in 1884 a local priest realised it was an ancient synagogue. By this time animosity towards the Jews had long since dissipated and the government declared it a national monument. After the horrendous treatment that the Jews suffered in the medieval period, modern day Spain has done its best to make amends. In 2015 the Spanish government launched what they called an "historic rehabilitation". This entitled any Jew with an ancestral connection to Spain, from prior to the expulsion, to claim automatic citizenship. To be fair to Spain, it wasn't the only European country to evict Jews in the middle ages, but it *is* the only country that has tried to atone in this way. Over 4,000 people have acquired Spanish citizenship under this law, and from a low of zero, there are now an estimated 50,000 Jews in Spain.

I left the synagogue and walked the short distance to the *Mezquita*, undoubtedly the most famous building in the city. Its official name is the *Mezquita-Catedral de Córdoba* (the Mosque-Cathedral of Córdoba), which tells you quite a lot about why it's such an interesting building.

I approached the grand wall I'd been looking for the previous night *(that's not just a wall, it's a muralla,* I thought to myself.) It was hard to take in the whole building; it was a huge sandstone edifice with a tall traditional-looking cathedral tower at one end. Viewing the *Mezquita* in the light for the first time, I could see the mosque-like decoration and detailing along the side. I'd never really seen anything like it on a cathedral before. Islamic-style arches, pillars and tiling ran along the length of the wall. The inside of the arches looked like they'd been bricked up, as if someone had tried to integrate them into the flat wall of the cathedral. Nevertheless, they were still clearly visible.

After the Moors arrived in the 8th century Córdoba began to grow in importance. The Emir decided to build a large mosque, based on the design of the Great Mosque of Damascus. Thousands of people were employed in its construction; marble and stone were quarried from the surrounding mountains, and mines were dug for the required metals. Factories and industry emerged as the city began to boom.

Over the next two centuries, the Moors' empire, Al-Andalus, developed rapidly, and nowhere more so than Córdoba. By the year 1000, when the Moors territory stretched nearly to the French border in the north, Córdoba was the most populous city in Europe, with half a million inhabitants. Furthermore, those citizens had a higher degree of literacy and education than anywhere else in the continent. Córdoba boasted hundreds of public baths, a dozen libraries, paved streets and even a form of street lighting (whereas Paris and London were little more than small towns at the time), but the crowning achievement of it all was this building in front of me now.

I entered the *Mezquita* and was struck by the incredible interior. I wasn't ready for it at all. I'll level with you. I'd been in Spain for well over two months now, and I had been inside a *lot* of cathedrals. I was like a hard-bitten detective who thought he had seen it all. Soaring high-vaulted ceilings? Tick. Immense golden altarpieces? Yep.

Majestic stained-glass windows? Been there, done that. I was cathedraled out. I'd hit the end of the road, nothing could shock me anymore.

On one side was a vaulted ceiling and dome with a traditional altar piece. Impressive enough, but it was a typical scene, nothing out of the ordinary. *Seen one, seen 'em all.* File this one under: classic medieval gothic cathedral. Case closed. Or so I thought. I turned to walk to the other side of the building, and I approached the prayer hall. There I stumbled across something I'd never seen before: hundreds of free-standing pillars forming colourful red and white arches. They were unmistakeably Islamic in appearance, and they were everywhere, a forest of them. I drew nearer and inspected one of the pillars up close. It was made from beautiful swirled grey marble, supporting a double stone arch, one stacked on top of the other, creating a pleasing geometric effect.

When the Muslim poet and philosopher Muhammad Iqbal visited the Mezquita in 1931 he described it as having "countless pillars like rows of palm trees in the oases of Syria". Iqbal believed that to the people of al-Andalus the beauty of the mosque would have been "so dazzling that it defied any description." I wasn't inclined to disagree. It was fabulous. I wandered between the pillars marvelling at the symmetrical pleasure of it all. Supposedly the arches were based on those in *The Dome of the Rock,* the famous Islamic shrine in Jerusalem. It was fascinating to think of the links between this building and the temples of Damascus and Jerusalem. Over 1,000 years ago, this place in the heart of Spain was regarded as just as much a part of the Islamic world as the Middle East.

That was not to last though, and following the *Reconquista* (Córdoba fell to a Christian King in 1236) the Mosque was converted into a Catholic cathedral. Although the minaret was turned into a traditional cathedral tower, many of the other features of the Mosque were kept and integrated into the cathedral. The biggest alteration was the insertion of a traditional nave. When King Carlos V saw the cathedral for the first time after the conversion he was said to have commented, "they have taken something unique in all the world and destroyed it to build something you can find in any city." Maybe he was cathedraled out too. I think he was a little harsh though. The Mezquita's mix of cathedral and mosque in one building is what makes it so fascinating, and such a perfect testament to the unique history of this area.

I made my way out, and found a table at a nearby restaurant. The sun was shining and I ordered the *Menú del día* (Menu of the day). The *menú* is a fixed-price three-course meal served by most restaurants, but only at lunchtime. It typically includes bread and a drink (sometimes a whole bottle of wine is placed on the table), and is priced around €10. The quality varies a lot, but even at the ropier end of the scale, it represents fantastic value. There is a legend that the dictator Franco mandated that all restaurants offer a *menú del día* at lunchtime so that even poor folks had the chance to eat well. That doesn't seem exactly true, although it's probable that the *menú del día* tradition evolved from the *"plato único"* law which was enforced up until the 1940s. This required restaurants to offer a certain dish on the menu at a maximum set price.

I'd been in Spain for a long time, and except for the home-cooked meals at the families I'd stayed with in Barcelona and Sevilla, I ate out a lot, and I almost always went for the *menú del día.* I could eat well, and having a three-course meal always felt like a treat. Besides, €10 was a steal. In the evening you couldn't get a *menú del día*, and you couldn't eat for anything like the same price. A decent meal with drinks was at least 20 to 25 euros. By my calculation inflation seemed to be running at about 300% between the early afternoon to the mid-evening. I know it's always more expensive to eat out in the evening whatever country you are in (although I have no idea why) but the difference in Spain felt absurd. One evening I ordered a *ración* (small plate) of calamari in a restaurant and it was €11. I had been in the very same restaurant the week before feasting like Henry VIII, commanding the waiter to bring me this, that and the other, and it had cost €10. The only difference? It was lunchtime.

I chatted to the waiter, asking him some questions about the different courses. I had already chosen, but I thought I'd take the free language practice. I ordered, and once he'd left, I looked out at the people passing by. I had an afternoon to kill, so I opened my map up, and considered my options. Something caught my eye. *Two euros off entry*. Could I? Should I? The coupon for the torture museum was staring at me. I thought for a moment, it didn't sound that appealing... but I read the details anyway. Its official name was the Museum of the

Spanish Inquisition, although the small picture of a chair with spikes sticking out rather suggested it might major on the torture aspect. On the other hand, it was already cheap, *and I had a coupon.* So, on some level it had two things going for it.

An hour later, and against my better judgement, I found myself approaching the entrance to the museum. It looked dark inside but I handed over my coupon and money anyway. I walked through the curtain and entered. I was surrounded by all manner of torture instruments. In one corner there was a full-size rack. Next to it was a cabinet full of thumb screws. On the opposite side of the room was a something that looked like the sarcophagus, the type of upright coffin I associated with mummies. The only difference was it had spikes covering the inside of it. Presumably some poor unfortunate was forced inside it and then skewered. I looked at the label. It was called an Iron Maiden. *How appropriate,* I thought. Arguably, being inside that would be even worse than having to listen to one of their albums. Arguably.

I looked around in vain for a description or history of the Spanish Inquisition. There wasn't one, so I went into the next room. Another room of torture devices. I didn't really want to read any of the descriptions, they were all so gruesome. I didn't like it at all. Who would? I vaguely remembered that I had been in a torture museum before, and I hadn't liked it then either. At least in this one my displeasure was discounted. Literally.

I don't know why, but torture museums are surprisingly popular, or if not popular, then surprisingly prevalent. Here's a list of places that have torture museums: Amsterdam, Prague, London, Budapest, Bruges, Zagreb, Vienna, Lucca and Berlin. That's almost certainly not comprehensive, just the suggestions from Google's autofill once I started typing "torture museum".

Since not many people would actually want to see someone being tortured, and even fewer would want to be tortured themselves, it's baffling why there are so many torture museums. I'm not even sure people like going to them – Amsterdam's gets 2.5 stars on Tripadvisor, Vienna's the same. The torture museum in San Gimignano (somewhere in Italy, apparently) gets 1 star from one reviewer, who has titled her review: "Torturous". She says, "There are actually two Museums of Torture in this tiny city, and apparently a torture museum in every town in Europe we visited... visiting was neither a pleasurable, or illuminating, experience." I'm not sure why we think visiting torture museums *will* be a pleasurable experience, but we do it anyway, like continuing to scoff cheese or pringles way after the point you know you're full. Sometimes in life our rational brain is fully disengaged.

I continued looking around, learning nothing about the Spanish Inquisition, although I was surprised by just how many ways they had concocted to torture people. They were certainly strong on ideas and innovation, if not on empathy or morals.

In the next room we moved on to torture in the rest of Europe. Here there were some amusing torture implements (it was a low bar). They seemed to be inspired by the maxim, "let the punishment fit the crime". One was called "The Barrel Pillory", designed especially for disruptive drunks. The drunkard was forced to wear a wooden barrel with their head sticking out of the top and arms out of the side which "left him free to roam about to be ridiculed and scorned". To be honest, if the guy was that much of a boozer, I doubt being forced to wear a barrel would stop him going back to the pub. If anything, it might be a badge of honour. You certainly wouldn't enter into a drinking contest with anyone wearing a barrel. Another instrument was known as the "Noise Maker's Fife", and was for those caught making too much noise (swearing, partying, playing a musical instrument). The miscreant's fingers were locked into a metal flute-like device that was attached to a metal collar on the neck. Harsh, yes, but if you've ever experienced the misfortune of inconsiderate noisy neighbours, you might think differently.

I made my way out, through the completely unnecessary gift shop. €60 for a replica miniature wooden rack? €80 for a little wooden chair with real spikes? I mean who the hell would buy that, and what would you do with it if you did? I couldn't think of one appropriate place for it. It would look pretty strange on the mantlepiece, and stranger still in a child's doll house. To be blunt, it would also be a pretty weird *gift*. *"I saw this miniature torture chair, and thought of you."* would be easy to take the wrong way. In fact, the only suitable place for these bizarre little replicas is the gift shop of a torture museum. And that is where I was happy to leave them. I browsed for a moment longer, pausing in bemusement at the postcards with pictures of the highlights of the torture museum and then headed for the exit. I emerged back out into the sunshine, and wandered towards the old town once more.

Chapter 20 - Reunion

I was back in the car and heading into the countryside once more. Thankfully the route out of Córdoba was a lot easier than the route in. Once I was on the highway my thoughts flitted between the looming wedding speech, and oddly enough, the torture museum. For some reason my mind seemed to be associating the two. While arguably the speech wouldn't quite be *torture,* I wasn't looking forward to it. It was only a week away now, but fortunately I had just finished the rough draft. I would open with a stock joke (thanks, Google) then launch into a story that I'd never told Jack before... an admission of something. I figured some dramatic tension in the room might raise the stakes a little. Then there was the standard merciless ribbing of the groom. I wasn't sure if they did that at Spanish weddings, but what the hell, Jack was British, so he was getting it. Then a few comments about how Jack met his new wife, followed by the toasts. *Classic.* Plus, it had 17 gags in it. I'd counted.

Overall, I thought it was pretty good. There was just one problem: it was still in English. The whole *translating it into Spanish thing* was yet to be done.

I had considered running the entire speech through Google's Translate software, but I knew deep down that I shouldn't. It was completely unreliable, and I would end up sounding like a malfunctioning robot. No, the best thing was to translate it myself. After all, my Spanish *was* improving. All this practice was paying off. In his book "Outliers" Malcolm Gladwell says that being good at something simply comes down to practice. He argues that we massively overestimate the importance of natural talent, and underestimate practice. He even puts a figure on how long it takes to excel at something – 10,000 hours apparently. From musicians, to computer programmers, to golfers, the truly exceptional ones tend to have that amount of practice under their belt.

I think the same probably goes for languages. English speakers often say they would like to learn a foreign language, but unfortunately, they just don't have the talent for it. It's more likely they haven't devoted the time to it. A weekly French class just isn't sufficient to get good at the language (although it's probably still worth taking, as you will improve, and there's an enjoyment in learning itself).

If I had realised nothing else, it was that truly learning a foreign language takes time. That said, there is an *element* of natural talent to learning languages. I have a friend who can speak Chinese, French and Spanish, all to a good level. He must have an aptitude for languages. Or he's lying - it's very difficult to tell if someone is good at speaking Chinese when your ability to speak Chinese is the square root of zero.

I think anyone can become competent at a foreign language if they put the time in. Using Spanish every day, as I had done for two and a half months, I had finally got a flow to my speaking. I still made mistakes, but in general whole sentences came out without really thinking about it.

In conversation I still frequently found I didn't have the word I needed in my vocabulary, but I had learnt to work around it. I could make myself understood. One study says that once you know between 1,000 and 3,000 words of a foreign language you can have basic conversations and navigate everyday situations like shopping and public transport. By the time you know 4,000 you can discuss more specialised subjects like your profession, news and current events, give opinions and talk about abstract things. I think I was there, but I wasn't yet clear how many words I needed for the "telling jokes competently in wedding speeches" level. I was worried that was still beyond me.

**

With only a week left in Spain, my wife, Robyn, had arranged to join me for a short road trip before Jack's wedding. I drove back to Seville and parked up at the airport, arriving just before her flight landed. It would take a while for her to get through arrivals, so I got myself a coffee and waited. I considered writing a sign to hold up, like I was her chauffeur. That would be amusing. I could even spell her name wrong. I'm sure that would get a laugh. *Would it though?* I hadn't seen her in over two months, and she probably wasn't after a gag, or prank. Pretending I'd forgotten her name probably wasn't wise. Funny, yes. Wise, probably not.

She came through the gate about forty-five minutes later, and it was good to finally be re-united. We hugged and walked out to the car.

"How was the flight?" I asked.

"Fine, it wasn't long, and we had some good views over the mountains before we landed." She took in the surroundings, and the feeling of being outside, "It's so nice and warm," she lingered on the last word.

"It certainly is." I paused, and then announced proudly, "I've written the speech! It has 17 jokes in it."

"Ok, that's good," she looked at me sceptically.

"Although nine of them are about how much Jack likes booze."

"Right," she replied.

"Is that too many?"

"I don't know, maybe," she said. She sounded a little irritable.

"It's only just over half. And I think it's ok, because he *really* does like booze, doesn't he?"

"Can we just sort out getting our stuff into the car?" she replied.

"Are you in a mood?" I asked.

"No!"

"You sound like it," I noted.

"I'm not, but I will be!" she replied. So, she *was* in a mood. It's almost like I knew it before she did.

I decided I would help her out and change the subject to something she would prefer to talk about. "It's nice and warm here, isn't it?" I remarked.

"Yes! Good for us! Good for holidays!" she said smiling, and hugged me.

We spent a pleasant day and night in Ronda, scene of a magnificent and dramatic gorge. There wasn't much to do beyond looking at the gorge, and looking at the coach parties who had come to look at the gorge, but it was worth an overnight stop.

The next day we drove south, passing more olive groves and the amusingly named *Morón de la Frontera* (Moron of the border). I wondered if that was a reference to a specific "village idiot": someone who was such a clown that the whole village had been renamed in his honour. Or perhaps he was a moron, notorious in the local area, already living on the border, but nevertheless had a village grow up around him.

Unfortunately, I read later *Morón* simply means hillock in Spanish. I wondered if I'd mis-read, but it did indeed say hillock, not pillock. The name of the town was simply *the hillock of the border,* so disappointingly was not inspired by a celebrated local dimwit. The border in the name (and in several other town names in the area) was the 13th century divide between the Muslim and Christian Kingdoms. During the *Reconquista,* the area was the site of several battles and continuous skirmishes. Once the Moors left Spain, the idea of a border (or frontier) in Andalusia was lost, but the name of the towns stayed the same.

On we drove to Jerez, officially known as *Jerez de la Frontera* (Jerez of the border). Jerez is famous for two things: sherry and horses, and we intended to get our fill of both. Well, perhaps not a *fill* of horse, but we certainly hoped to clap eyes on a few.

We parked up at our hotel and went for a little walk around downtown. Luckily, we'd managed to time our arrival with that of the *Feria* (fair), one of the biggest in the South of Spain. It's a week-long celebration of horses (of which more later), flamenco and drinking.

It was mid-afternoon, and unseasonably hot, close to 35 degrees celsius, despite only being mid-May. We found an outdoor table at a café and people-watched as a large group arrived. The women mostly wore red flamenco dresses, the men were all in black. One man had a guitar and almost as soon as he sat down he started strumming a flamenco rhythm. Two of the group got up: a dark-haired woman with huge red hoop earrings, a white blouse, red sash around her waist and polka dot skirt. Her dancing partner was dressed in black, and adorned with the typical moustache that marked a certain sort of suave older Spanish gentleman.

The duo walked away from the table and into the pedestrianised street as the guitarist played. As one the group stood up from the table and began clapping out a rhythm, and a moment later they broke into song. Meanwhile the pair had reached the middle of the street and were ready to begin. They struck a flamboyant pose and held it for a few seconds, before they began to dance.

It was flamenco, but partner-style, rather than the traditional sort with just a lone female dancer.

They began dancing faster, picking up the rhythm that was being strummed. The man twirled the woman, her skirt twisting as she moved. They hit a pose at the end of one step, each sticking an arm into the air, rhythmically curling and flexing their outstretched hands, as their bodies remained frozen. The group at the table continued to sing and clap.

Before long, people from other tables and passersby joined the dancing duo, until there were a dozen couples in the street. I was surprised, as I didn't know where they had all come from, and also, because I thought spontaneous dancing in the street only really happened in musicals, rather than real life.

After a couple of songs, the guitarist finished and the group and dancers broke into applause. Those that had been walking by continued on their way, as if nothing had happened, and the group sat back down at their table.

"That was strange. It must be because it's festival week, right?" I asked.

"I guess so," Robyn replied.

"But we've got no frame of reference really. I mean we're one day in, and we have already seen spontaneous dancing in the street. So, it *could* be just what people do in Jerez. Just normal behaviour. From our sample size, we would have to say it's an everyday occurrence. Literally every day."

"Well, yes I suppose."

"Can you imagine how I've had to keep these sorts of thoughts to myself for the last two months?"

"Must've been hellish," she said, sardonically.

"No, it was ok. I wrote most of them down. You'll be able to read them all at some point," I said smiling, and she laughed.

In the evening we had a restaurant reservation, and we decided (perhaps unwisely) to go to a bar first. It was unwise because the restaurant, like much of Jerez, specialised in sherry; so pre-dinner drinks ran the risk of over-egging the pudding, or indeed, *over-sherrying the trifle*, so to speak.

Our hotel had recommended the restaurant *La Carbona* as it specialised in local produce and dishes. It also offered a five-course tasting menu with sherry pairing i.e. five sherries, each matched to a course. Wine pairing was common enough, *but sherry pairing?* We had never heard of such a thing so were keen to give it a go.

We arrived after our pre-dinner drink at the bar, and entered the restaurant. It was a lovely open big space, with white-washed walls, and huge wooden beams. There was a well in the middle of the dining area, which was a first, and lots of upturned barrels acting as tables in the bar area. I wasn't surprised to learn that the building had formerly been a sherry *bodega* (cellar) before its evolution into a restaurant.

We took our seats at our table and happily chose the five-course tasting menu, even though some of the dishes were a mystery to us. While each description had been translated from Spanish into English, some words had clearly proved too hard to translate; the *"Pastel de Caballa en escabeche de vinagre de Jerez, cebolla morada y manzana",* became "Mackerel cake in an escabeche of sherry vinegar, purple onion and apple". Quite apart from the merits of a mackerel cake (surely an outlier in the cake family?), I'm still at a loss as to what an escabeche is. That said, there were so many elements going on in that dish, that it seemed fine to let the odd unintelligible ingredient go.

I was also impressed that, in addition to the five glasses of sherry that came with the menu, the chef had managed to wangle some type of sherry into three of the five courses themselves. That was dedicated. Bordering on obsessive.

Jerez is synonymous with sherry – in fact the name sherry is an anglicisation of Jerez. In Spanish Jerez is pronounced *"Hereth",* but with a harsher, throatier sound to the H. Unsurprisingly, the English traders who developed a taste for the local tipple were having none of it and changed the name to the much simpler "sherry". However, you can still just about hear the resemblance between the two names.

The production of wine in the Jerez area began during the Romans, and continued through the rule of the Moors, although in 966, Al-Hakam II, the second Caliph of

Córdoba, decided to stop the manufacture of alcohol, and ordered the destruction of the vineyards. However, the inhabitants of Jerez appealed, arguing that the vineyards also produced raisins which fed the empire's soldiers. In a big concession the Caliph spared two-thirds of the vineyards.

After the raisin-hungry Moors had left Spain sherry production flourished, and by the 16th century it had a reputation as one of the world's finest wines. Supposedly, when Ferdinand Magellan equipped himself for his voyage around the world in 1519, he spent more on sherry than on weapons (but then again, maybe he was just a piss artist).

Sherry vineyards (much like the vineyards of La Rioja) were devastated by the phylloxera virus. In 1894 the virus spread rapidly, and many sherry producers went out of business before they were able to bring in resistant vines. The after-effects were severe. Sherry had been made with 100 varieties of grape, but after the virus hit (and ever since) it's only been made with three. That said, with the aging and fortification process, there are still many different varieties. All sherry has one thing in common though: if it is labelled as sherry it must come from the area surrounding Jerez, as the drink has protected status in Europe. However, given how much was on the menu in this restaurant, I was surprised any sherry was making it out of the city at all.

Despite my scepticism the mackerel cake was delicious, as were the artichoke and prawns, the fish with spinach noodles, and the steak frites. Now we were on to dessert.

"It's a far cry from a hotdog on a pier, isn't it Robyn?"

"I have to agree, it is," she said, looking up from her plate.

I was referring to our long road trip across the USA, where we tried all manner of gourmet delights, one speciality from each state we visited. Although, thinking back, most of the foods we ate could be categorised in two broad churches: "fried meat" and, "things with cheese on". Many dishes even combined the two.

I took another mouthful of my dessert, and then another sip of sherry. It was my fifth glass. "I don't think we ever had sherry in the US though," I said.

"True. We're making up for it now though."

"Yes, it's like a year's worth in one meal. And I must say, I really didn't think they could get sherry in to the dessert, but you know what, I hold my hands up, I was wrong," I said, regarding my ice cream with raspberry coulis and sauce of fino sherry.

"This is probably more sherry than I've ever had in my life," Robyn said.

"In one sitting?"

"Possibly in total," she replied.

I nodded, not confident I could disagree. "Can you imagine them interviewing a prospective chef for this place? They would have to be a true believer. Think about it. First question would probably be: *What are your feelings on sherry?*

Hmmm, yeah, it's fine. I don't mind it, take it or leave it, I guess...

Right, so if I told you that sherry will have to feature in every dish you make, would that be a problem for you? Because, we'll be honest, this is kind of a deal breaker for us."

She laughed, and took another sip of sherry.

Chapter 21 – One Horse Town

The following morning we had tickets to the horses; no, not the ones that run around a course, carrying tiny men in colourful jerseys, in a manner that encourages you to throw good money after bad, but instead, the famous horses of Jerez.

Robyn had always liked horses and seeing them here was her idea. I wasn't nearly so bothered. I wanted to stay in bed a bit longer, as I had succumbed to the Magellan-esque quantities of sherry I'd imbibed the previous evening.

"What's so special about these horses then? I asked, rubbing my eyes.

"They're world famous. Jerez has one of the most well-known riding schools in the world."

"Right, but what do these horses do exactly? Are they fast?"

"No, they're not fast. In fact, I don't think they run at all."

"They don't run!? The tickets are 25 euros each! I should bloody well hope they do."

"They don't run. They dance."

"Dance? A dancing horse? How preposterous," I considered it for a moment, "What type of music do they dance to?"

"R&B mostly. A little bit of jazz," she replied.

"Really? Jazz?"

"No, you fool, of course not. Get up."

An hour or so later we were at the *Real Escuela Andaluza del Arte Ecuestre* (Royal Andalusian School of Equestrian Art). It was another hot day under a blue sky. We had an hour or so before the show began and wandered around the school complex, looking at the buildings and horses in pens. As the fair was going on in the city, a lot of the other visitors were in traditional Andalusian costume and eye-catching flamenco dresses. I saw a lot of polka dots. Not much used elsewhere in fashion, but still very big in the flamenco world it would seem.

Jerez has long been associated with horses. In fact, the fair (of which, more later) is dedicated to them, and known as the *"Feria del caballo"* (the horse fair). The story of the equestrian school begins at the fair. In 1973 Don Alvaro Domecq Romero brought his show "How the Andalusian horses dance," to the fair and won the prestigious *"Caballo de oro"* (Golden Horse) – a statue of a golden horse, not a real golden horse, unfortunately. Following his win, he decided to found a school to conserve the skills and abilities of the Andalusian horse. Numbers had dropped dramatically in the twentieth century and Don Alvaro wanted to protect the breed. The Andalusian horse has always been renowned as, "strongly built, and compact yet elegant... Throughout its history, it has been known for its prowess as a war horse, and was

278

prized by the nobility." Unfortunately, Don Alvaro had other ideas for them, namely, a lot of dancing.

We continued to wander around, looking at the blacksmiths and saddlery where they manufactured and maintained horse harnesses. It was interesting to see such traditional crafts still taking place. Outside, and in front of the pens, there were insightful signs explaining the traditions of Spanish horsemanship and dressage, and even the history of horses themselves. I learnt that there are no wild horses anymore. 15,000 years ago wild horses were widespread in Europe, Asia, North America, but around 8,000 years ago they process of extinction began, and they were domesticated in large numbers by humans.

There are two types of "wild" horse now – feral horses (e.g. the Mustang in the US) which live in the wild, but whose ancestors were domesticated horses. Typically, they descend from herds which got lost or escaped. Now they just rove around the wilderness, running free, which is pretty wild, I guess. The largest population is in Australia where 400,000 Brumby horses live feral, carting about, doing who knows what. The second type of wild horse is the *Przewalski* breed, which was the last true wild horse. It roamed the Mongolian steppe until it went extinct in the late 1960s. However, a small herd of 13 *Przewalski* horses were captured in 1945 and were then kept in captivity. In the 1990s the *Przewalski* horse was reintroduced to its natural habitat in Mongolia. There's now a herd of over 300 living in the wild there, all descended from that original group of 13. Since the *Przewalski* horse was never domesticated, that herd has a claim to be the only wild horses left in the world. The whole story also underlines the importance of conserving endangered species before it's too late.

Following the first successful reintroduction in Mongolia a decision was taken to place another herd of *Przewalski's horse* somewhere else in the world. Where do you think they put them? China? Russia? You could probably spend the rest of your life guessing and you still wouldn't get it.

They put them in Chernobyl. That's right, the Russian Academy of Sciences successfully lobbied to put a herd in the "Chernobyl Exclusion Zone", the 1,000 square miles of uninhabitable, sealed-off territory, that surrounds the decaying nuclear plant, in a deliberate effort to prevent any human interference. I can see the logic, but I'm not sure of the wisdom of putting wild horses in a radioactive zone. The last thing we need are wild horses, out of sight, mutating, no doubt gaining superpowers, and then wreaking their revenge on humankind for all that horse-taming we've done over the years. I'm not saying it's likely, but someone should think these things through. And these animals are dangerous – they aren't cuddly, slow-moving pandas. Quite the opposite, *"Przewalski horses live in family groups, whose leader is a strong stallion with absolute power."* What? Have these scientists not seen *Planet of the Apes*? It's pretty much impossible to avoid, they keep remaking it. Just don't say you weren't warned.

In better news, in 2011 the status of *Przewalski's horses* was upgraded from "critically endangered" to merely "endangered". Every single one alive today descends from that last herd of 13, but there are now over 2,000 *Przewalski horses*: the majority in zoos, but several wild herds too.

Back at the equestrian school it was time for the show, and we proceeded to the purpose-built arena: a large U-shaped riding ring, the floor covered in sand, surrounded by tiered seating rising up on three-sides. It reminded me of the time I saw fake medieval-style jousting in the US.

"Do you think they will do any jousting in the show, Robyn?"

"Almost certainly not," she said, as she picked up the show leaflet, and turned it over looking for the English section. "Here you go," she said and began reading, "*How the Andalusian Horses Dance* is an equestrian ballet accompanied by quintessential Spanish music and 18th century styled costumes, all put together and choreographed using movements based upon Classical Dressage, *Doma Vaquera* (country-style riding) and traditional equestrian chores."

"Sounds like a chore to me," I muttered. She shot me a disapproving look and I smiled.

Moments later the music started and the murmuring amongst the audience ceased. A single besuited rider emerged on a fine chestnut brown horse. He cantered around, before stopping and saluting the royal box (well, a little balcony which featured a portrait of the

King). He disappeared, and half a dozen grey horses were led out by pairs of men who walked slowly behind them. The lady next to me was trying to take surreptitious photos, in that manner that you do when you've been told not to take pictures.

In the ring the men began encouraging the horses to rear up and walk on their hind legs. Several of the horses could only manage a couple of seconds before dropping back down to all-fours, while others could balance perfectly, standing and paddling their front legs in the air. Their composure and strength was admirable. However, I couldn't decide whether seeing some horses struggle meant that seeing the ones who could do it was more impressive, or whether the ones not doing it were letting the whole side down a bit. *How do the Andalusian Horses Dance? On their own and inconsistently,* it would seem.

The music stopped, and the horses were led away. I wondered whether they were being rewarded with a system of performance-related hay. If so, some of the horses would not be eating well tonight. The next part of the show began, and a carriage led by three stallions entered the ring. The shining black carriage with large colourful, yellow wheels carried two immaculately dressed men sitting in the front. Both wore intricately detailed red jackets and smart, flat-topped, flat-brimmed, grey hats. Two identically-dressed ladies sat in the back in bright blue flamenco-style costumes. The horses had splendid black coats, and wore harnesses covered in bells.

The coachman, who held the reigns, encouraged the horses into a canter. The other three people were just passengers really, which is not a bad way to make a living I guess. The coachman cracked his whip, and the horses began to go faster. They had to corner sharply, given their pace and the confines of the ring, but they didn't slow. Two more horse-drawn carriages appeared and the three began to weave in and out of each other in an impressive piece of choreography.

The lady next to me continued with her sneaky photography, until one of the ushers appeared at the end of our row, pointed at her camera, and gave an exaggerated wag of the finger. The lady mimed an overly-expressive, *"Oh, I didn't realise,"* type gesture. The usher was unyielding, and answered her with another wag of the finger, and the woman, defeated, put her camera away.

The final section of the show involved some classical dressage. If you don't know what that means, don't worry, it's just very dainty trotting. First one horse came out and ran around in a very deliberate, flouncy, bouncy style, and then he was joined by two more horses, and they proceeded to delicately walk around the arena too. Their movement appeared both tentative and precise. It reminded me of that moment when you step on to a tiled floor in bare feet, and it's either way too cold or way too hot, so you try and creep around on tip toes. The more I watched it though the more I saw their movements were actually very controlled, and rather graceful. A little poncey, sure, but very elegant too. As it went on the horses' movements became more complicated, walking diagonally, and then almost sideways, all in perfect synchronicity and in time to the music. It became almost mesmerising. Finally, the music stopped, and the horses did too. The crowd signalled their hearty approval (despite the lack of jousting), and a few minutes later we were back outside in the heat and sunshine.

It was mid-afternoon now, and hot, but the fair was on and there were more horses to be seen. *Ferias* (fairs) are a big thing in Spanish culture, particularly in Andalusia. Most cities and towns in the region host a week-long event, normally in the Spring or Summer. Seville's *Feria de Abril* (April Fair) is the biggest, but Jerez's is also significant, and has a history dating back nearly 800 years. When Alfonso X completed the reconquest of Jerez from the Moors in 1264 he instituted two annual duty-free fairs in the city to commemorate the victory. The Spring one gained regional recognition, and developed into a commercial livestock fair. Later, Gypsies (who have been resident in Andalusia since the 15th century, and are credited with developing flamenco) brought their performing horses to the fair and local wine producers began to set up stands. The emphasis switched to entertainment, and the fair gained its horse theme. In the modern day a funfair was added, along with flamenco and musical performances, but the focus remained on the horses.

We walked over from the Equestrian school to the fairground. It was huge – over 52,000 square metres in size - and contained 200 hundred *casetas* (stands). The sun was shining, and we entered the park through two ornate arches. We took in the scene: the brilliant blue sky was in sharp relief to the golden sandy ground. The *casetas* stretched as far as the eye could see; long lines of them, interspersed with palm trees. They formed a distinct avenue, and horse-drawn carriages ambled up and down. It was mid-afternoon, and very hot, close to forty degrees. There weren't many people walking around, but several of those who were carried umbrellas to shield themselves from the fierce sun.

We entered a *caseta,* a large tent, open at the front, full of benches and with a bar in the back. Robyn sat down, and I made my way towards the bar. As I did so, I noticed waiters making their way between the tables. I was pleasantly surprised, as this wasn't something you would see at a festival in the UK, instead you are normally required to muscle through a crowd of people to get to the bar; at which point you must desperately try to catch the eye of an over-worked bartender, and if you manage that, all you win is an opportunity to pay three times the going rate for a type of beer that you would never contemplate ordering in your local pub in the first place.

I returned to the table and moments later a waiter approached. He spoke quickly, in a kind of *time-is-money, let's go,* style.

"¿Qué desean tomar?" (What will you have?), he asked rapidly.

I had plenty of time, so I decided to practice my Spanish and string out our interaction a little, *"Pues, ¿Qué recomendarías?* (Well, what would you recommend?)

"¿Para tomar? ¿O para comer?" (To drink, or to eat?) he said, quick-fire.

"Los dos. ¿Qué es tipico?" (Both, what's typical?)

"Bueno, lo tipico aquí para tomar es el rebujito. Es fino y le echamos limon. Muy fresco. Para comer le recomiendo pescaíto frito o montaditos." (Ok, well to drink, a rebujito, which is sherry and lemonade, and really refreshing. To eat, I recommend little fried fishes or a little sandwich), he said, rattling along at a pace I struggled to keep up with.

He looked at me expectantly. It's always awkward to ask for a recommendation and then say something other than, "Sounds lovely, I'll have that." Presumably, because if you say, "Ok, well, I'll have something else," then the unspoken subtext is, *"What you just recommended sounds disgusting, and even though nothing on the menu appealed to me, I will go back to that, rather than eat whatever grotesque concoction you just tried to force on me."* So, yes, asking for a recommendation can be a high stakes gamble.

In this case, even though I had my doubts, I acquiesced and nodded, *"Vale, tomaremos dos rebujitos y un plato de pescaíto frito."* (Ok, we'll have two rebujitos and a plate of fried fish).

"Muy bien," (Very good) he said, and disappeared.

I was a little wary of the *rebujito,* as we don't tend to mix wine (or sherry) with soft drinks, even though I had been in Spain long enough to know it was common here.

This was the first time I had heard of a *rebujito* (a speciality of Andalusia) but I thought it was worth a try, and Robyn agreed. Besides, it had to be better than the drink *calimocho*. It's very popular, especially amongst the young, but to the uninitiated sounds frankly disgusting. *Calimocho* (or *kalimotxo* in Basque, where it originated) is equal parts cola and red wine, and that's it. Yet it's the late-night drink of choice for many.

In Spain it's very common to see youths emerging from a mini-market with a two-litre bottle of cola and a couple of cartons of cheap Don Simon red wine, on their way to a park, square or riverbank to drink into the night. During my two and a half months in Spain I'd had *calimocho* a couple of times, out in bars. In fact, it reminded me of a cocktail I had made at a friends' wedding once. *The Bradwell,* as I dubbed it, was a mixture of the only two things left at the end of the party: gin and cola. It didn't go down well, but perplexingly, unlike *The Bradwell*, *calimocho* is very popular indeed.

The *rebujito* came in two small cups, and was fresh tasting, just as the waiter had promised. The name stems from the Spanish verb *arrebujar*, which means "to jumble up," or mix up. The *-ito* means little, so it literally translates as "little jumble", or "little mix-up", which is rather sweet. I noted that our plate of food, *pescaíto frito* (small fried fishes), used the same suffix of *-ito*, as *pescado* (fish) became *pescaíto* (little fish). The adding of *-ito* to words is common in Spain, and even more so in some Latin American countries. It was endearing really, as it suggested the dishes were small and delicate. This was a particular contrast for me after having spent so much time in the US, where the opposite tendency with food is more common, e.g. the *Big Daddy* from KFC, the *Son of Baconator Combo* from Wendy's, or the *Zinger Fully Loaded,* also from KFC. They sound more like obstacles on an assault course, or the final boss in a video game, rather than options at a restaurant.

We continued making our way between different *casetas,* sampling different food and drink as we went. As it grew later the fairground grew busier and the atmosphere livelier. Here and there people strummed guitars while others broke out in dance, as we had witnessed the previous day. Strings of lights came alive as dusk fell, and it was clear people were set in for the night. Knowing the Spanish, that would mean the small hours, but Robyn and I had a long drive the next day, so we left them to it and wandered back towards the city.

***

The following day we set out in the car towards Granada. It would be my final stop on the journey, and it also meant the wedding was just a few days away. I tried not to think about it. It was an issue for Saturday Rich, and I was Tuesday Rich. Let him worry about it. I was fine, or that's what I kept telling myself anyway.

It was a drive of a little over three hours to Granada, but we wanted to detour to one of Andalusia's famous *pueblos blancos* (white towns). They are a series of towns and large villages found inland, mostly around the *Sierra de Grazalema* Natural Park. Their uniform white buildings, set amongst craggy hills, supposedly made them a photographer's dream. We picked the town that involved the smallest detour, Setenil de las Bodegas, and set the satnav. It was famous for two things; firstly, its role in the *Reconquista,* the Christian reconquest of Spain, and secondly, for houses built into the rocky walls of a gorge.

Legend has it that the name Setenil de las Bodegas derived from the Roman Latin phrase *septem nihil* (seven times nothing). This refers to the Moorish town's resistance against the Christian reconquest; allegedly it was only captured after seven sieges. It was first besieged unsuccessfully in 1407, and it took until 1484 for Christian forces to expel the Moorish rulers. You would have to say the Christians were rather ungracious in victory when they renamed the town in commemoration of its defeat. They even chose to mock the town's heroic resistance during the seven previous sieges, choosing "seven times nothing" as the source of the new name. It's only one step up from renaming the place, "Losertown". But as we have seen (and shall see once more in Granada), the reconquest of Spain was an ungracious time, with little love lost between the competing factions. The fall of the town was one of the last steps in the Christian reconquest of Spain. Around five centuries after it had begun, Setenil de las Bodegas fell, and eight short years later, the Moors were driven from Spain completely.

After a drive through more rolling olive groves, we approached the town. We could see the sunshine bouncing off the white cluster of buildings. As we got closer we entered the cleft of the gorge. The town was cut in two by the river and we continued following the satnav, heading towards its centre. I was driving, and starting to feel a bit apprehensive about entering the unfamiliar town, as I remembered my multiple circuits around the one-way system of Córdoba. More worrying though were the increasing number of road signs that I didn't understand.

"Robyn, do you think it's ok to ignore road signs?"

"What do you mean? When?"

"I mean here in Spain. I understand some of them, and most of the rest you can kind of work out, but I would say there's the odd gap in my knowledge. Here and there."

"Go on," she said, warily.

"The speed limit signs are fairly self-explanatory. Sure, you've got to remember the old kilometres-not-miles per hour trick. I did get caught out that time I was doing 40 miles per hour by the school, but generally I get it right," she looked shocked, and I quickly clarified, "Joking, I'm joking."

"Right, what's the problem then?"

"These *"Calle estrecha"* signs," I said, and gestured to one of them. "They're everywhere. I know *calle* means street, but *estrecha,* I can't remember that word. *Estrecha? estrecha?* Sounds like straight. Maybe it means straight street?"

"Why would they have a sign saying straight street?"

"That was what I was wondering. It's not the type of thing they usually put up signs about. Although maybe they would if it was the straightest street in the world."

We rounded a gentle bend, and kept driving.

A minute later it became painfully obvious what *estrecha* meant. As we continued towards the centre of town, inbetween the white-washed stone walls of the buildings, the street became narrower and narrower (but not any straighter).

"I think *estrecha* might mean narrow," I said, stating the obvious. She nodded, choosing to say nothing. The street narrowed further (and let me say at this point that a street has to be pretty bloody narrow in Spain before they put a sign up). Naturally, it was also one-way, and it wasn't possible to turn around anyway. The only course of action was to continue. I drove slower and slower.

By now I was genuinely worried I was going to scrape the car. The walls of the buildings seemed to be closing in. I wondered if we had accidentally entered an MC Escher drawing and the street would keep narrowing until it reached a vanishing point.

Best not to admit my worries, I thought. I had got us into this mess and admitting to that wasn't on my agenda. "This is a situation isn't it!" I said, cheerily. Robyn merely cocked an eyebrow in response. "Don't fancy driving, do you?" I asked, only half-joking. She laughed, and I slowed down further. The road rose above us, and if anything, it looked narrower still. "Maybe I should reverse or something?"

"I don't think that would be any easier," she replied, and I agreed.

I slowed the car to a crawl. At the top of the rise, I could see the street narrowed to a slender gap, before emerging on to another road. "If we can make it through that gap, it should be fine. Could you get out and fold the wing mirrors in?" I asked. Robyn agreed, and got out. As she was about to get back in, I stopped her, "Would you mind staying out to guide me through?"

She looked up the rise, "I think that's a good idea, but I'm not sure it's going to fit though."

"It'll be fine," I said, racking my brain to remember what the excess fee for damage was on the car hire agreement.

She walked ahead of me, and up the rise, as I inched along in the car behind her. If she'd carried a little red flag, it would have been exactly like Victorian times, where a man walked ahead of every new-fangled car to warn everyone that it was coming through. Except in this case I didn't want anyone to look at us.

She reached the top, looked both ways and gave the thumbs up. If I could get out onto that road, it would be ok. I considered flooring it to get it over and done with, but that didn't seem wise. Instead, I edged up the rise and towards the final two buildings on the corner of the road. Robyn watched me as I went, pointing a little to the left, and then a little to the right, and I adjusted accordingly. As I went up, her face tensed up in a grimace with each revolution of the wheels, until I stopped completely. Tentatively, she beckoned me onward and I crept forward. Suddenly her face broke into a grin and I realised my folded-in wing mirrors had passed the narrowest point. Like the head of a baby during birth, the car had finally emerged.

Robyn got back in the car, "Well... that was close. It was practically touching the wing mirrors on both sides."

"Lesson learned. Don't ignore the *Calle estrecha* road signs!"

"That's not the lesson!"

"No?"

"Don't ignore *any* of the road signs! That's the lesson!"

"What? Even the ones with the little black cross in the red circle? I see them all the time. Or the one of the funny picture of a bull in a red triangle? I'm pretty sure those are just decorative." She rolled her eyes and then laughed.

After the trauma of the drive, the houses built into the rock didn't seem quite so dramatic. Nevertheless, we went for a pleasant walk around town, first dining on a tasty menú del día outside in the sunshine. In the early afternoon we walked along the river and admired the houses built under an overhanging ledge of the rock face.

Parallel to the river bank there was a street so far under the ledge that the overhanging rock created a roof over the street. It was very unusual to see buildings constructed like that, and a real accomplishment too. It's hard enough screwing a shelf into a brick wall. I can't imagine how hard it would be to build a house into rock. The houses do have some advantages though: they stay cool in the fierce Andalusian summer, and warm in the cold mountain winters. It still seems a strange choice of house, and that the owners might prefer one of the beach houses on the nearby Costa Del Sol. Perhaps it's because beach or no beach, it's always better to build your house on rock, rather than on sand.

Chapter 22 – The Palace

Jack stood in front of the mirror, tying and untying his tie for the fourth time. He was wearing his formal groom's outfit, and more nervous than I had ever seen him.

"How does it look?" he asked.

"It looks fine, mate! You'll be the best dressed cocktail waiter at this thing." He shot me a look to show he was unimpressed. "I'm joking! You look good. Although I'm not sure about your cummerbund."

"Why? What's wrong with it?"

"I just don't think you're the cummerbund sort."

"This isn't helpful Rich. You're not being helpful."

"Oh, come on, it's only the dress rehearsal. And besides, you want to talk about helpful? How about asking me to do half my best man's speech in a language I don't speak? That wasn't exactly helpful was it?"

"Pffff." He gave a dismissive flick of the hand, "how's that going anyway?" he asked, doing his tie for the fifth time.

"Well, it hasn't been *easy.*"

"No?"

"No! Of course not! How's your Spanish anyway?"

"It's not really an issue. Sofía's English is perfect. I would learn, but there's no point really. You know how it is."

"Not really. I've had to learn!"

"It's a project. You love projects! It's basically a gift. I've given you a big old gift. More or less," Jack said, beaming.

"Right. Well, I guess you'll be getting your *gift* in 48 hours time."

"Is it a big gift?"

"It's the speech."

"Right. I'm getting the speech...*and*..." he lingered, and in response I rolled my eyes. He continued, enjoying himself, "Maybe you lost the gift list. Not to worry. I've got it on my phone. I'll just pop you over a little email now. Not a problem at all."

"Shut up," I said, and he grinned. I gestured at his suit, "Your tie looks wonky, by the way." He scowled and turned back to the mirror once more.

***

It was Friday now, and the wedding was tomorrow. We had been in Granada for three days already. It was a unique place. The old half of the city, known as Albaicín (or Albayzín in Arabic), was full of labyrinthine streets which wound their way up the hillside. It was the type of place that was easy to get lost in, but generally a pleasure to do so, unless you had somewhere to be, or realised you were at the bottom of the hill when you should be at the top.

Albaicín was the ancient Moorish quarter of the city and the Moorish influences were still evident. The streets were narrow, cobbled and generally only fit for pedestrians. Fortunately, we had returned the rental car already. Regardless, when I saw a *"calle estrecha"* sign, I still felt a shiver pass over me. That said, it would have to be a seriously narrow street to prevent me, an average-sized man, from being able to pass through, so I concluded I was safe.

Robyn and I had spent a pleasant day wandering around, and up and down, and round and round the old town. We passed doorways with characteristically Islamic-style detailing and hanging baskets full of colourful pink and blue flowers. Even better were the delightful little plazas where we could stop for a *café con leche* and a look at the map (for the millionth time). Eventually we gave up with the map and just wandered. In the afternoon, back down at the bottom of the hill, we found ourselves on a long street filled with cafés and teashops. Many of them were Moroccan or North African, and people sat outside with hookah pipes, so we took a table and ordered one. Hookah pipes, the tall, thin pipes for smoking flavoured tobacco through a glass-basin of water, originated either in Persia, or India, although I had always associated them with North Africa. I wondered whether the people running the teahouses were descended from the Moors, or were more recent immigrants. From their accents it seemed to be the latter, but it was interesting to think that they were following in the footsteps of other North Africans who had made this city what it was, hundreds of years earlier.

The following day we went to the jewel in the crown of Moorish Spain: the palace and fortress complex known as the Alhambra. It was the day before the wedding, and in keeping with tradition, Jack wasn't meant to see Sofía, so he had accompanied myself and Robyn. Helpfully, he had borrowed his future-in-laws' car, so it was up to him to deal with the dreaded *calle estrechas.*

"So, I guess you've been to the Alhambra before then?" I asked Jack, as we approached the visitor car park.

"Why would you say that?"

"Because you're marrying a girl from Granada and the Alhambra is *the thing* in Granada."

"I haven't actually. Never felt the need, I suppose."

I was bemused, but unsurprised, "You won't be acting as our tour guide then?"

"I could do. I'm happy to make a load of stuff up if you want. Actually, I do know one fact. Do you know why it is called Alhambra? Well, *Al* means *the* in Arabic, and they also raised a lot of pigs up here, and that's where the *ham* part comes from."

"Really??" said Robyn.

Jack laughed, and I gave her a disappointed shake of the head, as if to say, *never believe a word this man says.*

"Oh," she was disappointed. "You moron," she said to Jack, assessing the situation accurately.

We got out of the car, and proceeded with our pre-bought tickets past the long line of people. It was a huge site, situated on top of the steep hill. We had caught views of it the previous day from the hillside of the Albaicín district, and it looked magnificent. An imposing, yet beautiful set of buildings, both a palace and a castle, and one of the most iconic places in Europe. Originally built as a small fortress in the year 889 (towards the beginning of the Moors rule in Spain), it was later rebuilt and expanded in the 13th century as the Moors concentrated their powerbase in Andalusia, during the Christian reconquest.

We wandered through the buildings, starting with the royal palaces. The walls and archways were decorated with highly-detailed white stucco plaster and Islamic arches that I had seen so frequently throughout Andalusia. However, this was even finer than the Alcázar in Seville, in both size and beauty.

We passed into a splendid square known as the "Court of the Lions", named for a large fountain basin that was carried on the backs of a dozen lions (statues, not real ones, fortunately). The whole courtyard carried layers of symbolic meaning. The twelve lions represented the twelve original tribes of Israel, harking back to the Koranic and biblical legends that would have been so important to the royals of the time.

The fountain and patio were surrounded by a ring of thin stone columns, which were said to represent the palm trees that encircle an oasis in the desert. The idea of an oasis was symbolically important, as it was closely related with the idea of paradise in the Moors' imagination. Furthermore, the courtyard was divided into four parts, symbolising the four corners of the world, each irrigated by a water channel that represented the four rivers of paradise. The whole courtyard was therefore the physical embodiment of paradise. I thought it was nice, but I hadn't imagined so many tourists, or selfie-sticks for that matter, in paradise.

We moved through more hallways and rooms, many intricately decorated. Often the ceilings were ornate and things of beauty too. One in particular was made of wood, and all of it elaborately carved.

Much of the Alhambra has been reconstructed and renovated, but I'm in favour of that. It brings it alive: much more so than if it were in ruins. It was enjoyable to walk through the regal rooms, and pass out into the gardens, imagining the royals that would have lived there 700 years before. It felt like walking through living history. This type of experience is one of the greatest joys of travelling in Europe. I had travelled with Robyn and Jack separately in the US, and while that has its charms, for history you can't beat Europe.

The Alhambra was full of stories too. The Hall of the Abencerrages was so-called in honour of a rather gruesome legend. The Abencerrages were a family of aristocratic Moors living in Granada. In the 15th century one of their young men fell in love with one of the royal ladies, and took to climbing into her window at night time. On hearing about this the king was enraged, and hatched a plan. He invited the whole Abencerrage family for a banquet in one of the halls of the Alhambra. Once they were dining, his guards shut the doors and allowed a rival family to kill them all. All thirty-six Abencerrages were massacred, most beheaded. From then on, the Hall carried their name. Unsurprisingly, the King received a much lower RSVP rate to his subsequent banquets. Despite the horrible tale, it was another beautiful room. It was a perfect square, and its main feature was the ceiling where an incredibly intricate carving of an eight-point star framed a beautiful dome.

Another thing that interested, intrigued and amused in equal measure were the information signs. On the one hand they contained some fascinating facts about life in the Alhambra, but on the other, the English translations were so bad they were amusing. You know the type of thing. The sort of mistranslations often found in China, where they are known as *Chinglish*. For instance, a sign in a clothing shop saying, *"Let us help you try out clothes. Please don't touch yourself."*

These signs weren't quite on that level, but nevertheless, there were some gems. My favourite was one indicating that a path was blocked. The English translation read, *"The itinerary was be detoured by labours of maintenance. Sorry, the inconveniences."* Wow. Even Google Translate isn't that bad. I had no idea how they had come up with such a weird translation. Perhaps they had done a word for word literal translation. Or perhaps an over-confident workman had volunteered. One whose English didn't quite match up to his promises. I particularly liked the line, *"Sorry, the inconveniences,"* as though *the inconveniences* were people, and they were signing off their apology. I'm guessing if the inconveniences *were* people, then apologising would be all they would ever do. Any time they got involved in any kind of project, I would guess. And you might think this was a hastily knocked-up handwritten sign. Nope. It was permanent. Made from perspex.

I sympathised though. It is hard to translate, and you can never check your own work. You can look at something again, but you don't have the feel of a language the way a native speaker does. Often the only solution is to directly translate word for word, but sometimes that just doesn't work. The structure of sentences often aren't the same. For instance, take the rather offhand saying, "What difference does it make?" If you translate that word for word then you arrive at, *"¿Que diferencia hace?"* That's just wrong and apparently sounds awful to a Spanish speaker. Instead, they say *"¿Qué más da?"* which is fine if you know it, but impossible to guess, and very different to the word for word translation from English. If you were translating the other way, word for word from the Spanish into English, then their version of the saying translates

302

something like, "What more gives?" which, as you can tell, doesn't really make sense.

There is no shortcut to these translations, other than practice, and being wary of translating word for word. That was why I had got one of Sofía's family to check my speech the previous day. I didn't want to sound like a confused three-year old, or worse, accidentally insult the bride. Insulting the groom – I was happy with that – but not the bride, I knew what my life was worth. As it was, Sofía's sister had been kind enough to go through the speech, and while there were plenty of corrections, he was very kind. Almost too kind. I was paranoid. Anyway, the proof was in the pudding, and tomorrow I would find out for real.

We continued wandering through the Alhambra, and along the ramparts of the castle. I've already described the advanced civilisation that the Moors built in Spain, particularly here in the South, but Granada was unique. Following the big push of the Christian Reconquest, most of Spain was reclaimed by 1236, when Córdoba fell, but Granada survived as a city-state with a Muslim Moor ruler for another 250 years. It's surprising to me that the Christian Kings reconquered so much and left this little island of a city alone. There are many reasons: the powerful fortress of the Alhambra was one, but more important was that the rulers of Granada could see which way the wind was blowing. As Ferdinand III, King of Castile, took Córdoba, the Nasrids, who ruled Granada, aligned themselves with him, even paying tributes to his kingdom. Once the Nasrids were no longer a threat (and indeed protected by Ferdinand), they were free to continue running their city state. In fact, Granada was a useful connection for Ferdinand to the Muslim and Arab trade centres in Africa and Asia, especially for gold, silk, and dried fruits.

Granada, under the Nasrids, was a cosmopolitan city with many religions and ethnicities, and had Jewish and Christian quarters. It was renowned as a centre for artisans and craftsmen, and key in the development of the *mudejar* style of architecture which fused Islamic and Christian heritage and stylings.

That said, all good things must come to an end. In the late 15th century, the zealots were in control, and there was a drive to purify Spain as a solely Catholic country. The Moorish enclave of Granada could no longer be tolerated. Ferdinand and Isabella, the power couple of their era, known as "Fernabella" (by me anyway), launched the Granada War in 1482. Ten years later, they were triumphant, and the last Moorish Emir in Spain admitted surrender. Emir Muhammad XII capitulated on the terms set out in The Alhambra Decree of 1492. This explicitly protected the rights of Muslim citizens to continue to practise their faith openly and unhindered. In reality, the conclusion of the war saw the end of the *"convivencia"* philosophy (live and let live) between religions and ethnicities in Spain.

The fall of Granada and the completion of the Reconquest emboldened the country's religious leaders. They persuaded the King to finally outlaw Judaism, following centuries of persecution of the religion. And now, despite the explicit protections of the Alhambra Decree, Islam was in their sights too. In 1499 one of Spain's high-ranking religious leaders, Cardinal Cisneros, accompanied the Spanish Inquisition to Granada. He was disappointed at the slow rate of conversion of non-Christians in the city, and determined to do something about it.

The Bishop of Granada favoured peaceful and slow conversions: explaining the 'truths of Catholicism' to Muslim residents. Cardinal Cisneros felt differently. He described this as, "giving pearls to pigs," and instead, upon arrival in the city, ordered forced baptisms and mass conversions. He also commanded that all Arabic manuscripts found in Granada would be burned. The outrage felt by Muslims across Andalusia sparked uprisings, first in Granada itself, and then in the surrounding mountains. Within a year though, the rebellion was violently suppressed, and this was just what Cardinal Cisneros needed: an excuse to tear up the Alhambra Decree. All remaining Muslims were given a choice: Christian baptism or exile from Spain. By 1526 this "choice" was mandatory for all Muslims across Spain.

Many Moors stayed on in Spain though by converting, some in name, and some in spirit. Today, more than 10% of people from the South of the country have some North African ancestry, and Andalusians in particular are renowned for their darker skin tone, hair and eye colour.

As we left the Alhambra, I reflected on the strength of regional identity in Spain. It's not an especially big country, 46 million people or so, only the seventh biggest country in Europe, yet it seems more fragmented and diverse than most. It's not unified by geography: not being an island like the UK, or ringed by mountains like Switzerland, it doesn't have a single unifying language like France, or the Netherlands, nor does it have a sense of a glorious history (invented or real) like Russia or Germany.

During the journey I had met many Spaniards who expressed a regional identity before their national identity. This was more common in the Basque Country and Catalonia, but even in Madrid and Andalusia, people talked about their region much more than I was used to in the UK. In England, there's a big divide between North and South, and pride in certain cities, but it's not nearly as pronounced as in Spain.

One person I had met in Bilbao was telling me about his sense of being Basque, and talk turned to football, which can be a great barometer of identity. I asked him what the reaction had been in Bilbao to Spain winning the football World Cup in 2010. "Not much," he replied, "Almost nobody was wearing a Spain shirt during the tournament or after the victory." I couldn't believe it. This was the World Cup, the biggest event in football, possibly the biggest event in sport. Spain had never won before, and players from the Basque Country were *in* the Spain squad, yet people weren't celebrating it. It's even more surprising for me, as an England fan. We have such little success in sport that if our national *table* football team won their world cup, we would be getting the flags out and holding street parties. But here, regional identity is more important, and for some people it goes so far as to be in direct opposition to feeling Spanish.

To explain this identity issue I would point to two factors; first, and most important, is language. The sense of regional identity is much stronger in the regions that have their own language. Secondly, the history - specifically the feudal kingdoms that existed in one form or another for centuries. They predate the nation of Spain, and since Franco's death they have been constitutionally enshrined as the modern day autonomous communities. In that sense Spanish people are similar to Americans, who often have a keen sense of connection to their home state, and less similar to British people, who tend to have more of a national identity, than a regional one (as our regions are less strongly defined).

Another factor that strengthens regional identity is that people in Spain seem to move around the country less. That's just a personal observation, but I was struck by how many Spaniards I met who had never left the place they grew up. Unlike British people, Spaniards don't tend to move to a different city for University, and they often live with their parents for longer, which keeps them rooted in their home city. Whatever the reasons behind it, as a traveller, I liked the regional differences that I had found on my journey.

That evening, Jack, Robyn and I dined in a small restaurant in the Albaicín district. We were directly across the valley from the Alhambra, and had a great view of it.

"Big day tomorrow boss, isn't it?" I said to Jack.

"Yes, but for you as well, I would say," Jack shot back.

"Bigger for you though," I insisted.

"But yours is a big speech. A whopper," he replied.

"Stop bickering," said Robyn, and looked at us pointedly. "Now, what have you chosen to eat?"

"This is an important meal. Your last supper," I said to Jack.

"Zip it," Robyn interrupted, and I did as I was told.

I looked at the menu again, "I am going to have fish, maybe a vegetable side. We can split a fried rice if you want, Robyn?"

"Sure, I'm having chicken, so let's share the rice."

A moment later the waiter came over, and we ordered. At Jack's insistence, I ordered for all of us, *"Para él espaguetis, para ella el pollo, y para mí, la trucha con ajo blanco, espinaca y arroz frito,"* (For him, spaghetti, she'll have the chicken, and for me, fish with garlic and spinach, and fried rice.).

"Muy bien," (Very good), said the waiter and exited.

"Excellent work Ricky! You've got the lingo down!" said Jack. He even sounded a little impressed.

"Muchas gracias," I said, putting on my most Spanish of Spanish accents.

A few minutes later the food arrived, but it was not what I was expecting. The spaghetti, fish and chicken were present and correct, but the other two dishes, the garlic and spinach, and the fried rice, were present, but definitely not correct. *Why?* Because they were soup. They were both soup. Separate soups.

"Have I missed something here?" I said, gesturing at the bowls.

"You've got a lot of soup there, haven't you mister? You likes your soups don't ya? Two of 'em," said Jack, deliberately unhelpfully.

I grabbed the menu, and looked at the names of the dishes again. Both were exactly what I thought they had been.

"Look here," I said, pointing, *"Ajo blanco y espinaca* – that literally means white garlic and spinach, and the other one, *arroz frito*, that means, and has always meant, fried rice!"

"It doesn't matter. We can just send them back," said Robyn.

I carried on, "It doesn't say soup anywhere on this menu! How are you meant to know what's a soup? White garlic and spinach? How are you supposed to figure out

309

that's a soup? Secret soup, isn't it? And this fried rice?" I said, pointing at the soup, "Where's the fried rice?" I stuck a spoon in the bowl and dug down. Like the seabed shifting, I dredged up a layer of rice. "Ok, fine there's fried rice *in it,* but I can't help but feel like the "soup" element is the most important part. It's not some unimportant ingredient or garnish. It. Is. A. Soup."

Jack peered in closely at it, "Yes boss, it's a soup."

I ignored him, "So white garlic and spinach is actually white garlic and spinach soup, except with a silent soup. Maybe the rule is that soup can be anywhere. *Surprise! Soup!* Anything can be a soup. No longer imprisoned to the starters section, it can be lurking anywhere on the menu, literally anywhere."

The truth is I was annoyed and frustrated. I had been here three months. I had learnt so much Spanish, and what had it amounted to? Two unwanted, surprise bowls of soup. Why did it have to be so hard? I didn't even know the basics. Why did I have to be so useless?

"Just send them back," Robyn said, and placed a gentle hand on top of mine.

"Fine," I said, and looked round for the waiter. *"¡Oye!"* (Listen!) I said, and he walked over. *"Lo siento, pero no sabía que estos platos eran tipo sopa, pensaba que estaban cocinados differente."* (Sorry, but I didn't know these dishes were soup. I thought they were different).

"¿Diferente? ¿Cómo qué?" (Different? Like what?) he said, a touch defensively.

"¿Ajo y espinaca? Verdura? ¿Pensaba el arroz frito era, y no sé por qué, era arroz frito, no una sopa." (Garlic and spinach? Vegetables? And I thought the *Fried rice* would be, and I don't know why, I thought it would be fried rice, not soup).

"Son platos típicos." (They are a common dish).

"Entiendo, me equivoqué y no las quiero." (I understand, but I made an error, and I don't want them.)

"¿No? No pasa nada. ¿Quiere arroz y verduras al vapor?" (No? Oh, no worries. Do you want vegetables and rice?)

"Sí, por favor." (Yes, please.) I said, and the waiter strolled away.

"Wow, nice work Rich," said Jack. This time he really did seem impressed.

"Well, hang on." I said.

"Did you get them changed?" Robyn asked.

"No, unfortunately we have to pay for both soups. But he did take them away, so at least we don't have to look at them."

"Oh, never mind. That's fine. Doesn't matter," she said.

"I'm joking!" I said, smiling, and she playfully punched me on the arm, and all three of us laughed.

I felt pleased. Making mistakes is just part of learning a language. That doesn't really stop, no matter how much you learn. I once read that fluency was an unrealistic goal in language learning. Complete fluency is reserved for native speakers. It's not what you should judge yourself against. Learning a language is about understanding, and making yourself understood. Of course, you might still get caught out by surprise soup lurking on the menu. That means you're still learning. But you are getting to know another culture: opening up new avenues, making new connections, meeting people and exploring new places. As I looked out at the Alhambra, and saw it turning pink in the rays of the setting sun, I wondered if there was a finer place anywhere else in Spain to finish a journey like this one.

Epilogue

It was 10pm and I still hadn't given my speech.

I was sitting at the top table, a large circle, with Robyn to my left, and Jack to my right. Jack's parents were there too, as were Sofía, her sister and mother. I had no idea how Spanish weddings worked, and I wasn't sure Jack did either. So far, the day had been a mix of fun and waiting around, with a few little ordeals thrown in for good measure. Exactly like any other wedding then, I suppose.

Robyn and I had accompanied Jack to a grand building downtown for the short and simple ceremony. I didn't really have a role to play there, except to try and make Jack feel as nervous as possible. Although even *I* felt a little mean doing that, and besides, it wasn't necessary, he was making himself nervous. Eventually, I did give him some reassurance, reasoning it was, *"unlikely she would back out now. Too much money down the drain already."* Apparently, I, *"wasn't helping. Not even a little bit,"* according to Jack. From then on, I stuck to the more encouraging and straightforward, *"you'll be fine, mate,"* which seemed to do the trick.

The service was modest and to the point. It was a civil ceremony and the man officiating was kind enough to translate some of his sections into English for those guests who didn't speak Spanish. However, he did have the thickest Spanish accent I had ever heard. It was so thick that half the time he was speaking English I wondered if he had switched back to Spanish. Twenty minutes after the ceremony had begun, Jack kissed Sofía, and they were married.

As the newlyweds exited the church we threw rice *(arroz)* at them. Fortunately for them, it was actually *arroz*, and not soup. We took photos outside the grand *Ayuntamiento* (Town Hall) building. It was the perfect backdrop in brilliant white, under the blue skies, as spring turned into summer. The couple smiled and chinked their flutes of champagne, twirling and hugging as the photographer requested.

The fiesta element of the wedding didn't begin until 4pm. Jack and Sofía had arranged a party at a grand house in the mountains outside the city. After the photos, and celebratory champagne, we had a couple of hours to relax and make our way to the venue.

The previous day Jack had asked me a favour, "Richie boy, I'm going need you to help me out tomorrow."

"Of course, I'm the best man. It's part of the deal, isn't it?"

"Sure. But there's something specific I need. It's Sofía's mother, Camila, you see. She's a bit of a... how shall we say... liability. So, I want you and Robyn to go in the car with her, and Sofía's two sisters, to drive to the venue tomorrow. Penelope, Sofía's sister's going to drive. It's not going to be an issue. But I want my best man on this. *Best man.* Get it?"

"Yep. I get it. It won't be a problem."

And how those words came back to haunt me, louder and louder, during the two-hour car journey that Jack had promised me would take no more than forty minutes. To be fair to Jack, he had done everything he could to account for the "liability" of his mother-in-law, but it still wasn't enough.

After the ceremony we accompanied Sofía's two sisters and mother to a multi-storey car park, where Jack had arranged the rental of a swanky BMW for us. After all, it wasn't just the bride's big day, it was her mother's too. Penelope took the driver's seat, and I noted Sofía's mother, Camila, didn't hesitate in taking the front passenger seat. Robyn, myself and the other sister, Veronica, squeezed into the back.

Jack had pre-programmed the in-car satellite navigation system to guide us straight to the venue, but the problems started before even we got to that part. On approaching the car, Penelope tried to remotely unlock it, but only succeeded in setting off the alarm. My first observation was the swankier the car was, the louder the alarm. Camila, in mumzilla mode, grabbed the car key and tried the patented technique of mashing all the buttons at once. It didn't help.

Later, I wondered if the alarm was just the car's way of warning us of the hellish journey to come. If it was, we did not heed its advice.

Perhaps it was the alarm that spooked Penelope. She was not an especially confident driver anyway. In fact, knowledge of how cars work was not her strong suit either. Normally, starting a car and pulling away is an almost unconscious, automatic process. Generally, it's a manoeuvre undertaken by a single person. Typically, the driver. Here it was more of a team event. It also involved an element of increasing pressure. Like a challenge in the Crystal Maze. If it was set in a multi-storey car park.

Getting the handbrake off became a joint project. As usual Camila volunteered her services, but they were rendered useless by the fact that they were useless. Camila instructed her other daughter, Veronica, to solve the issue, which would have been fine if Veronica knew how to solve it. She didn't. But in all the button pressing, the brake unlocked, and we were off, if two huge lurching stalls constitutes being off. The first one forwards, and then one more in reverse for good measure. That said, it really woke everyone in the car up, even if it did raise more questions about Penelope's suitability as designated driver. But, she was *our* driver, and we were sticking with her.

Once out of the space, the car park itself was a fresh challenge. Each time Penelope pulled the huge boat of a car around one of the tight corners of the multistorey, she squealed, and truth be told, it wasn't long before I found those little shrieks oddly reassuring. She was invested here, and clearly didn't want to crash. Camila, who I quickly learnt was a pointer, wasn't helping matters with her wild and expressive gestures, or with her shouts of *¡Cuidado, Penelope!* (Careful, Penelope!) each time dear Penelope let out one of her characteristic squeals.

316

Miraculously we emerged from the multistorey and then the fun really began. Penelope followed the directions from the car's satellite navigation but within fifteen minutes, it was clear we were going in a circle. A little bit of in-car tension ensued, until Veronica suggested we use her phone for directions, and she turned on her navigation app. Camila, who spoke not a word of English, and had a thick Andalusian accent, was also involved. I wasn't sure how, but if I had to do a post-mortem of it all, like an air crash incident investigation, I would place a fair amount of blame at her door.

Camila took Veronica's phone and positioned it in front of the display in the middle of the dashboard, and Penelope drove onwards. Fifteen minutes later we were still in the city (not just the same city, the same neighbourhood, it seemed). Something was up. Camila and Penelope began speaking in rapid Spanish. I could only catch some of it. From what I could understand, one or two key roads were closed, and Penelope had concluded that the phone navigation wasn't leading us anywhere either.

Plan A (the in-car navigation system) and Plan B (the phone's navigation app) were a bust, but Penelope had her own solution: shouting at Camila while following some directions from the in-car navigation system, and some from the phone. Unsurprisingly, this "mix and match" approach to following directions was as unsuccessful as you would think it would be.

Robyn and I had exchanged a quiet look long before which translated as "We should remain quiet and stay out of this." Both parties were happy with this arrangement, and we drove onwards, towards the one-hour mark.

After pulling over several times to ask passersby for directions we eventually made our way out of the city and to the reception venue. Our forty-minute journey had become a two-hour marathon. A real saga for the ages. By which I mean it felt like a Saga trip that went on for ages.

In the evening, and back at the top table, Jack had given his speech, Sofía had given hers, even Camila had given one. But I hadn't given mine, and another course had been served.

"Why haven't I done my speech yet? Why are we doing them separately anyway? That's not how it normally works," I said to Jack.

"To be honest boss, they don't really do speeches at weddings here. That's what Sofía tells me, anyway. I don't think they even normally have best men. But you know, we're sticking with our traditions. We didn't beat them in the war for nothing, did we?"

"What war?"

"Spanish Armada. Sent them packing, didn't we?"

"Oh yeah. Fair enough," he was distracting me though and I returned to the topic in hand, my speech, "Jack, if we are talking about traditions, the tradition

318

would be for me to speak *before* the meal! I would be done by 5pm and free to enjoy myself," I complained.

"It's a new tradition then. You go on last. You can't argue with traditions, even new ones. Something old, something new, something borrowed, boss is over-due... and feeling blue," he said, happy-as-could-be.

I didn't have long to wait though, once the last course was taken away, Jack gave me the microphone and the floor was mine. I stood to my feet slowly, and the crowd clapped wholeheartedly.

"Ladies and gentlemen," I cleared my throat, and looked down at my notes, *"If there's anybody here this evening who's feeling nervous, apprehensive and queasy at the thought of what lies ahead...... it's probably because you have just married Jack. Sorry Sofía, it's too late now."*

The small English section of the group laughed, and the time had almost come to switch to Spanish. *"But now for the benefit of most people here, I am going to speak in Spanish. Rest assured the jokes are very funny, so feel free to join in and laugh, even if you don't understand them."* The English people giggled, and I took a breath. The moment had finally arrived.

I looked up, towards the back of the room. Dozens of tables filled my view. There was a light shining on me, and all I could see were dark blurry shapes of people. I cleared my throat once more and began, *"¿Dónde debo empezar?"* (Where should I start?), and before I had even finished the question, the Spanish section cheered.

Acknowledgements

Thanks first to my wife, brother, and Mum for reading the early drafts of this. Your suggestions and improvements have no doubt immeasurably improved the book. Thanks also to my wife for putting up with me being away and going to Spain for such a long period.

¡Muchas gracias! to all the Spanish people I spoke to, particularly those who talked with me towards the beginning, when I was frankly, pretty bad. Thankfully, I got better, and I hope you enjoyed chatting with me, as much as I enjoyed chatting with you. Special thanks too to Alba for correcting the Spanish in the text.

I also would like to say how much I appreciate those who reviewed my first book *Drive-Thru USA* on Amazon or Good Reads. I read every review, as most authors do, and it's really satisfying to see that someone has enjoyed the book. It's great motivation to keep writing, and I rely on recommendations and reviews from people like yourself to help other people discover the book! If you did enjoy this one, then please do write a review on Amazon.

Thanks for reading, and happy travels!

Also by Rich Bradwell

Drive-Thru USA:
A tale of two road trips

Join Rich Bradwell on his epic journey across the US as he travels the length and breadth of the country, from the Florida Keys to Death Valley to the Rocky Mountains. Accompanied on the drive by his long-suffering wife, Robyn, and haunted by a shambolic cross-country trip with his idiotic friend Jack ten years earlier, he covers over 10,000 miles and follows the famous Route 66. He also goes looking for the very best food that this amazing country has to offer. From feasting on lobster on the rocky shores of Maine, to tracking down America's first pizzeria, no culinary stone goes unturned. On his quest, he finds the origin of hot dogs and the best barbecue in the south, he even tries soup made from peanuts.

In between he also falls in love with a clown and escapes alien abduction...ok, so that doesn't happen, but he does win a poker tournament in Las Vegas, hides from forest hippies in Georgia and falls out with an Australian. Rich's hilarious journey is littered with insights into a land best understood with one hand on the wheel and the other on a burger.

'Hilarious! This is an adventure that makes you want to hit the road and drive' Shutter Safari

'Funny and perceptive, filled with insights and tales of amazing food' thewiredjester.co.uk

'I really enjoyed this book, I found it by accident and was delighted I did! Great read' Amazon.co.uk review

Available to buy at Amazon UK and Amazon USA.

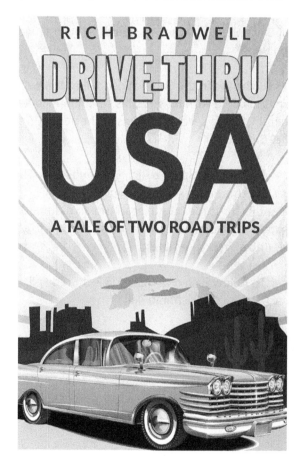

The Author

Rich was born in the early 80s and began his working life as a journalist in the city of London writing for a financial magazine. When he realised that he could write about travel instead of complex loans and financing, he quit. Since then he's tried to spend as much time travelling as possible.

Rich lives in the South West of England, where he spends his time with his wife, his cat and his collection of books, including several editions of the adventures of *Pablo Diablo.*

My Reign in Spain is Rich's second book. The first was *Drive-Thru USA: A tale of two road trips* which told the story of Rich's three month road trip across the USA and Canada with Jack, and another cross-country trip with his wife, Robyn, ten years later.

To follow Rich on Twitter: @RichBradwell
www.twitter.com/richbradwell

If you want to get in touch, then email
richbradwell@gmx.com

Made in the USA
Monee, IL
26 November 2020